C# Weekend Crash Course™

Stephen Randy Davis

Hungry Minds™

Best-Selling Books • Digital Downloads • e-Books • Answer Networks • e-Newsletters • Branded Web Sites • e-Learning

New York, NY • Cleveland, OH • Indianapolis, IN

C# Weekend Crash Course™

Published by
Hungry Minds, Inc.
909 Third Avenue
New York, NY 10022
www.hungryminds.com

Library of Congress Control Number: 2001089351

ISBN: 0-7645-4789-5

Printed in the United States of America

10 9 8 7 6 5 4 3 2 1

1B/RY/RS/QR/IN

Distributed in the United States by Hungry Minds, Inc.

Distributed by CDG Books Canada Inc. for Canada; by Transworld Publishers Limited in the United Kingdom; by IDG Norge Books for Norway; by IDG Sweden Books for Sweden; by IDG Books Australia Publishing Corporation Pty. Ltd. for Australia and New Zealand; by TransQuest Publishers Pte Ltd. for Singapore, Malaysia, Thailand, Indonesia, and Hong Kong; by Gotop Information Inc. for Taiwan; by ICG Muse, Inc. for Japan; by Intersoft for South Africa; by Eyrolles for France; by International Thomson Publishing for Germany, Austria, and Switzerland; by Distribuidora Cuspide for Argentina; by LR International for Brazil; by Galileo Libros for Chile; by Ediciones ZETA S.C.R. Ltda. for Peru; by WS Computer Publishing Corporation, Inc., for the Philippines; by Contemporanea de Ediciones for Venezuela; by Express Computer Distributors for the Caribbean and West Indies; by Micronesia Media Distributor, Inc. for Micronesia; by Chips Computadoras S.A. de C.V. for Mexico; by Editorial Norma de Panama S.A. for Panama; by American Bookshops for Finland.

For general information on Hungry Minds' products and services please contact our Customer Care department within the U.S. at 800-762-2974, outside the U.S. at 317-572-3993 or fax 317-572-4002.

For sales inquiries and reseller information, including discounts, premium and bulk quantity sales, and foreign-language translations, please contact our Customer Care department at 800-434-3422, fax 317-572-4002 or write to Hungry Minds, Inc., Attn: Customer Care Department, 10475 Crosspoint Boulevard, Indianapolis, IN 46256.

For information on licensing foreign or domestic rights, please contact our Sub-Rights Customer Care department at 212-884-5000.

For information on using Hungry Minds' products and services in the classroom or for ordering examination copies, please contact our Educational Sales department at 800-434-2086 or fax 317-572-4005.

For press review copies, author interviews, or other publicity information, please contact our Public Relations department at 317-572-3168 or fax 317-572-4168.

For authorization to photocopy items for corporate, personal, or educational use, please contact Copyright Clearance Center, 222 Rosewood Drive, Danvers, MA 01923, or fax 978-750-4470.

Hungry Minds™ is a trademark of Hungry Minds, Inc.

About the Author

Stephen R. Davis, who goes by the name of Randy, has been a programmer and author for almost 20 years. He is currently a senior consultant with Valtech, a global consulting, training, and mentoring company (www.valtech.com).

Randy can be reached at www.stephendavis.com.

About the Contributor

Richard Lassan is a Senior Consultant with GA Sullivan in the Nashville, Tennessee, office. Richard has been actively involved in software development for the past fifteen years. His first computer was the TI994A, and from there he moved on to the Commodore 64, the Apple II, and finally the IBM PC. Richard currently spends his time learning .NET and writing and evangelizing about the benefits of building applications with .NET. He can be reached at rickl@gasullivan.com.

About the Series Editor

Michael Lane Thomas is an active development community and computer industry analyst who presently spends a great deal of time spreading the gospel of Microsoft .NET in his current role as a .NET technology evangelist for Microsoft. In working with over a half-dozen publishing companies, Michael has written numerous technical articles and written or contributed to almost 20 books on numerous technical topics, including Visual Basic, Visual C++, and .NET technologies. He is a prolific supporter of the Microsoft certification programs, having earned his MCSD, MCSE+I, MCT, MCP+SB, and MCDBA.

In addition to technical writing, Michael can also be heard over the airwaves from time to time, including two weekly radio programs on Entercom (http://www.entercom.com/) stations, including most often in Kansas City on News Radio 980KMBZ (http://www.kmbz.com/). He can also occasionally be caught on the Internet doing an MSDN Webcast (http://www.microsoft.com/usa/webcasts/) discussing .NET, the next generation of Web application technologies.

Michael started his journey through the technical ranks back in college at the University of Kansas, where he earned his stripes and a couple of degrees. After a brief stint as a technical and business consultant to Tokyo-based Global Online Japan, he returned to the States to climb the corporate ladder. He has held assorted roles, including those of IT manager, field engineer, trainer, independent consultant, and even a brief stint as Interim CTO of a successful dot-com, although he believes his current role as .NET evangelist for Microsoft is the best of the lot. He can be reached via email at mlthomas@microsoft.com.

Credits

Senior Acquisitions Editor
Sharon Cox

Project Editors
Mildred Sanchez
Eric Newman

Technical Editors
Pierre Boutquin
Richard A. Lassan

Copy Editors
Maarten Reilingh
Eric Newman

Senior Vice President, Technical Publishing
Richard Swadley

Vice President and Publisher
Joseph B. Wikert

Project Coordinator
Dale White

Graphics and Production Specialists
Beth Brooks
Sean Decker
Joyce Haughey
Jill Piscitelli
Laurie Petrone
Betty Schulte
Erin Zeltner

Quality Control Technicians
Carl Pierce,
Charles Spencer

Permissions Editor
Carmen Krikorian

Media Development Specialist
Megan Decraene

Proofreading and Indexing
TECHBOOKS Production Services

to Drs. Madeleine Duvic,
Jennifer Cather, and Estil Vance

Preface

C# *Weekend Crash Course*™ teaches the reader C# (pronounced "C-sharp") in one busy but rewarding weekend.

What Is C#?

C#, Microsoft's new programming language, is the flagship of the .NET (pronounced "Dot Net") Internet initiative.

A simple Web page is very easy to build. Almost any public domain Web page editor lets you put text up on your site, add links to other pages, and slap your name on a banner across the top. A more complicated Web page — one that loads information from a database, for example — is very difficult to write, however.

Microsoft created the .NET initiative to simplify the creation of smart Web pages that can pull up maps or telephone numbers, to name just a few, dynamically based upon the user input. Some smart pages need a significant amount of software intelligence.

Pre-Internet languages are ill adapted to perform these features. Some very clever programmers figured out ways to build smart pages using conventional functional languages like C; however, such attempts were just a hack. .NET was designed from the ground up to provide elegant solutions to Internet problems.

.NET and C# were created to address another, more subtle problem. The Internet has turned into an invaluable asset to every businessperson, software developer, parent, and taxi driver. However, to date the Internet has not become much of an asset to most software programs.

It's not that programs haven't been written to use the Internet — the problem is that programs don't use the Internet routinely. Programs don't access modules located on remote computers in the same casual way they do when they access modules on the local machine.

.NET provides this capability. With .NET, programs can access modules on other machines as easily as those on their on. A built-in lookup feature makes it easy to find the modules you are looking for out there in the Internet jungle. Automatic versioning makes sure that your program retrieves the proper version of the module and avoids the so-called "DLL hell" of different applications' overwriting each others' system modules. .NET's built-in security makes sure that others aren't intercepting your remote data streams. Support for the XML standard for Internet exchange greatly simplifies the exchange of data with other types of machines.

It wasn't that many of these features aren't already available with some other new languages. In particular, the Java language, from Sun Microsystems, offers excellent Internet support. However, the difference between C# with .NET and Java is easily stated: "Java says, rewrite everything, run everywhere; C# says rewrite nothing, and run it on operating systems that support the .NET libraries."

Many companies already have a huge investment in existing software. Forcing these companies to completely rewrite their current applications — which are serving their needs quite well, thank you — is a hard sell. .NET allows for the gradual conversion of existing applications to the Internet.

Finally, all of the .NET languages integrate seamlessly. A C# module can invoke Visual Basic .NET without skipping a beat. This complete integration allows a company to slowly migrate existing applications written in a languages such as Visual C++ over to the easier to learn and maintain C# language.

C# vs. Visual C#

Microsoft designed C# to be an open language — it bundled up the C# grammar and key components of the environment and offered them to the European Computer Manufacturers Association (ECMA) for certification as an international standard. (ECMA was founded in 1961 to help create standards in the information systems industry, including those for computer languages.)

In theory, ECMA certification means that any company can write its own C# development package. A number of companies have created their own development environments for other programming languages. These same companies may decide to adapt their tools to C#.

C# Weekend Crash Course teaches you C#. It is written to be largely environment agnostic. Of course, every program in the book has been tested to work with Visual C#; however, these same programs should work in any other company's C# environment as well.

The Object-Oriented Paradigm

C# Weekend Crash Course presents more than just the C# language. You need to learn the object-oriented paradigm in order to make complete use of the power of C#. Object-oriented programming is not all hype — it really is a different approach to programming compared with earlier programming styles. Object-oriented programs are easier to write and maintain by providing a software paradigm that is closer to the way people think.

This book uses numerous examples to teach you object-oriented along with C#.

Who

C# Weekend Crash Course is intended for the beginner through the intermediate reader.

This book serves the beginner by not assuming any knowledge of programming or programming concepts. The first few lessons go over real-world, non-techie explanations of what programming is.

This book is also great for the home programmer. The multiple examples demonstrate programming techniques used in modern, high-speed programs.

Serious programmers or students should add C# to their quiver of programming skills as well. The ability to speak knowledgeably of C# can make the difference between getting that job and not getting it.

What

The reader will need a C# development environment in order to follow along in the book and develop programs. For most readers, this means purchasing a copy of Visual C#, which comes bundled with Visual Studio .NET. In addition, the reader will need a PC with enough horsepower to install and execute Visual Studio .NET. For the most part, that means:

- At least a 500MHz Pentium II processor. (You can get by with less, but the response time may become intolerable.)

- At least 256MB of RAM — more if you can get it. Visual Studio .NET has a large appetite for memory.

- 2GB of free disk storage. Visual Studio .NET seems much less sensitive to available disk space. The example programs contained on the enclosed CD-ROM take up a minimal amount of space.

- A CD-ROM drive. The Visual Studio .NET package is delivered on a set of four CD-ROMs.

Power users can gain access to C# by downloading the .NET Software Development Kit (SDK) from the Microsoft Web site. The SDK provides the .NET libraries along with a command-line C# compiler. Programmers edit their files using some other editor and then build them by entering commands on the command line of an MS-DOS window.

The power and memory requirements for the SDK C# compiler are less than those for Visual Studio .NET.

C# Weekend Crash Course provides step-by-step instructions for creating and building the more complicated programs in the book using the SDK compiler.

C# Weekend Crash Course is committed to supporting other C# environments as they become available. Check out www.stephendavis.com **for details.**

How

C# Weekend Crash Course follows a one-weekend format. Start on Friday evening, conclude on Sunday afternoon.

This one-weekend format is ideal for:

- the student who wants to catch up with the rest of the class,
- the one-time programmer who wants to brush up on his or her skills, and
- anyone who wants to learn C# while the kids are off at Grandma's house

Of course, you can proceed through the book at a more leisurely pace, if you prefer. Each section of four to six sessions can be read independently.

**20 Min.
To Go**

You should be able to complete each of the 30 sessions in 30 minutes. Time markers in the margin, such as the one shown here, help keep you on track.

Each session ends with a set of review questions to allow you to gauge your comprehension of the material. A set of more involved questions is provided in an appendix intended for the days following to help drive home knowledge gained during the weekend session.

How This Book Is Organized

C# Weekend Crash Course consists of 30 sessions in six parts.

Friday evening: Getting started

This section introduces you to basic programming language concepts. It begins with the classic "Hello, world" program written C# style and continues by examining simple mathematical and flow control operations. The features of C# presented in this section are almost indistinguishable from those of its cousins C++ and Java.

Saturday morning: Object-based programming

The C# language is built around the class concept. You'll spend this morning getting used to the care and feeding of the basic C# class.

Saturday afternoon: Object-oriented programming

This section starts by describing how object-oriented programming languages describe the way we think. It then goes on to teach you the features you will need to convert the simple class into an object oriented workhorse.

Saturday evening: Controlling access to objects

C# outfits its classes with a number of features to allow programmers to compartmentalize their class information. This section teaches you how to use these features to make your object-oriented programs easier to write and easier to maintain.

Sunday morning: C# techniques

This section expands on both the object-oriented and the control access features of C#. The numerous examples in this section show you how to combine the features from previous sections with good programming techniques to create classes that can take care of themselves.

Sunday afternoon: Advanced techniques

This final section presents some features that you can pass over in your first reading if you feel swamped. However, you'll want to return to master these extra features of the language before you start writing your own professional-quality programs.

Getting Help (with C#, That Is)

I maintain a Web site, www.stephendavis.com, containing a set of Frequently Asked Questions (FAQ). If there's something you can't figure out, try going there — maybe I've already answered your question. In addition, I include a list of any mistakes that might have crept into the book. Finally, and I do mean finally, there's a link to my e-mail address in case you can't find the answer to your question on the site.

What's Left?

Nothing. Go to the first page and start the clock. It's Friday evening — you have two days.

Acknowledgments

I find it very strange that only a single name appears on the cover of any book, but especially a book like this. In reality, many people contribute to its creation. I would like to thank the editorial staff at Hungry Minds, but for whose involvement this would have been a poorer work.

I would like to thank Valtech for the use of their equipment, time, and encouragement. I've never met a more talented group of guys.

Most of all, I thank my wife, Jenny, and son, Kinsey, for their patience and devotion. I hope we manage to strike a reasonable balance; however, I seem to have sent my son up the wall. I mean literally, up a wall. He has taken on rock climbing and he's quite good at it. In addition, he received his black belt in TaeKwonDo and earned three state championship titles in his class. Jenny continues to study gerontology and is qualified in Elder Care and Activities. Do you think she's trying to tell me something?

Contents at a Glance

Contents

C# Weekend Crash Course™

☑ **Friday**

☐ Saturday

☐ Sunday

Part I — Friday Evening

PART

I

Friday Evening

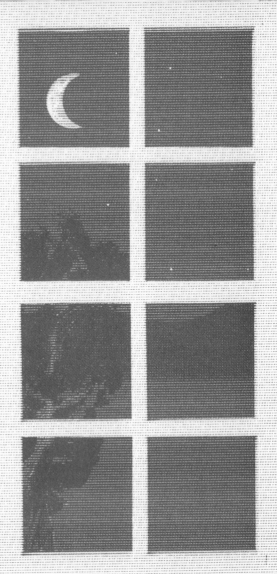

Introducing C# Programming

Session Checklist

✔ Reviewing the origins of C#

✔ Entering your first C# program

✔ Executing your program

✔ Examining the highlights of this simple program

**30 Min.
To Go**

I 've always believed that you can't understand where you're going without knowing where you came from. (I've always believed a whole lot of other things, some of which turned out to be true.) This session begins with a quick review of what makes up a computer language. The session continues by examining the sources of C# before concluding with our first C# program.

Computer Languages

Before we can examine a computer language like C#, we need to know what a computer language is and how it is used to create programs like WinZip or Microsoft Word.

Programming languages

What is a programming language? Let me give it a try: A computer programming language is a set of commands used to implement a computer program. This definition is not enlightening partly because it uses *computer* and *program* on both sides of the definition. Okay. What's a program?

Webster's New Collegiate Dictionary lists a number of definitions for the word *program*. The sixth in this list is "a logical sequence of coded instructions specifying the operations to be performed by a computer in solving a problem or processing data."

The language that the computer processor itself understands is extremely limited and complicated. While it is possible to write a program in computer processor language, commonly known as *machine language*, it is almost never done anymore.

Instead, programmers create their programs in a language that is not nearly as free as human speech but a lot more flexible and easy to use than machine language. A tool known as a compiler converts this higher-level language into a machine language file before it can be executed.

Enter C#

The C# programming language is one of those intermediate languages that programmers use to create executable programs. C# seems ideally designed to occupy the gap between the powerful but complicated C++ and the easy-to-use but limited Visual Basic.

C# is:

- **Flexible:** C# programs can execute on the current machine or can be transmitted over the Web to be executed on some distant computer.
- **Powerful:** The command set for C# is essentially the same as that for C++ with the rough edges filed smooth.
- **Easy to use:** C# modifies the commands responsible for the majority of C++ errors to make them safer.
- **Visually oriented:** The C# library provides the help needed to readily create complicated display frames with drop-down menus, tabbed windows, grouped push buttons, scrolling sliders, and background images, to name just a few.
- **Internet friendly:** C# plays a pivotal role in Microsoft's new Internet-based .NET (pronounced "dot net") strategy.
- **Secure:** Any language intended to be used on the Internet must include some type of security to protect against malevolent hackers, and C# does.

Your First Program

Human programs can take us only so far. Look at a C# program. This version of the ubiquitous "Hello, world" program prompts you for your name and then spits it back at you with suitable salutations attached.

The following steps walk you through the process of creating a C# program using the popular Visual Studio .NET implementation of C#. The details will be different for other C# development tools.

Installing your C# compiler

You will need to install your C# environment before you can start creating C# programs. Follow the installation instructions that came with your compiler. If you are using Microsoft's compiler, note that Visual C# is part of the Visual Studio .NET package.

Creating the project

In many environments, including Visual C#'s, you must create a *project* before you can start to enter your C# program. A project is like a bucket. You throw all of the files that go into making your program into the project. When you tell your compiler to build the program, it begins sorting through the project. It will re-create any machine instruction files it needs to in order to re-create the program.

When using Visual Studio, select File ⇨ New... ⇨ Project to create a new project. Visual Studio presents you with a window of icons representing the different types of projects you can create. From the window that appears, click on the Console Application icon.

The default name for your first application is ConsoleApplication1. The default location for this file is somewhere deep in your My Documents folder. Maybe it's just because I'm difficult (or maybe it's because I'm writing a book), but I like to put my programs where I want them, not necessarily where Visual Studio wants to put them. To change the default directory for your program, click the Browse button and navigate to some existing directory. Type in the name field in order to change the name of the project that you're about to create. (It's allowed but probably not a good idea to embed blanks within your project name.)

Click OK. After a bit of disk whirring and chattering, Visual Studio generates a file called Class1.cs. (If you look in the window labeled Solutions Explorer, you will see some other files — ignore them for now.) C# source files carry the extension .cs. The name Class1 is the default name for this file.

Creating your source file

**20 Min.
To Go**

Edit the source file until it appears as follows. (If you are using the Visual Studio environment, your initial source file is called Class1.cs. Some environments require that you manually create an initial source file. Follow the instructions that came with your compiler.)

> **At this point, don't be concerned about the double (//) or triple (///) slashes (which denote comment lines), and don't worry about one space versus two spaces, but do pay attention to capitalization.**

```
namespace HelloWorld
{
    using System;

    public class Class1
    {
        // This is where our program starts
        public static int Main(string[] args)
        {
            // prompt user to enter her name
            Console.WriteLine("Enter your name, please:");

            // now read the name entered
            string sName = Console.ReadLine();
```

```
// great the user with her name
Console.WriteLine("Hello, " + sName);

// wait for user to acknowledge the results
Console.WriteLine("Hit Enter to terminate...");
Console.Read();

return 0;
            }
        }
    }
```

Once your version of `Class1.cs` appears like the one above, save your results. In Visual Studio, select File ⇨ Save All.

The complete `HelloWorld` program can be found on the companion CD for this book.

Building the program

Somewhere within your Visual Studio development environment is a menu selection that says Build, Build Project, Build Solution, or some other phrase to that effect. Visual Studio uses the Build ⇨ Build menu option. Your C# compiler should respond with some type of progress message. Visual Studio displays the following in the Output window:

```
- Build started: Project: HelloWorld, Configuration: Debug .NET -

Preparing resources...

Build complete — 0 errors, 0 warnings
Building satellite assemblies...

——————— Done ———————
Build: 1 succeeded, 0 failed, 0 skipped
```

To *build* a program means to convert (*compile*) all of the files that make up your C# program into a machine language program.

You will get a series of error messages if the build step fails for any reason — for example, if you entered the program incorrectly. If you just can't seem to find the problem, you can copy the program files in the `HelloWorld` directory off of the accompanying CD-ROM.

Executing the program

You may now execute your program. From within Visual Studio .NET, choose Debug ⇨ Start without Debugging. The program immediately prompts you for your name. As soon as you press the Enter key on the keyboard, the program responds as follows:

```
Enter your name, please:
Stephen
```

```
Hello, Stephen
Hit Enter to terminate...
```

You can also execute the program directly from the DOS prompt or by double-clicking the name of the program in Windows Explorer.

The executable that this program generated is designed to execute from the command prompt of an MS-DOS window, a so-called *console application.* Technically this is a Windows program because the DOS window is executing under Microsoft Windows and because at its core the program relies upon Windows functionality. However, this is not what you would commonly think of as a *Windows application.*

Learning to program Windows, even using a powerful tool such as C#, is a complicated task. Entire books have been written on just one aspect of Windows programming. Teaching you Windows programming and C# programming at the same time is too much for one book or for one person.

Don't start creating true Windows applications until you feel comfortable with the C# language itself.

A Review of the Program

Let's take this first C# program apart one section at a time in order to understand how it works.

10 Min.
To Go

The program framework

All of the programs that we will generate for this book are based on a block labeled Main() (a block is a section of C# code surrounded by open and closed braces).

```
public static int Main(string[] args)
{
    // ...our program goes here...

    return 0;
}
```

I hate to do this to you, but you'll have to accept the remaining lines in HelloWorld.cs as a framework in which our programs execute. The meaning of these statements will be explained as you work your way through the sessions of this book.

The very first line added to HelloWorld.cs appears as follows:

```
// This is where our program goes
public static int Main(string[] args)
```

Any line that begins with a // or /// is free text and is ignored by C#. Consider // and /// to be equivalent for now.

Why include lines in your program that the computer ignores? It isn't always easy for the human reader to understand a C# program as written. Adding extra explanatory text, which programmers call *comments*, makes the job much easier. Comment early and often. It'll help you and others to remember what you meant when you wrote all those C# statements.

The meat of the program

The real core of this program is embodied in the following statements embedded within the block of code marked with Main():

```
// prompt user to enter her name
Console.WriteLine("Enter your name, please:");

// now read the name entered
string sName = Console.ReadLine();

// greet the user with her name
Console.WriteLine("Hello, " + sName);
```

The program begins executing with the first C# statement, Console.WriteLine. This command writes the character string Enter your name, please: to the console.

The next statement reads in your answer and stores it in a *workbox*, sName. (I'll have more to say about these storage locations in Session 2.) The last line attaches the string Hello in front of your name and outputs the result to the console.

The final three lines wait for the user to press the Enter key on the keyboard to make sure that she has time to read the output of the program before proceeding.

```
// wait for user to acknowledge the results
Console.WriteLine("Hit Enter to terminate...");
Console.Read();
```

The Origins of C#

Readers completely new to programming will want to continue on to Session 2; however, those of you who are familiar with the programming scene might be wondering about how C# came to be. Why do we have C#? What was wrong with C++? What about Java?

Sometime in the early 1990s, Microsoft realized that it was falling behind the curve with respect to the Internet craze, which was just then getting started. Microsoft was slow to react to what it had misjudged to be just some techie toy. (Of course, at the time they were right — the Internet *was* just some techie toy; however, as my third-grade teacher used to say, "He has potential.") It was time to take action.

First, Microsoft needed a browser (the program you use to access Web sites). Microsoft's browser was Internet Explorer, commonly known by its initials, IE. The initial versions of IE weren't so great, but by version 3.0, IE had caught up with its rival browser from Netscape.

Sun's Java versus Microsoft's Visual J++

A programmer can write an interactive Web page using almost any language, including C++. However, C++ lacks features critical to Web development. In addition, C++ with its tortured syntax is very complex for the average programmer. Certain aspects, such as memory management, are difficult even for the seasoned veteran.

Realizing the limitations of C++, Sun Microsystems created the Java programming language. Java borrows heavily from the C++ language; however, Java is easier to use and adds important features that support Internet development.

Microsoft recognized that Internet programmers were adopting Java in droves. Again, it was time to respond. There was no time to develop a new programming language. For once, Microsoft decided to go along with the rest of the industry — it licensed Java. That is, it bought the rights to use the source code to the Java compiler and libraries.

Licensing Java from Sun turned out to be a mistake — a costly one at that. Sun made Microsoft sign a deal that in order to use Sun's core code, Microsoft couldn't change the Java language in any way. They couldn't add to or remove any features from their implementation. Microsoft compounded that error with a second mistake almost as bad as the first — the contract Microsoft signed with Sun was understandable.

Microsoft had been working on its second-generation Internet tool suite known as .NET. Microsoft began adding features to its version of Java, which it dubbed J++, in order to support .NET. Unfortunately for Microsoft, this violated the contract that it had signed with Sun.

Sun sued Microsoft. After unsuccessfully arguing the point, Microsoft decided to abandon Visual J++ 6. Microsoft didn't recall Visual J++ — they just stopped selling it anymore. (As an aside, this didn't do much for sales of the book *Programming Visual J++ 6*, which I had just written.)

Microsoft went back to the drawing board and created its own C++ descendant, which became C#.

You can do only so much with a simple browser. Netscape introduced a *scripting* language called JavaScript that could be used to jazz up Web pages. Web designers were able to combine these scripting languages with standard Web page instructions (called HTML, by the way) to make some pretty interesting Web pages — good enough to display ads for credit cards with a low, low 18% introductory rate, for example.

Simple Web pages, even those containing fancy scripts, were too limiting for the type of Web development that most Web designers wanted. Developers needed a programming language designed for the Internet in order to build really neat interactive Web pages, so Microsoft developed its own (see sidebar).

Done!

REVIEW

It's been said before, and it bears restating: A computer is a very fast, very stupid slave with a limited vocabulary. Computers do exactly what you tell them to do. Their native language is too difficult for programs used by humans. Higher-level intermediate languages like C++, Basic, and Java were created to simplify the programmer's job. The C# language is the newest in an evolutionary line of programming languages that start with C and stretch through C++ and Java.

C# is powerful, easy to use, and ideal for Internet applications.

QUIZ YOURSELF

1. What is a compiler? (See "Programming languages.")
2. Name three advantages of C# over other programming languages. (See "Enter C#.")
3. What is a comment (to a programmer) and what is it used for? (See "A Review of the Program.")

Mathematical Operations

Session Checklist

✔ Performing integer arithmetic in a program

✔ Examining the limitations of integer arithmetic

✔ Finding a cute little number that might just solve our arithmetic problems

**30 Min.
To Go**

The C# program in Session 1 prompted the user for her name and then spit that name back to the console. This isn't particularly useful, because if you're able to remember your name long enough to type it in, then you probably don't need to be told by the program what it is.

This session begins by looking at some "real" programs — programs that actually do something.

The Fahrenheit to Celsius Conversion Program

The United States has not been quick to adopt some world standards for measurement, including temperature. For example, the United States uses the Fahrenheit scale whereas the remainder of the world has adopted the Celsius scale.

In this section we create a program to convert a temperature in degrees Fahrenheit into degrees Celsius. I will use this example to describe some of the arithmetic operations in C#.

The following C# program displays the Celsius equivalent of a Fahrenheit temperature entered from the keyboard.

If you are using Visual Studio .NET, you will notice that I have removed sections of code outside of the Main() framework. Code outside of the Main() framework doesn't do anything.

```
// IntegerTemperature - this program prompts the user for
//                      a temperature which is assumed to
//                      be in degrees Fahrenheit. The
//                      program converts the temperature to
//                      degreesCelsius and outputs the
//                      result.
namespace IntegerConvert
{
    using System;

    public class Class1
    {
        public static int Main(string[] args)
        {
            // prompt user to enter temperature
            Console.Write("Enter temp in degrees Fahrenheit:");

            // read the number entered
            int nFahr;
            string sFahr = Console.ReadLine();
            nFahr = Int32.Parse(sFahr);

            // convert that temperature into degrees Celsius:
            // first remove the 32 degree offset from 0 Celsius
            int nBaseFahr;
            nBaseFahr = nFahr - 32;

            // now reflect the fact that one degree Celsius is
            // equivalent to almost 2 degrees Fahrenheit
            int nCelsius;
            nCelsius = (nBaseFahr * 100)/(212 - 32);

            // output the result
            Console.WriteLine("Temperature in degrees Celsius = "
                              + nCelsius);

            // wait for user to acknowledge
            Console.WriteLine("Hit Enter to terminate...");
            Console.Read();
            return 0;
        }
    }
}
```

The `ConvertTemperature` program uses the same framework described in Session 1. The body of the program is included between the braces ({}) immediately following the line

```
public static int Main(string[] arg)
```

The program prompts the user to enter a number representing the temperature in degrees Fahrenheit using the command

```
// prompt user to enter temperature
Console.Write("Enter temp in degrees Fahrenheit:");
```

The function `Write()` does not add a line feed at the end as `WriteLine()` does. The next statement is a little more involved. The line

```
int nFahr;
```

declares a variable of type int.

What is a variable?

The term *variable* is borrowed from the world of mathematics; the meaning of *variable* is not that different in the programming world. C# variables are little boxes where the program can save values.

For example, the mathematician might say

```
n = 1
```

meaning that from this point forward, when the mathematician says *n,* you should read 1.

When the C# programmer says

```
int n;
n = 1;
```

he means carve off a small amount of storage to which he assigns the name n and stores the value 1 in that location. This is completely analogous to selecting a toolbox, giving it the name *n* (not a very imaginative name for a toolbox, but a name nonetheless), and storing a 1 (whatever that might represent) in the toolbox *n*.

The mathematician says that "n is equal to 1," meaning that the term *n* is equivalent to 1. Programmers must be precise in their terminology. The C# programmer says that "1 is assigned to *n,*" meaning that the value 1 is stored in the variable *n*. The equals symbol (=) is called the *assignment operator* and not the equals operator. The assignment operator takes the value on its right and stores it in the variable on the left.

What is an int?

Mathematicians deal with concepts. They can make up variables anytime they want — a single variable may have different meanings throughout the same equation. Computers are not nearly as flexible.

C# variables have a fixed type. The most common type is int, which stands for *integer*. Integers are the counting numbers like 1, 2, 3, and so on, plus the negative numbers -1, -2, -3, and so forth.

Once a variable has been declared as int, it can hold and regurgitate integer values, as the following example demonstrates.

```
// declare a variable n
int n;

// declare an int variable m and initialize it
```

```
// with the value 2
int m = 2;

// assign the value stored in m to the variable n
n = m;
```

Converting temperatures

After declaring the int variable nFahr, the program continues by reading in a value from the keyboard and storing it:

```
// read the number entered
int nFahr;
string sFahr = Console.ReadLine();
nFahr = Int32.Parse(sFahr);
```

The expression Int32.Parse() **converts the string read in from the keyboard into the 32-bit** int **format. There are other sized integer types.**

Rules for declaring variables

A variable may be initialized to a value as part of the declaration.

```
// declare another int variable and give it
// the initial value of 1

int o = 1;
```

Initialize a variable when you declare it. In most, but not all, cases, C# will initialize the variable for you, but don't rely on that fact.

Variables may be declared (almost) anywhere within a program. However, a variable may not be used until it has been declared and set to some value. Thus the following two assignments are not legal:

```
// the following is illegal since m is not assigned
// a value before it is used
int m;
int n = m;

// the following is also illegal as p has not been
// declared before it is used
p = 2;

int p;
```

Finally, you cannot declare the same variable twice.

The computation continues using the following equation:

```
int nC = (nFahr - 32) * 5 / 9
```

For reasons that will become clear later in the session, I've divided the subtraction part from the fraction. (I've also removed the comments.)

```
int nBaseFahr;
nBaseFahr = nFahr - 32;
int nCelsius;

nCelsius = (nBaseFahr * 100)/(212 - 32);
```

Finally, the program outputs the results as follows:

```
// output the result
Console.WriteLine("Temperature in degrees Celsius = "
                   + nCelsius);
```

Executing the ConvertTemperature program

Executing the program generates the following results:

```
Enter temp in degrees Fahrenheit:100
Temperature in degrees Celsius = 37
Hit Enter to terminate...
```

You may not immediately recognize that result. Let's try a well-known value:

```
Enter temp in degrees Fahrenheit:212
Temperature in degrees Celsius = 100
Hit Enter to terminate...
```

I continue to execute the program with different inputs until I'm sure that the program is working as it should.

Representing Fractions

The IntegerConvert program declares a single type of variable: int. The int variables worked just fine for this program, but they don't work properly in every case. C# provides a few other variable types to partially circumvent these problems. The remaining sections in this session examine these other variable types.

The properties of an int

The majority of simple variables are of the type int. However, C# provides a number of twists to the int variable type for special occasions. All integer variable types are limited to whole numbers. The int type suffers from other limitations as well. For example, an int variable can store values only in the range of minus 2 to plus 2 billion.

Two billion inches is greater than the circumference of the Earth.

For those readers for whom 2 billion is not quite enough, C# provides an integer type called `long` (short for *long integer*) that can represent numbers as large as I can imagine.

```
long lAVeryLargeInteger = 4000000000; // declare a long int;
```

The only problem with a `long` is that it consumes 16 bytes (64 bits), twice as much as a "normal" int.

The actual range of `long` is plus or minus 90,000,000,000,000,000,000. No kidding.

C# also supports integer variables with smaller ranges, which take up correspondingly less room. These are shown in Table 2-1. In general, you should choose the `int` type variable that provides the optimal size-versus-range ratio for your need. If you don't particularly care, just stick with `int`.

Table 2-1   *Integer Variable Types*

Type	Size (in bytes)	Range	Code Example
sbyte	2	–128 to 127	sbyte sb = 12;
byte	2	0 to 255	byte b = 12;
short	4	-32 thousand to 32 thousand	short sn = 12,3456;
ushort	4	0 to 64 thousand	ushort usn = 62,345,678;
int	8	-2 billion to 2 billion	int n = 1,234,567,890;
uint	8	0 to 4 billion	uint un = 3,234,567,890U
long	16	-10^{20} to $+10^{20}$ ("a whole lot")	long l = 123,456,789,012L
ulong	16	0 through $2 * 10^{20}$	long ul = 123,456,789,012UL

Notice that constants are a value also. By default, a simple constant such as 1 is assumed to be an `int`. Constants other than an `int` must be marked as such. For example, 123U is an *unsigned* integer, `uint`.

Most of the integer variables are called *signed*, meaning that they can represent a negative value. The unsigned integers can represent only positive values, but you get twice the range in return. As you can see from Table 2-1, most of the unsigned integer varieties start with a u while the signed types generally don't have a prefix.

Demonstrating the limitations common to all integer types

**20 Min.
To Go**

Many calculations involve fractions that cannot accurately be represented by simple integers. The problem can be demonstrated by a slight modification to our conversion program.

The expression for the formula to convert Celsius to Fahrenheit temperatures is as follows:

```
nCelsius = (nFahr - 32) * (5 / 9)
```

The ConvertTemperatureWithRoundOff version of the conversion program uses this equation exactly as written to perform the conversion. The relevant sections of the program are shown here.

```
public static int Main(string[] args)
{
  // prompt user to enter temperature
    Console.Write("Enter temp in degrees Fahrenheit:");

  // read the number entered
  string sFahr = Console.ReadLine();
  int nFahr;
  nFahr = Int32.Parse(sFahr);

  // convert that temperature into degrees Celsius
  int nCelsius;
  nCelsius = (nFahr - 32) * (5 / 9);

  // output the result
  Console.WriteLine("Incorrect temperature in degrees Celsius = "
                    + nCelsius);

  // wait for user to acknowledge
  Console.WriteLine("Hit Enter to terminate...");
  Console.Read();
  return 0;
}
```

The entire version of the ConvertTemperatureWithRoundOff **program can be found on the CD.**

Executing the program with the same input used with the original ConvertTemperature program generates peculiar results:

```
Enter temp in degrees Fahrenheit:100
Incorrect temperature in degrees Celsius = 0
Hit Enter to terminate...
```

What went wrong?

Integer roundoff

The ConvertTemperatureWithRoundOff program generates results that clearly are incorrect. In fact, the program outputs zero for all input.

To see how this comes about, consider the ratio 5 / 9. Mathematically, the result of this division should be 0.555.... Unfortunately, int variables can store only the whole part, which is zero. The fractional part (0.555...) is dropped off. Obviously, anything multiplied by zero is zero.

Representing fractional values

The limitations of an int variable can be unacceptable at times. The range isn't generally a problem — the double zillion range of a 64-bit integer should be enough for anyone. The fact that an int is limited to whole numbers is a bit harder to swallow.

Thankfully, C# offers a set of floating point variable types that can represent fractional values. The set of floating point types is shown in Table 2-2.

Floating point numbers owe their name to the fact that the decimal point is allowed to "float" between the digits from left to right like 10.0 to 1.00 to 0.100. Cute, but descriptive.

Table 2-2   *Floating Point Variable Types*

Type	Size (in bytes)	Range	Accuracy	Code Example
float	8	10^{-45} to 10^{38}	6 digits	float f = 1.2F;
double	16	10^{-324} to 10^{308}	15 digits	double d = 1.2;

The Accuracy column in Table 2-2 refers to the number of significant digits that a floating point variable type can represent. For example, 5/9 might appear as the following when expressed as a float:

0.5555551457382

Based on the number of digits of accuracy from Table 2-2, we know that all of the digits after the last 5 are incorrect. A float variable is said to have six significant digits of accuracy, meaning that numbers after the sixth digit should be ignored.

The same number might appear as follows when expressed as a double:

0.55555555555555557823

The double packs a walloping 15 significant digits.

All floating point variables are signed (that is to say, there is no such thing as a floating point variable that can't represent a negative value).

Floating point ConvertTemperature

The following example uses the floating point type when converting from Fahrenheit to Celsius. The relevant sections of the floating point version of the temperature conversion program, ConvertTemperatureWithFloat, appear as follows:

```
public static int Main(string[] args)
{
  // prompt user to enter temperature
  Console.Write("Enter temp in degrees Fahrenheit:");

  // read the number entered
  string sFahr = Console.ReadLine();
  double dFahr;
  dFahr = Double.Parse(sFahr);

  // convert that temperature into degrees Celsius
  double dCelsius;
  dCelsius = (dFahr - 32.0) * (5.0 / 9.0 );

  // output the result
  Console.WriteLine("Temperature in degrees Celsius = "
                + dCelsius);

  // wait for user to acknowledge the results
  Console.WriteLine("Hit Enter to terminate...");
  Console.Read();
  return 0;
}
```

The program actually uses the double **variable type; however, programs that use either** double **or** float **are said to be floating point programs.**

The complete ConvertTemperatureWithFloat **program can be found on the CD.**

The results of executing the program are:

```
Enter temp in degrees Fahrenheit:100
Temperature in degrees Celsius = 37.777777777777779
Hit Enter to terminate...
```

Examining the limitations of floating point variables

You might be tempted to just use floating point variables all the time because they solve the truncation problem so nicely. Sure, they use up a bit more memory, but memory is cheap these days, so why not? Floating point variables have limitations as well as advantages when compared with integer variables.

Counting

You cannot use floating point variables where the ability to count is important. The problem is that floating point numbers are often not exactly even.

For example, 12.5 might be represented as 12.500001. For most people, that little extra bit (no pun intended) on the end is of little consequence. However, as I point out in Session 1, the computer takes things extremely literally. To C#, 12.500000 and 12.500001 are not the same at all.

Thus, if you add 1.0 to 1.0, you can't tell if the result is 2.0 or 2.000001. C# avoids the problem by restricting counting to those types shown in Table 2-1.

Calculation speed

It used to be that a processor such as the x86 varieties used in Windows-based PCs could perform integer arithmetic much faster than arithmetic of the floating point persuasion. In those days, a programmer would go out of her way to limit a program to integer arithmetic.

The difference in addition speed on my Pentium III processor on my simple (perhaps too simple) test of about 300,000,000 additions and subtractions carefully chosen to avoid cache effects was about 3 to 1. That is to say, for every `double` addition performed, I could have done 3 `int` additions. (Computations involving multiplications and divisions may show different results.)

Not so limited range

It was also the case at one time that a floating point variable could represent a considerably larger range of numbers than an integer type. It still can, but the range of the `long` is large enough to render the point moot.

Even though a simple `float` can represent a very large number, let me reiterate that the number of significant digits is limited. Thus, 123,456,789F is the same as 123,456,000F.

Combining Integers and Fractions into Decimals

As you have seen, both the integer and floating point types have their problems. What you really want is a variable type that

**10 Min.
To Go**

- Acts like a floating point in that it can store fractions

- Acts like an integer in that computations are exact: 12.5 is really 12.5 and not 12.500001

Fortunately for us, C# provides such a variable type called decimal. decimal variables can represent any number between 10^{28} and 10^{-28} — that's a lot of zeros!

Using decimal to calculate interest

Here's a new program to demonstrate the decimal variable type. (I'm getting tired of converting temperatures, so let's perform a currency calculation.)

The choice of currency was not random. The decimal **variable type has a number of uses, including in the banking industry, where rounding off can cause real problems.**

The following CalculateInterest program inputs a principal followed by the interest and then calculates the total of the principal plus the interest.

Session 3 contains CalculateInterestTable, **a much more useful version of this program.**

```
// CalculateInterest - calculate the interest amount
//                     paid on a given principal.
//                     A much more useful version appears
//                     in CalculateInterestTable

namespace CalculateInterest
{
    using System;

    public class Class1
    {
        public static int Main(string[] args)
        {
            // prompt user to enter source principal
            Console.Write("Enter principal:");
            string sPrincipal = Console.ReadLine();
            decimal mPrincipal = decimal.Parse(sPrincipal);

            // enter the interest rate
            Console.Write("Enter interest:");
            string sInterest = Console.ReadLine();
            decimal mInterest = decimal.Parse(sInterest);

            // calculate the value of the principal
            // plus interest
            decimal mInterestPaid;
```

```
        mInterestPaid = mPrincipal * (mInterest / 100);

        // now calculate the total
        decimal mTotal = mPrincipal + mInterestPaid;

        // output the result
        Console.WriteLine();  // skip a line
        Console.WriteLine("Principal    = " + mPrincipal);
        Console.WriteLine("Interest     = " + mInterest
                          + "%");
        Console.WriteLine();
        Console.WriteLine("Interest paid = "
                          + mInterestPaid);
        Console.WriteLine("Total        = " + mTotal);

        // wait for user to acknowledge the results
        Console.WriteLine("Hit Enter to terminate...");
        Console.Read();
        return 0;
      }
    }
  }
```

CalculateInterest begins by prompting the user for the principal and interest of a bank loan (presumably). It then calculates the interest amount by multiplying the interest times the principal (remember that 10 percent interest is really 0.10, because *percentage* means "divide by one hundred"). Finally, the total paid is the sum of the original principal plus the interest.

On output, the statement Console.WriteLine() with no arguments simply writes a blank line in order to divide sections of output.

The following shows the results for a sample execution of the program:

```
Enter principal:1234
Enter interest:12.5

Principal    = 1234
Interest     = 12.5%

Interest paid = 154.25
Total        = 1388.25
Hit Enter to terminate...
```

Comparing decimals with integers and floating point types

It would seem that the decimal variable type has all of the advantages and none of the disadvantages of both ints and doubles. decimal variables have a very large range, they don't suffer from round-off problems, and 25.0 is 25.0 and not 25.00001.

The decimal variable type has two significant limitations, however. First, a decimal is not considered a counting number, because it may contain a fractional value. This becomes important in Session 4.

The second problem with `decimal` variables is equally (or more) serious. Computations involving `decimal` values are significantly slower than those involving either simple integer or floating point values. On my crude benchmark test of 300,000,000 additions and subtractions, the operations involving `decimal` variables were some 50 times slower than those involving simple `int` variables. I suspect that the relative computational speed gets even worse for more complex operations. Also, most computational functions such as calculating sines and exponents are not available for the `decimal` number type.

It is clear that the `decimal` variable type is most applicable in applications such as banking where accuracy is extremely important but where the actual number of calculations is relatively small.

Numeric Constants

There are very few absolutes in life; however, I'm about to give you a C# absolute: *Every expression has a value and a type.*

It's easy to see that in a declaration such as `int n` the variable n is an `int`. Further, it's reasonable to assume that the type of a calculation n + 1 is an `int`. However, what type is the constant 1?

The type of a constant depends on two things: its value and the presence of an optional descriptor letter at the end of the constant. Any integer type less than 2 billion is assumed to be an `int`. Numbers larger than 2 billion are assumed to be a `long`. Any floating point number is assumed to be a `double`.

Table 2-3 demonstrates constants that have been *declared* to be of a particular type. The case of these descriptors is not important. Thus, 1U and 1u are equivalent.

Table 2-3	*Types of Constants Declared Using Suffixes*
Constant	**Type**
1	int
1U	unsigned int
1 L	long
1 UL	unsigned long
1.0	double
1.0F	float
1M	decimal

Changing Types

Humans don't usually treat different types of counting numbers differently. A normal person (as distinguished from a geek) doesn't think about the number 1 as being signed, unsigned, short, or long.

Although C# does consider these types to be different, even C# realizes that there is a relationship among them. For example, the following is allowed:

```
int nValue = 10;
long lValue;
lValue = nValue;  // this is OK
```

An int variable can be converted into a long because no value of an int can't be stored in a long. C# makes the conversion for you automatically.

A conversion in the opposite direction can cause problems, however. For example, the following is illegal:

```
long lValue= 10;
int nValue;
nValue = lValue;  // this is illegal
```

The problem is that there are values which can be stored in a long but which do not fit in an int (4 billion, for example). C# generates an error in such a case. C# cannot make the conversion because data may be lost during the conversion, resulting in a very subtle bug.

But what if you know that the conversion is okay — even though lValue is a long, its value can't be greater than 100 in this particular program (for example). In that case, converting the long variable lValue into the int variable nValue would be perfectly okay.

You can tell C# that you know what you're doing by means of what is known as a *cast*.

```
long lValue= 10;
int nValue;
nValue = (int)lValue;  // this is now OK
```

A *cast* is the name of the type that you want contained in parentheses and placed immediately in front of the value you want to convert. This cast says "go ahead and convert the long lValue into an int — I know what I'm doing."

Casts can also be applied to convert a floating point number into a counting number:

```
double dValue = 10.0;
long lValue = (long)dValue;
```

In fact, all numeric types can be converted into all other numeric types through the application of a cast.

Done!

REVIEW

C# programs are based on data stored in individual locations called variables. The most common variable type is the int (integer) type. int variables are ideal for counting applications but cannot be used to represent fractions. The double type can handle fractional values with extreme precision but cannot be used for counting purposes. The decimal variable type combines many of the advantages of int and double variables; however, arithmetic involving decimal values takes the computer a long time to perform ("long" here is relative). Finally, variables, constants, and arithmetic expressions all have a type in addition to their value. A constant 1 is either an int (1), a double (1.0), or a decimal (1M), to name a few.

QUIZ YOURSELF

1. What does the WriteLine() command do? What is the difference between Write() and WriteLine()? (See "The Fahrenheit to Celsius Conversion Program.")

2. What is the potential problem using an integer variable when converting a Fahrenheit temperature into Celsius? (See "Demonstrating the limitations common to all integer types.")

3. What one absolute statement can you make about all C# expressions? (See "Numeric Constants.")

4. Can one type of variable be converted into another? How? (See "Changing Types.")

Controlling Program Flow

Session Checklist

✔ Making decisions "if" I can

✔ Deciding what "else" to do

✔ Performing arithmetic with TRUE and FALSE values

**30 Min.
To Go**

Session 2 demonstrated how a program can take user input, do some set of operations, and spit the results back out to the user. With no way to control what the program does based upon user input, these programs are necessarily fairly trivial. What we need is the ability to branch control down a different path when certain conditions are met.

Making Decisions in the World

You make literally thousands of decisions as you move through even a single day. You put on a sweater if the temperature is cool or put on a coat if it's really cold. You stop if the light is red and go when it's green (and go really fast when it's yellow).

We need that same capability in our C# program if we are to create useful programs.

The basis of all C# decisions is the if statement:

```
if (some comparison)
{
    // ...do something...
}
// control passes to this statement whether the comparison
// is true or not
```

A pair of parentheses immediately following the keyword contains some comparison. Immediately following the comparison parentheses is a block of code set off by a pair of braces. If the comparison turns out to be true, then the program executes the code within the braces. If the comparison turns out to be untrue, then the program jumps to the statement immediately following the closed brace.

The statement is more easy to understand with a concrete example.

```
// make sure that a is not negative:
// if a is less than 0...
if (a < 0)
{
    // ...then set a to 0
    a = 0;
}
```

This segment of code makes sure that the variable a is greater than or equal to zero. The statement says "if a is less than 0 then assign 0 to a."

Technically the braces are not required. if(comparison) statement; **is treated exactly as if it had been written** if(comparison) {statement;}. **General consensus and my preference are to always use braces, which adheres to good programming standards.**

Table 3-1 shows the comparison operators that are defined in C#.

Table 3-1 *Logical Comparison Operators*

Operator	Result Is True If...
a == b	a has the same value as b
a > b	a is greater than b
a >= b	a is greater than or equal to b
a < b	a is less than b
a <= b	a is less than or equal to b
a != b	a is not equal to b

20 Min. To Go

CalculateInterestWithTest

You can use the if statement to make a small improvement to the CalculateInterest program that you created in Session 2. That program accepted as valid input whatever the user gave it. In general, such blind acceptance is a bad idea. You know that neither the principal nor the interest rate can be negative. So, you can add a test to make sure that the user hasn't entered a bad value:

```
// CalculateInterestWithTest -
//              calculate the interest amount
//              paid on a given principal. If either
//              the principal or the interest rate is
```

```csharp
//               negative, then generate an error message.
namespace CalculateInterestWithTest
{
  using System;

  public class Class1
  {
    public static int Main(string[] args)
    {
      // prompt user to enter source principal
      Console.Write("Enter principal:");
      string sPrincipal = Console.ReadLine();
      decimal mPrincipal = decimal.Parse(sPrincipal);

      // make sure that the principal is not negative
      if (mPrincipal < 0)
      {
        Console.WriteLine("Principal cannot be negative");
        mPrincipal = 0;
      }

      // enter the interest rate
      Console.Write("Enter interest:");
      string sInterest = Console.ReadLine();
      decimal mInterest = decimal.Parse(sInterest);

      // make sure that the interest is not negative either
      if (mInterest < 0)
      {
        Console.WriteLine("Interest cannot be negative");
        mInterest = 0;
      }

      // calculate the value of the principal
      // plus interest
      decimal mInterestPaid;
      mInterestPaid = mPrincipal * (mInterest / 100);

      // now calculate the total
      decimal mTotal = mPrincipal + mInterestPaid;

      // output the result
      Console.WriteLine();  // skip a line
      Console.WriteLine("Principal    = "
                         + mPrincipal);
      Console.WriteLine("Interest     = "
                         + mInterest + "%");
      Console.WriteLine();
      Console.WriteLine("Interest paid = "
                         + mInterestPaid);
      Console.WriteLine("Total         = " + mTotal);
```

```
        // wait for user to acknowledge the results
        Console.WriteLine("Hit Enter to terminate...");
        Console.Read();
        return 0;
    }
  }
}
```

This version calculates interest to be paid in the same way as the earlier CalculateInterest program. The only difference here is that if the user mistakenly enters a negative value for either the principal or the interest, the program generates an error message and sets the corresponding value to zero. (Setting a variable to a valid value ensures that problems won't arise during calculations that follow in the program.) Problems you may encounter include division by zero and arithmetic overflow exceptions.

 The complete CalculateInterestWithTest **program can be found on the CD.**

 I cover exceptions in Session 25.

Executing the program with illegal input generates the following:

```
Enter principal:1234
Enter interest:-12.5
Interest cannot be negative

Principal    = 1234
Interest     = 0%

Interest paid = 0
Total        = 1234
Hit Enter to terminate...
```

What else can I do?

if statements are required to implement a number of arithmetic functions. For example, the following code segment stores the greater of two numbers a and b in the variable max:

```
int max;
// if a is greater than b...
if (a > b)
{
    // ...save off a as the maximum
    max = a;
}

// if a is less than or equal to b...
if (a <= b)
```

```
{
    // ...save off b as the maximum
    max = b;
}
```

The second statement is unnecessary because the two conditions are mutually exclusive. The else keyword defines a block of code that is executed if the block is not.

The code segment to calculate the maximum now appears as follows:

```
int max;
// if a is greater than b...
if (a > b)
{
    // ...save off a as the maximum; otherwise...
    max = a;
}
else
{
    // ...save off b as the maximum
    max = b;
}
```

If a is greater than b, then the first block is executed; otherwise, the second is executed.

Embedded if statements

The CalculateInterestWithTest program is a distinct improvement over the original CalculateInterest because it warns the user of illegal input; however, continuing with the interest calculation even if one of the values is illegal doesn't seem quite right. It causes no real harm here, because the interest calculation takes little or no time, but some calculations are not nearly so quick. In addition, why ask the user for an interest rate after she has already entered an invalid value for the principal? Obviously (to us if not to her), the results of the calculation will be invalid no matter what she enters next.

What would be better is for the program to perform the interest calculation only if both values are correct. This will require two statements, one within the other.

 A statement found within the body of another statement is called an embedded statement.

The following subsection of the program CalculateInterestWithEmbeddedTest uses embedded statements to exit the program as soon as a problem with the input has been detected.

```
public static int Main(string[] args)
{
    // prompt user to enter source principal
    Console.Write("Enter principal:");
    string sPrincipal = Console.ReadLine();
    decimal mPrincipal = decimal.Parse(sPrincipal);
```

```csharp
      // if the principal is negative...
      if (mPrincipal < 0)
      {
        //...generate an error message...
        Console.WriteLine("Principal cannot be negative");
      }
      else
      {
        // ...otherwise, enter the interest rate
        Console.Write("Enter interest:");
        string sInterest = Console.ReadLine();
        decimal mInterest = decimal.Parse(sInterest);

        // if the interest is negative...
        if (mInterest < 0)
        {
          // ...generate an error message as well
          Console.WriteLine("Interest cannot be negative");
          mInterest = 0;
        }
        else
        {
          // both the principal and the interest appear to be
          // legal; calculate the value of the principal
          // plus interest
          decimal mInterestPaid;
          mInterestPaid = mPrincipal * (mInterest / 100);

          // now calculate the total
          decimal mTotal = mPrincipal + mInterestPaid;

          // output the result
          Console.WriteLine();  // skip a line
          Console.WriteLine("Principal    = "
                          + mPrincipal);
          Console.WriteLine("Interest     = "
                          + mInterest + "%");
          Console.WriteLine();
          Console.WriteLine("Interest paid = "
                          + mInterestPaid);
          Console.WriteLine("Total         = " + mTotal);
        }
      }
      // wait for user to acknowledge the results
      Console.WriteLine("Hit Enter to terminate...");
      Console.Read();
      return 0;
    }
```

The complete `CalculateInterestWithEmbeddedTest` **program can be found on the CD.**

The program first reads the principal, as in earlier versions. If the principal is negative, the program outputs an error message. Only if the principal is not negative (greater than or equal to zero) does the program continue by asking for the interest rate. Only if this number is non-negative does the program calculate the interest payment.

Examples of the three cases are shown here. First, entering a negative principal results in the following output:

```
Enter principal:-1234
Principal cannot be negative
Hit Enter to terminate...
```

Second, entering a correct principal but a negative interest rate generates the following:

```
Enter principal:1234
Enter interest:-12.5
Interest cannot be negative
Hit Enter to terminate...
```

Only by entering both a legal principal and a legal interest rate do I see the desired calculation:

```
Enter principal:1234
Enter interest:12.5

Principal     = 1234
Interest      = 12.5%

Interest paid = 154.25
Total         = 1388.25
Hit Enter to terminate...
```

Indenting code for readability

An `if` statement does not cause the source code to indent. Indenting is added by the programmer to make the programs easier to read. I prefer two spaces per indention.

**10 Min.
To Go**

Most programming editors support auto indenting whereby the editor automatically indents as soon as one enters the command. If you are using one of the Visual Studio editors, select Tools ⇨ Options. Now select the Text Editor folder. From there select C# ⇨ General. Finally, click on Tabs. On this page you will want to enable Smart Indenting and set the number of spaces per indent.

You can see that with all that indenting going on, programs of more than modest complexity can spread completely across the page from left to right even with only two spaces per level of indentation. In later sessions you will see a number of ways to avoid this problem.

Performing Boolean Arithmetic

Table 3-1 lists the operators that can be used in a conditional statement. However, remember that every expression in C# has a value and a type. The value of an operator is True or False, but what's the type? It turns out that the type of a comparison expression is called bool.

The term bool **refers to Boolean, which is the calculus of logic first described by the mathematician George Boole in the nineteenth century.**

You can declare a variable of type bool as follows:

```
bool bContinue;
bContinue = nYear < nDuration;
// ...later on...
while (bContinue)
{
    // ...continue on, but somewhere you need to recalculate
    // bContinue or else the while loop is infinite
}
```

I'll cover loops in Session 4, including the above-mentioned while **keyword.**

When the expression nYear < nDuration is evaluated, it has a value of either (True or False) which is of type (bool), and is assigned to the variable bContinue. This Boolean value can be used later as a conditional. The while loop executes as long as the variable bContinue contains a True.

There are two other Boolean operators: the compound AND (&&) and the compound OR (||). These operators work as follows:

```
if ((a < b) && (c < d))
{
    // ...execute if both a is less than b and c is less than d
}
```

Thus, the body of the statement is executed only if both conditions are true. Similarly:

```
if ((m < n) || (o < p))
{
    // ...execute if either m is less than n or o is less than p
    // or both
}
```

Variable naming

What's with all this nYear and bContinue? What's with the funny letter on the front? Many programmers (including me) prefer to prepend a letter to the variable name that indicates the type of the variable. Thus, anywhere within the code that I see nYear, I automatically know that nYear is of type int. Similarly, dValue is a double. This can help detect common errors. For example, if I say dValue = nYear I know that I'm converting an int into a double. Did I really mean to do that or is something wrong here?

Microsoft first started this practice back in the early C++ days. They called it Hungarian notation because it was started by a programmer of Hungarian descent. Microsoft has since stopped using Hungarian notation, but some of us continue the practice.

Hungarian notation is not as important as it once was if your compiler generates a warning when you mix incompatible variable types in a single expression. (Visual Studio .NET does generate mixed expression warnings.) However, compilers are generally silent about conversions that they consider to be "safe," such as assigning a short to an int. I still prefer to see all mixed mode expressions as I'm actually writing code, so I stick with Hungarian notation.

If a **is not less than** b, **then it doesn't really matter whether** c **is less than** d **or not — either way, the result is still** False. **Because of this, C# takes a shortcut: If** a **is not less than** b, **then C# does not even perform the second expression. Similarly, if** m **is less than** n, **then the OR expression is** True **no matter what** o **and** p **are, so why bother calculating them? This is called** *short circuit* **evaluation.**

For instance, in the following example we want to make sure that m < n AND o < p, so that the program will print out that we are a genuis. Failure of this if statement means that we are not a genuis.

```
if ((m < n) || (o < p))
{
    // ...execute if either m is less than n or o is less than p
    // or both
    Console.WriteLine("I am a genius");
}
else
{
    Console.WriteLine("I am not a genius!");
}
```

Done!

REVIEW

Programs adapt to users' wishes by making internal decisions. The C# language provides the statement, optionally followed by else, to allow a program to branch depending upon a conditional expression: True and the program takes one path, False and it takes another.

QUIZ YOURSELF

1. What control command is optional on the end of an if statement? (See "Making Decisions in the World.")

2. From a programmer's perspective, what are the positive and negative effects of indenting embedded clauses? (See "Indenting code for readability.")

3. What is a Boolean? What are the legal values of a bool variable? Name two operators that are legal for a bool variable. (See "Performing Boolean Arithmetic.")

4. Why do int variable names in this book start with an "n"? (See the "Variable naming" sidebar.)

SESSION

4

Program Loops

Session Checklist

✔ Looping through the same code

✔ Investigating scope rules

**30 Min.
To Go**

The if statement demonstrated in Session 3 allows the C# program to react to the user (or other) input during program execution. However, the CalculateInterest program is of only passing interest. It would be much easier to perform this simple interest calculation with a calculator or by hand on a piece of paper than it would be to find and execute a program to perform it.

What if we could calculate the amount of principal for each of a number of succeeding years? That would be more interesting. It would be easier to enter values into a C# program than to perform that type of compound arithmetic with a calculator.

Looping Commands

We need some type of loop command in order to repetitively perform an action such as calculating the interest for each successive year.

while

The C# keyword while introduces an execution loop:

```
while(comparison)
{
    // ...series of commands...
}
```

The series of commands within the braces is executed over and over as long as the comparison within the parentheses is true.

To be more specific, the comparison operation is performed. If the condition is true, then the code within the block is executed. Once the block of code has been executed, control returns back to the top and the whole process starts over again.

If the condition is not true the first time the while loop is encountered, then the series of commands is never executed.

We can use the while loop to repetitively perform the foregoing interest computation, resulting in a table of interest values, one for each year as shown in the following CalculateInterestTable program (the while loop section has been bolded here):

```
// CalculateInterestTable - calculate the interest
//            paid on a given principle over a period
//            of years
namespace CalculateInterestTable
{
  using System;

  public class Class1
    {
    public static int Main(string[] args)
    {
      // prompt user to enter source principal
      Console.Write("Enter principal:");
      string sPrincipal = Console.ReadLine();
      decimal mPrincipal = decimal.Parse(sPrincipal);

      // if the principal is negative...
      if (mPrincipal < 0)
      {
        //...generate an error message...
        Console.WriteLine("Principal cannot be negative");
      }
      else
      {
        // ...otherwise, enter the interest rate
        Console.Write("Enter interest:");
        string sInterest = Console.ReadLine();
        decimal mInterest = decimal.Parse(sInterest);
        // if the interest is negative...
        if (mInterest < 0)
        {
          // ...generate an error message as well
          Console.WriteLine("Interest cannot be negative");
          mInterest = 0;
        }
        else
        {
          // both the principal and the interest appear to be
          // legal; finally, input the number of years
```

```csharp
        Console.Write("Enter number of years:");
        string sDuration = Console.ReadLine();
        int nDuration = Int32.Parse(sDuration);

        // verify the input
        Console.WriteLine();   // skip a line
        Console.WriteLine("Principal    = "
                        + mPrincipal);
        Console.WriteLine("Interest     = "
                        + mInterest + "%");
        Console.WriteLine("Duration     = "
                        + nDuration + "years");
        Console.WriteLine();


        // now loop through the specified number of years
        int nYear = 1;
        while(nYear <= nDuration)
        {
          // calculate the value of the principal
          // plus interest
          decimal mInterestPaid;
          mInterestPaid = mPrincipal * (mInterest / 100);

          // now calculate the new principal by adding
          // the interest to the previous principal
          mPrincipal = mPrincipal + mInterestPaid;

          // round off the principal to the nearest cent
          mPrincipal = decimal.Round(mPrincipal, 2);

          // output the result
          Console.WriteLine(nYear + "-" + mPrincipal);

          // skip over to next year
          nYear = nYear + 1;
        }
      }
    }
    // wait for user to acknowledge the results
    Console.WriteLine("Hit Enter to terminate...");
    Console.Read();
    return 0;
    }
  }
}
```

The entire version of the `CalculateInterestTable` **program can be found on the CD.**

The output from a trial run of CalculateInterestTable appears as follows:

```
Enter principal:1234
Enter interest:12.5
Enter number of years:10

Principal    = 1234
Interest     = 12.5%
Duration     = 10years

1-1388.25
2-1561.78
3-1757
4-1976.62
5-2223.7
6-2501.66
7-2814.37
8-3166.17
9-3561.94
10-4007.18
Hit Enter to terminate...
```

Each value represents the total principal after the number of years elapsed. For example, the value of $1,234.00 at 12.5 percent compounded annually is $3,561.94 after nine years.

Most of the values show two decimal places for the cents in the amount. Because trailing zeros are not displayed, some values show only a single or even no digit after the decimal point. Thus, $12.70 is displayed as 12.7.

The CalculateInterestTable program begins by reading the principal and interest values from the user. Unlike its predecessors, CalculateInterestTable also prompts for the number of years over which to iterate.

Before entering the while loop, the program declares a variable nYear that it initializes to 1. This will be the "current year" — this number will change "each year" as we loop. If the year number contained in nYear is less than the total duration contained in nDuration, then the principal for "this year" is recalculated by calculating the interest based on the "previous year." The calculated principal is output along with the current year offset.

The statement decimal.Round() **rounds off the calculated value to the nearest fraction of a cent.**

The key to the program lies in the last line within the block. The statement nYear = nYear + 1; increments the nYear by 1. Thus, if nYear begins with the value 3, its value will be 4 after this expression. This incrementing moves us along from year to year.

Once the year has been incremented, control returns to the top of the loop, where the value nYear is compared with the requested duration. If the current year is less than 10, the calculation continues. After being incremented 10 times, the value of nYear becomes 11, which is greater than 10, causing the loop to terminate; and then program control passes to the first statement after the while loop. The program stops looping.

The counting variable nYear **has to be declared and initialized before the actual** while **loop (in other words, do not declare the variable inside the loop). In addition, the** nYear **variable must be incremented generally as the last statement within the loop. This means you have to look ahead to see what variables you will need. This pattern is easier once you have written a few thousand** while **loops, as I have.**

For a number of reasons, you cannot declare nYear within the loop itself as shown in the following example:

```
while (nYear < 10)
{
    int nYear = 1;
    // ...whatever...

    nYear = nYear + 1;
}
```

The main problem is that nYear is not declared when it is first used in the condition statement nYear < 10. A second problem is that the variable nYear is re-created and re-initialized to 1 after every loop so that it never increases.

It is a common mistake to forget to increment the counting variable. In this case, had I left off the statement nYear = nYear + 1; then nYear would always be 1 and the program would loop "forever." This is called an infinite loop. The only way to exit an infinite loop is to terminate the program (or reboot). Infinite loops are very common, so don't be embarrassed if you get caught in one.

do...while

One small variation is the do...while loop. In this case, the condition is not checked until the end of the loop.

```
int nYear = 1;
do
{
    // ...some calculation...
    nYear = nYear + 1;
} while (nYear < nDuration);
```

The primary difference is that the do...while loop is executed at least once no matter what the value of nDuration is. In practice, the do...while loop is fairly uncommon.

10 Min.
To Go

Scope Rules

One last point to make about looping commands before I move on. A pair of open and closed braces constitutes what is known as a block of code. The code contained within that block is somewhat separated from the surrounding code. For example, any variable contained within that block is accessible only to other statements within the block. This is easier to explain by example:

```
int n = 1;
{
  int m = 0;

  // code contained within this block has access to both
  // n and m, however...
  m = m + n;
}

// ...the following is illegal since m is only known
// within the block
m = m + n;
```

This segment begins by declaring the variable n, which it initializes to 1. The segment then goes on to define a new block. The first statement within the block defines a new variable m. The following addition makes use of both variables.

Once the program exits the block (that is, continues executing beyond the closed brace), the variable m no longer exists — it simply goes away. If the program were to somehow reenter the block, however, m would be redefined and reinitialized to our favorite value of 0.

The braces following a control such as an if or a while also form a block. A variable declared within this block is accessible only from within the while loop. Thus, the following example borrowed from Session 3 is illegal:

```
// determine the larger of two variables m and n
if (n > m)
{
  int nMax = n;
}
else
{
  int nMax = m;
}

// the following doesn't compile because nMax
// isn't accessible outside of the while block
Console.WriteLine("The greater value is " + nMax);
```

The problem is that nMax is declared within the if block. By the time the program reaches the WriteLine, nMax is no longer defined. The following version, which defines nMax outside of the if blocks, works as expected:

```
// determine the larger of two variables m and n
// (define nMax outside of the blocks
int nMax;
if (n > m)
{
  nMax = n;
}
```

```
else
{
  nMax = m;
}

// the following works as expected
Console.WriteLine("The greater value is " + nMax);
```

Defining a variable within a `while` block introduces a second type of problem, as the following code segment demonstrates:

```
// count the number of attempts to do something
int nTries = 1;
int nMaxTries = 10;

while(nTries < nMaxTries)
{
  // define a counter and increment it
  int nCount = 0;
  nCount = nCount + 1;

  // perform some undefinined operation...

  // now output the result along with the counter
  Console.WriteLine(nCount);

  nTries = nTries + 1;
}
```

Rather than display an incrementing value, the program segment outputs the number 1 over and over. On each iteration of the `while` loop, the program exits and then reenters the block. The program re-creates and reinitializes nCount on every pass.

Done!

REVIEW

Just as important as the ability to branch the flow of program execution is the related capability of a program to loop through a section of code until some condition is satisfied. A program can process checks until there are none left without knowing how many checks there are or calculate interest for *N* number of years where *N* is provided by the user at runtime.

QUIZ YOURSELF

1. Name the loops that can be used in C# programming? (See "Looping Commands.")
2. What are the two special controls that can be used in loops? What are they used for? (See "Special Controls.")
3. What do we mean by the scope of a variable? (See "Scope Rules.")

PART

I

Friday Evening
Part Review

1. The C# compiler can generate warnings for minor infractions instead of error messages. Why is it not a good idea to continue programming without "fixing" program warnings?

2. Why do good programmers include comments in front of each major block of code? Why do I prefer to include comments as I write a program rather than wait until the code already works?

3. Declare an integer variable nVar1 and a floating point variable var2.

4. What is the difference between an integer and a floating point? Cite a typical use for an integer variable and one for a floating point.

5. Write a small program ConvertFeet.cs that reads a length entered by the user at the console and converts it from feet into meters (assume that a meter is 3.3 feet — that's close enough).

6. What is the type of expression within a control — that is, what is the type of x in the statement if(x)?

7. Write a function double Abs(double) that returns the absolute value of the input variable.

8. What does the following function do?
```
bool IsEven(double x)
{
    double dHalf = x / 2;
    double dModulo = dHalf - (int)dHalf;
    return (dModulo == 0.0)
}
```

9. Why is it dangerous to use the equality operator == when comparing a double variable with a specific value?

10. Use the Abs() function you wrote in Problem 7 to write a safe comparison function IsEven().

11. Write a function CountTo10() that displays the integers 1 through 10.

12. Why is the following function an infinite loop even though dValue is sometimes odd within the loop?

```
void CountUntilOdd()
{
  double dValue = 0;
  while(IsEven(dValue))
  {
    Console.Write("x = " + dValue);
    dValue = dValue + 1.0;
    Console.WriteLine(" and then " + dValue);
    dValue = dValue + 1.0;
  }
}
```

13. What is the main difference between:

```
while(condition)
{
  Calculation();
}
```
            and
```
do
{
  Calculation();
} while(condition);
```

☑ Friday

☑ **Saturday**

☐ Sunday

PART

II

Saturday Morning

Common Operations

Session Checklist

✔ The most common looping command of all: the for loop

✔ Investigating a few other arithmetic operators

**30 Min.
To Go**

Yesterday you learned the very basics of C# programming, including the famous while loop. This session eases you back into the water by examining the rest of the control commands. The remaining sessions in this book make use of these common operations.

The for Loop

Session 4 introduced you to the concepts of branching and of looping. The while loop is the simplest and second most commonly used looping structure in C#. However, a looping structure known as the for loop is actually more common.

The for loop has the following structure:

```
for(initExpression; condition; incrementExpression)
{
    //...body of code...
}
```

When the program encounters the for loop, it first executes the initExpression expression. It then executes the condition. If the condition expression is true, then the program executes the body of the loop, which is surrounded by the braces immediately following the for command. Upon reaching the closed brace, control then passes to incrementExpression and then back to condition where the loop starts over again.

You can better see how the for loop works with an example:

```
a = 1;  // totally unrelated
for(int nYear = 1; nYear < nDuration; nYear = nYear + 1)
{
    // ...body of code...
}
a = 2;
```

Suppose that the program has just executed the a = 1; expression. Next the program would declare the variable nYear and initialize it to 1. That done, the program compares nYear with nDuration. If nYear is less than nDuration, the body of code within the braces is executed. Upon encountering the closed brace, the program executes the nYear = nYear + 1 clause before returning to the nYear < nDuration comparison.

This should look a lot like the while **loop that we built in Session 4. In fact, the definition of a** for **loop can be converted into the following** while **loop:**

```
initExpression;
while(condition)
{
    // ...body of code...

    incrementExpression;

}
```

Why do you need another loop?

So if there is an equivalent while loop, then why have the for loop at all? Generally, the sections of the for loop are there for convenience and to containerize the three parts that every loop should have: the setup, the conditional, and the increment. Not only is this easier to read, but it's also easier to get right. (Remember that the most common mistake in a while loop is forgetting to increment the counting variable.)

The for **loop is designed so that the first expression initializes a counting variable, and the last section increments it; however, the C# language does not enforce any such rule. The programmer can do anything she wants in these two sections — she would be ill advised to do anything but initialize and increment the counting variable, however.**

The increment operator

Notice how you've used the expression n = n + 1 on multiple occasions already and you've written only four programs. C# provides an increment operator that does nothing more than increment its argument by 1. Thus

```
int n = 5;  // declare and initialize n
n++;        // now increment it; equivalent to n = n + 1
            // at this point in the program, n is equal to 6
```

The increment operator is particularly convenient in a for loop:

```
for(int nYear = 1; nYear < nDuration; nYear++)
{
    // ...body of code...
}
```

In fact, the increment operator appears most often in for loops.

Pre- and post-increment

**20 Min.
To Go**

Believe it or not, there are actually two increment operators: *++n* and n++. The difference is subtle but important. Remember that every expression has a type and a value. In the following segment

```
int n = 1;
int m = n++;
```

clearly the type of the n++ expression is int; however, what is the value? That is to say, what is the resulting value of m? (Hint: The choices are 1 and 2.)

It turns out that in this case the value of m is 1. That is to say, the value of the expression n++ is the value of n before it is incremented. n++ is called the *post-increment* operator.

Either way, the value of n is 2 once the n++ expression has executed.

C# also provides operator *++n*, called the *pre-increment* operator. If we try the same trick with this operator we get different results:

```
int n = 1;
int m = ++n;
```

Now the value of m is 2, the value of n after it has been incremented.

Pre- and post-decrement

C# provides a pair of decrement operators corresponding to the increment operators but in the opposite direction. In the following code segment the value of m is 1 while the value of n is 0.

```
int n = 1;
int m = n-;
```

Here the value of m is 0. The value of n is 0, just as it was before.

```
n = 1;
int m = -n;
```

Special controls

Two special controls can be used within a loop: break and continue. Executing the break command causes control to pass outside of the current loop, whereas continue passes control back immediately to the while.

The break control

The following program BreakDemo demonstrates a use of the *break*. BreakDemo asks the user to input a value. It then returns the inverse of that value and asks again. The program terminates when the user enters a negative number. (It also exits if the user enters zero because we wouldn't want to take the inverse of zero!)

```
// BreakDemo - demonstrate the use of the break statement
namespace BreakDemo
{
  using System;

  public class Class1
  {
    public static int Main(string[] args)
    {
      // input a sequence of values
      Console.WriteLine("Enter a sequence of numbers");
      Console.WriteLine("The program outputs the inverse");
      Console.WriteLine("(Enter a negative number to exit)");
      while(true)
      {
        // read in another number
        Console.Write("Next value:");
        string s = Console.ReadLine();
        double d = Double.Parse(s);

        // exit if number is negative
        if (d <= 0.0)
        {
          break;
        }

        // output the inverse
        double dInverse = 1.0 / d;
        Console.WriteLine("Inverse is = " + dInverse);
      }

      // wait for user to acknowledge the results
      Console.WriteLine("Hit Enter to terminate...");
      Console.Read();
      return 0;
    }
  }
}
```

The entire version of the BreakDemo **program can be found on the CD.**

The BreakDemo program first explains to the user what's about to happen. It then enters a while(true) loop. This loop would be an infinite loop were it not for the next few lines that input a value from the user and check to see if it's negative. If it is negative, the program executes the break, which exits the loop.

The following is an example of the output from this program:

```
Enter a sequence of numbers
The program outputs the inverse
(Enter a negative number to exit)
Next value:1
Inverse is = 1
Next value:2
Inverse is = 0.5
Next value:3
Inverse is = 0.333333333333333
Next value:0.222
Inverse is = 4.5045045045045
Next value:-1
Hit Enter to terminate...
```

Why break?

The BreakDemo program demonstrates clearly the need for the break control. The problem is that the exit condition is not known at either the beginning or the end of the loop. The user hasn't entered a value at the beginning of the loop. By the time the program reaches the end of the loop, it's too late: The program has already displayed the inverse of the negative number, or, worse yet, it's tried to calculate the inverse of zero. The decision to exit has to be made somewhere within the loop. The break control is just the ticket.

Why have an increment operator, and why two of them?

The reason for the increment operator lies in the obscure fact that the DEC PDP-8 computer of the 1970s had an increment instruction. This would be of little interest today were it not for the fact that the C language, the original precursor to C#, was originally written for the DEC PDP-8. Therefore, because there was an increment instruction, n++ generated fewer machine instructions than n = n + 1. Given how slow those machine were, saving a few machine instructions was a big deal.

Today, our compilers are smarter and there is no difference in the time it takes to execute n++ and n = n + 1, so the need for the increment operator has gone away; however, programmers are creatures of habit and the operator remains to this day. You will almost never see a programmer increment a value in a loop using the longer but more intuitive n = n + 1. You will always see the increment operator.

Further, you will almost always see the post-increment operator instead of the pre-increment operator, though the effect in this case is the same. There's no reason other than fashion and the fact that it looks cooler.

The switch Control

10 Min. To Go

Often there are times when a given variable can have a number of different values. For example, nMaritalStatus (in the next code example) can be 0 for unmarried, 1 for married, 2 for divorced, or 3 for widowed. (I think I got them all.) To differentiate between these values we could use a series of if statements:

```
if (nMaritalStatus == 0)
{
  // must be unmarried
  // ...do something...
}
else
{
  if (nMaritalStatus == 1)
  {
    // must be married
    // ...do something else...

//..and so forth
```

You can see that these repetitive if statements can get old quickly. Not only that, the chain of if statements that indent their way across the page from left to right is difficult to read. Testing for multiple cases is such a common occurrence that C# provides a special construct to decide between a set of mutually exclusive conditions. This construct is called the switch statement:

```
switch(nMaritalStatus)
{
   case 0:
         // ...do the unmarried stuff...
         break;

   case 1:
         // ...do the married stuff...
         break;

   case 2:
         // ...do the divorced stuff...
         break;

   case 3:
         // ...do the widowed stuff...
         break;

   default:
         // goes here if doesn't pass any of the cases
         break;
}
```

The argument to the `switch` statement doesn't have to be a number:

```
string s = "Davis";
switch(s)
{
   case "Davis":
         // ...control will actually pass here...
         break;

   case "Smith":
         // ...do the married stuff...
         break;

   case "Jones":
         // ...do the divorced stuff...
         break;

   case "Hvidsten":
         // ...do the widowed stuff...
         break;
   default:
         // goes here if doesn't pass any of the cases
         break;
}
```

There are some restrictions, of course. The argument to the `switch()` itself may be any type of expression that evaluates to one of the value types. The various `case` values must refer to a value of the same type as the switch expression. In addition, the `case` values must be constant in the sense that their value must be known at compile time.

Value types are `int, long, string,` **and so forth.**

Done!

REVIEW

Though the common C# programming structures reviewed in this session are not fundamental, they can be helpful.

The `while` loop from Session 4 is the most fundamental loop control; however, the `for` loop provides the `while` loop a more convenient format for its most common variation. Added to that are more convenient increment and decrement operators to further streamline the looping business.

Finally, the `switch` statement is a convenient replacement for a set of like `if` statements.

QUIZ YOURSELF

1. What is the most common of all looping constructs? (See "The for loop.")
2. When n starts out as 5, what is the value of n++? (See "Why have an increment operator, and why two of them?")

Working with Arrays

Session Checklist

✔ Defining arrays of values

✔ Using the arrays to perform calculations

✔ Accessing arrays using the foreach construct

✔ Comparing an array of chars with a string

**30 Min.
To Go**

Variables containing single values are all well and good, but there are many occasions when a problem deals with a number of elements.

C# provides the array for storing assemblies of like values.

Introducing Arrays

Consider the problem of averaging a set of ten floating point numbers. Each of the ten numbers requires its own double storage (averaging int variables could result in rounding errors as described in Session 2):

```
double d0 = 5;
double d1 = 2
double d2 = 7
double d3 = 3.5
double d4 = 6.5
double d5 = 8
double d6 = 1
double d7 = 9
double d8 = 1
double d9 = 3
```

You would now need to accumulate each of these values into a common sum that you would then divide by 10 (the number of values):

```
double dSum = d0 + d1 + d2 + d3 + d4 + d5 + d6 + d7 + d8 + d9;
double dAverage = dSum / 10;
```

Listing each element by name is tedious. Maybe not so tedious when there are only 10 numbers to average, but imagine averaging 100 or even 1,000 floating point values.

The fixed-value array

Fortunately, it isn't necessary to name each element separately. C# provides a structure, known as an *array*, that is capable of storing a sequence of values. The previous code segment could be written as follows using an array:

```
double[] dArray = {5,2,7, 3.5, 6.5, 8, 1, 9, 1, 3};
```

The double brackets [] refer to the way individual elements in the array are accessed: dArray[0] corresponds to d0, dArray[1] corresponds to d1, and so on.

This array wouldn't be much of an improvement were it not for the fact that the index of the array can be a variable. Using the following for loop is easier than writing each element out by hand:

```
// FixedArrayAverage - average a fixed array of
//                     numbers using a loop
namespace FixedArrayAverage
{
  using System;

  public class Class1
  {
    public static int Main(string[] args)
    {
      double[] dArray =
              {5, 2, 7, 3.5, 6.5, 8, 1, 9, 1, 3};

      // accumulate the values in the array
      // in the variable dSum
      double dSum = 0;
      for (int i = 0; i < 10; i++)
      {
        dSum = dSum + dArray[i];
      }

      // now calculate the average
      double dAverage = dSum / 10;
      Console.WriteLine(dAverage);
```

```
            // wait for user to acknowledge the results
            Console.WriteLine("Hit Enter to terminate...");
            Console.Read();

            return 0;
        }
    }
}
```

Array bounds checking

The FixedArrayAverage program looped through an array of ten elements. Fortunately, the loop iterated through all ten elements. But what if you had made a mistake and didn't iterate through the loop properly? There are two cases to consider.

What if you had iterated through only nine elements? C# would not have considered this an error — if you want to read only nine elements of a ten-element array, who is C# to say any different? Of course, the average would be incorrect, but the program wouldn't know.

What if you had iterated through 11 (or more) elements? Now C# cares a lot. C# will not allow you to index beyond the end of an array. To test this, change the comparison in the for loop to the following: for(int i = 0; i < 10; i++), replacing the value 10 with 11 in the comparison. When you execute the program, you'll get the following error:

```
Exception occurred: System.IndexOutOfRangeException:
An exception of type System.IndexOutOfRangeException was thrown
at FixedArrayAverage.Class1.Main(String[] args)
in c:\c#\programs\fixedarrayaverage\class1.cs:line 19
```

(I have added newlines to enhance the readability.)

At first glance, this error message seems rather imposing. However, you can get the gist rather quickly: An IndexOutOfRangeException was reported. It's pretty clear that the program is trying to tell you that it tried to access an array beyond the end of its range — accessing element 11 in a ten-element array. (The message goes on to indicate exactly what line the access was made from, but we haven't progressed far enough in the book to understand the entire message completely.)

The error message shown here is generated through a mechanism known as the exception. Exceptions are explained in Session 25 and then amplified further in Chapter 26.

The complete `FixedArrayAverage` **program can be found on the CD.**

The program begins by initializing a variable dSum to 0. The program then loops through the values stored in dArray, adding each one to dSum. By the end of the loop, dSum has accumulated the sum of each of the values in the array. The resulting sum is divided by the number of elements to create the average. The output from executing this program is the expected 4.6. (I checked it with my calculator.)

The variable-length array

The array used in the example program FixedArrayAverage suffers from two serious problems. The size of the array is fixed at ten elements. Worse yet, the value of those ten elements is specified directly in the program.

A program that could read in a variable number of values, perhaps determined by the user during execution, would be much more flexible: Not only would it work for the ten values specified in FixedArrayAverage, it would work for any other set of values as well.

The format for declaring a variable-sized array is slightly different from that for a fixed-size, fixed-value array:

```
double[] dArray = new double[N];
```

where *N* is the number of elements to allocate.

The updated program VariableArrayAverage allows the user to specify the number of values to enter. Because the program retains the values entered, not only does it calculate the average, but it displays the results in a pleasant format.

```
// VariableArrayAverage - average an array whose size is
//                        determined by the user at run time.
//                        Accumulating the values in an array
//                        allows them to be referenced as often
//                        as desired. In this case, the array
//                        creates an attractive output.
namespace VariableArrayAverage
{
  using System;

  public class Class1
  {
    public static int Main(string[] args)
    {
      // first read in the number of doubles
      // the user intends to enter
      Console.Write("Enter the number of values to average:");
      string sNumElements = Console.ReadLine();
      int numElements = Int32.Parse(sNumElements);
      Console.WriteLine();
```

```
    // now declare an array of that size
    double[] dArray = new double[numElements];

    // accumulate the values into an array
    for (int i = 0; i < numElements; i++)
    {
      // prompt the user for another double
      Console.Write("enter double #" + (i + 1) + ": ");
      string sVal = Console.ReadLine();
      double dValue = Double.Parse(sVal);

      // add this to the array
      dArray[i] = dValue;
    }


    // accumulate 'numElements' values from
    // the array in the variable dSum
    double dSum = 0;
    for (int i = 0; i < numElements; i++)
    {
      dSum = dSum + dArray[i];
    }

    // now calculate the average
    double dAverage = dSum / numElements;

    // output the results in an attractive format
    Console.WriteLine();
    Console.Write(dAverage
               + " is the average of ("
               + dArray[0]);
    for (int i = 1; i < numElements; i++)
    {
      Console.Write(" + " + dArray[i]);
    }
    Console.WriteLine(") / " + numElements);

    // wait for user to acknowledge the results
    Console.WriteLine("Hit Enter to terminate...");
    Console.Read();
    return 0;
  }
 }
}
```

The entire version of the VariableArrayAverage **program can be found on the CD.**

Let's look at the output of a sample run in which you enter five sequential values 1 through 5 and the program calculates the average to be 3.

```
Enter the number of values to average:5

enter double #1: 1
enter double #2: 2
enter double #3: 3
enter double #4: 4
enter double #5: 5

3 is the average of (1 + 2 + 3 + 4 + 5) / 5
Hit Enter to terminate...
```

The VariableArrayAverage program begins by prompting the user for the number of values she intends to average. The result is stored in the int variable numElements. In the example, the number entered was 5.

The program continues by allocating an array dArray with the specified number of elements. In this case, the program allocates an array with five elements. The program loops the number of times specified by numElements, reading a new value from the user each time.

Once the values have been entered, the program applies the same algorithm used in the FixedArrayAverage program to calculate the average of the sequence.

The final section generates in an attractive format the output of the average along with the numbers entered. (Attractive to me — beauty is in the eye of the beholder.)

Using parentheses to change the order of evaluation

Notice the (i + 1) in the output string. Consider the case where i is equal to 4. Replacing i with 4 renders the following:

```
Console.Write("enter double #" + 4 + 1 + ": ");
```

This outputs the string

```
enter double #4 + 1:
```

With the parentheses, the expression (i + 1) is evaluated first. In the same case, where i is equal to 4, the expression

```
Console.Write("enter double #" + (4 + 1) + ": ");
```

becomes

```
Console.Write("enter double #" + 5 + ": ");
```

and generates the expected result:

```
enter double #5:
```

It's a little tricky to get display output just right. Follow each statement carefully as the program outputs parentheses, equal signs, plus signs and each of the numbers in the sequence.

The program terminates with the standard command prompt, which pauses the program until the user is ready for it to end.

One Last Looping Command: foreach

Notice in the two example programs that a for loop has to specify exactly how many elements are in an array. The program terminates if the for loop accesses elements that the array does not have — accessing the eleventh element of an array with only ten elements, for example.

But C# keeps track of the length of an array whether the array is declared statically (as in int array[4]) or dynamically (as in int array[N]).

Why can't C# figure out how many times to loop when accessing array members? In fact, the C# keyword foreach does exactly that. The typical loop appears as follows:

```
double dSum = 0;
for (int i = 0; i < numElements; i++)
{
   dSum = dSum + dArray[i];
}
```

The same loop using the foreach statement appears as follows:

```
double dSum = 0;
foreach (double dElement in dArray)
{
   dSum = dSum + dElement;
}
```

The first time through the loop, the foreach fetches the first element in the array and stores it in the variable dElement. On each subsequent pass, the foreach retrieves the next element. Control passes out of the foreach when all of the elements in the array have been processed.

Notice that no index appears in the foreach statement. This considerably reduces the chance of error.

Former C, C++, and Java programmers find the foreach **a little uncomfortable at first, because it is unique to C#; however, the** foreach **sort of grows on you. It is the easiest of all of the looping commands for accessing arrays.**

A String Versus an Array of Characters

The most basic character type is the char or single-character type.

Some people pronounce the "ch" in char like a "k" as in "characteristic" and some like a "ch" as in "charcoal." The latter is probably the more common, though I prefer the former.

A char is a variable designed to hold a character of the alphabet (be it Latin, Cyrillic, Arabic, katakana, or other), common symbols (comma, parenthesis, brace, and so forth), and a large number of kanji characters. A char variable is declared and (optionally) initiated as follows:

```
char c1;
```

or

```
char c2 = 'a';
```

The first declares a char variable c1 with an undetermined initial value. The second declares a variable c2 and initializes it to the character a. Note that in the code, a character is surrounded by single quotation marks.

A char variable has room for one and only one character. Thus, the following is not legal:

```
char c = 'ab';   // not legal since you can only store one
                 // character in a char variable
```

Arrays of char

An array of chars could be defined as follows:

```
char[] cArray = {'S', 't', 'e', 'p', 'h', 'e', 'n'};
```

Earlier languages such as C and C++ considered an array of chars to be the same thing as a string. However, C# considers them to be completely separate.

For example, you can use the foreach command to iterate through the characters in a char array. Thus, the following outputs my first name to the console:

```
foreach (char c in cArray)
{
    Console.Write(c);
}
```

You cannot use the foreach command on a string. The following generates an error when you try to compile the program:

```
string s = "Stephen";
foreach(char c in s)
{
}
```

Also, none of the operations defined for string variables may be used on an array of chars. Thus, the following is illegal (even though it might be true):

```
char[] cArray = {'S', 't', 'e', 'p', 'h', 'e', 'n'};
Console.WriteLine(cArray + " is great");
```

One confusing point is that both of the following Console.WriteLine **statements output the same string but for different reasons:**

```
char[] cArray = {'S', 't', 'e', 'p', 'h', 'e', 'n'};
Console.WriteLine(cArray);
Console.WriteLine("Stephen");
```

WriteLine() **knows how to iterate through the** cArray **using** foreach, **outputting each** char **separately.** WriteLine() **also knows how to output a string directly.**

The string type

The char variable is designed to handle a single character. A separate intrinsic type is the string. A string is a sequence of zero or more characters.

10 Min. To Go

Whereas a character value is surrounded by single quotation marks, the string is surrounded by double quotation marks. For example, the following declares and initializes the char variable c and the string variable s, respectively:

```
char c = 'c';
string s = "this is a string";
```

A C# string is not an array of char values. A string containing a single character is not the same as a char. In the following example, s and c are not equal:

```
char c = 'c';
string s = "c";
```

The string variable s cannot be converted into a char variable nor the other way around. They are simply not the same thing.

A string may contain no characters at all:

```
string emptyString = "";
```

The variable emptyString now points to a valid but empty string.

A good analogy is as follows: A char is to a string as a human is to a house. A house that has just me in it is not the same thing as me. Similarly, a house can be full of people or it can be empty, but it's still a house. And I can be only me.

In fact, strings are nothing new. You have already seen strings in action a number of times:

```
Console.WriteLine("this is a string");
```

The Console.WriteLine **operation outputs a string to the console.**

Operations on string variables

The string is not a counting type. There is no conversion between strings and `integers`, for example:

```
int nValue = (int)"1";   // not allowed
```

You can't add a number to a string in the arithmetic sense. For example, you can't use the increment operator on a string. However, there is a set of operations which do apply to strings. The most obvious is the assignment operator:

```
string s;

s = "this is a string";
```

Here we declare a string s with no initial value. In a subsequent operation we assign s the value of the string this is a string.

A string variable s that has yet to be initialized is not the same thing as a variable that points to an empty string, "".

The + operator is defined to concatenate two strings:

```
string s1 = "Stephen ";
string s2 = "Davis";
string sMyName = s1 + s2; // sMyName is now "Stephen Davis"
```

C# has overloaded the + operator: When applied to numbers, + means add, but when applied to strings, it means concatenate. This isn't a problem once you get used to it.

You can concatenate a number with a string as in the following:

```
int n = 10;
string s = "the value of n is " + n;
```

The resulting value of s is the value of n is 10. This extended + operator is what allows you to write statements such as:

```
// output the result
Console.WriteLine("Temperature in degrees Celsius = "
                + dCelsius);
```

This use of + is more of a convenience factor than anything else.

Done!

REVIEW

A simple variable provides room to store a single value. The array structure is much more flexible as it provides room to store a series of values (all of which must be of the same type). C# arrays may be fixed length (length known when program written) or variable length (length known when the program executes). Thankfully for us error-prone programmers, C# is clever enough to realize when we exceed the available space in an array. A special `foreach` looping control provides a convenient means for iterating through the members of an array.

Finally, you saw how an array of characters is in ways similar to but fundamentally different from a array of strings in C#. (This is in sharp contrast to C#'s predecessors, C and C++.)

QUIZ YOURSELF

1. Consider the following declaration (see "The fixed-value array"):
   ```
   int[] nArray = {1, 2, 3};
   ```

   a. How many elements are in nArray?

   b. What is the index of the first element in nArray?

   c. What is the index of the last element in nArray?

2. What is the advantage of the `foreach` control over the `for` control when iterating through arrays? (See "One Last Looping Command: foreach.")

The Object

Session Checklist

✔ Introducing the C# class

✔ Storing data in an object

✔ Assigning and using object references

**30 Min.
To Go**

Earlier sessions have limited themselves to the intrinsic variable types, such as int, double, and bool. Most programs require access to large sets of data. A C# array is ideal for storing a sequence of variables if all of the variables are of the same type. Arrays don't work well for grouping variables of different type, such as a string name combined with an int Social Security number. For this you need a structure known as the class.

This session introduces the C# class. In fact, you will be studying various aspects of the class for the rest of today.

Defining a Class

The array is very convenient for handling variables of a common type. The array is analogous to a row of houses all of the same type. The class is analogous to a house. This house is made up of a number of different types of things — a garage, a door, and windows, to name just a few.

An example of an Address class might appear as follows:

```
public class Address
{
    public int nAddressNumberPart;
    public string sAddressNamePart;
    public string sCity;
    public string sState;
    public int nPostalCode;
}
```

Why bother with classes?

The class construct has grown in importance in programming languages over time. If we look at the chain of major languages since 1960 or so, we see the following evolution:

- FORTRAN: No concept of a class.
- C: A limited class; it was possible to write programs that did not make use of classes.
- C++: A much more evolved class concept; it was still possible to write programs that didn't make use of classes, but only by limiting yourself to a subset of the language.
- Java: Not possible to code without making use of classes.
- C#: Not possible to code without making use of classes.

The class concept has grown in importance because programmers discovered that classes were very good at describing real-world objects. Suppose, for example, that I were writing a banking program that dealt with bank accounts. A bank account has features like an account holder's name, account number, balance, bank name, and so forth. In my heart I know that these properties belong together in a single structure because they all describe the same object — an account at my local bank. Holding a balance separate from the bank account number, for example, just doesn't make sense.

In C#, I might create a BankAccount class complete with a string describing the holder's name, an int with the account number, a double or a decimal variable containing the balance, a string with the bank name, and so on. A single BankAccount variable describes all of the relevant properties of a given bank account in my problem.

The argument of lumping together properties that belong together is persuasive, but there is a more subtle — in ways, more important — reason for dealing with classes: The more a computer language can mimic the problem environment, the easier it is to use.

For example, I could have created some "synchronized arrays" to describe the various properties of a bank account rather than create a BankAccount class. I could create an array of strings containing the names of bank account holders, a separate array of ints with bank account numbers, and a third array of double bank balances. I would then use some scheme for linking the name, bank account, and balance.

In my FORTRAN days, I had to use that type of approach to the problem. Such solutions are difficult to understand, however, because they do not adequately describe objects that we recognize from the problem. It is difficult to see a bank account concept buried in among three different types of arrays.

In short, the closer the program structures can be made to mimic the problem to be solved, the easier it will be to create and understand the program solution.

This Address class definition is the design of a particular type of house. The Address house plan has three strings and two living ints — this is sort of like saying that an Address-type house has two living rooms and three bedrooms each with their own name.

A class definition begins with the word class followed by the name of the class, in this case Address. Like all names in C#, the name of the class is case sensitive. C# doesn't enforce any rules concerning class names, but there is an unofficial rule that they must start with a capital letter.

The class name is followed by an open and closed brace set ({ }). Within the braces appears zero or more members. In this case, the class Address starts with an int member with the name nAddressNumberPart. The second member is the string sAddressNamePart, and so forth. (I explain the public attribute in Session 8.)

Creating an Object

20 Min. To Go

Defining a class is not the same thing as creating an object. For example, int is a class of sorts: It defines the layout for how data is to be stored. However, the following is not legal:

```
int = 10;   // this makes no sense
```

The problem, of course, is "which int"? The following code segment creates two objects n1 and n2 of class int and assigns them the values 10 and 20:

```
// create two objects of class int
int n1;
int n2;

// now populate the two objects with the values 10 and 20
n1 = 10;
n2 = 20;
```

Similarly, the following is not legal:

```
Address = 10;
```

You must first create an object of class Address:

```
// create two objects of class Address
Address addr1 = new Address();
Address addr2 = new Address();
```

The format of the two declarations is not quite the same. You don't say:

```
int m1 = new int();
```

Actually, this "class style" declaration is legal, just not necessary.

Once you have an object, you can populate it with values:

```
// create an object of class Address
Address addr = new Address();

// assign values to the members of addr1
addr.nAddressNumberPart = 123;
addr.sAddressNamePart   = "MyStreet";
addr.sCity              = "MyTown";
addr.sState             = "MyState";  // what else did you expect?
addr.nPostalCode;       = 123456;
```

In C# terms, we say that addr **is an object of class** Address**. We also say that an object is an** *instance* **of a class,** *instance* **here meaning "an example of" or "one of."** *Instance* **can also be used as a verb. Creating an object is also called** *instantiating* **the class.**

Now that an object of class Address exists, its members can be populated with data.

Accessing the members of an object

The following expression stores the number 123 in the nAddressNumberPart member of the object referenced by addr:

```
addr.nAddressNumberPart = 123;
```

Every C# operation must be evaluated by type as well as by value. The variable addr is an object of type Address; however, the variable addr.nAddressNumberPart is of type int (look again at the definition of the Address class). The constant 123 is also of type int so the type of the variable on the right matches the type of the variable on the left of the assignment operator =.

Similarly, in

```
addr.sCity = "Pleasantville";
```

the type of addr.sCity is string, which matches the constant string Pleasantville.

A simple address program

This simple AddressDataOnly program does the following:

- Defines the class Address
- Creates an object of class Address
- Stores values in the object
- Retrieves those values back out of the object for display

```
// AddressDataOnly  - declare a class Address which contains
//                    data members to describe a US address
namespace AddressDataOnly
{
  using System;

  class Class1
  {
    public static int Main(string[] args)
    {
      // create an object of class Address
      Address addr = new Address();

      // store values into the various members
      addr.nAddressNumberPart = 123;
      addr.sAddressNamePart = "My Street";
      addr.sCity = "Houston";
      addr.sState = "TX";
      addr.nPostalCode = 76001;

      // retrieve the values which make up the object
      Console.WriteLine(addr.nAddressNumberPart
                      + " "
                      + addr.sAddressNamePart);
      Console.WriteLine(addr.sCity
                      + ", "
                      + addr.sState
                      + " "
                      + addr.nPostalCode);

      // wait for user to acknowledge the results
      Console.WriteLine("Hit Enter to terminate...");
      Console.Read();
      return 0;
    }
  }

  // Address - define a "floor plan" for a US address
  class Address
  {
    public int nAddressNumberPart;
    public string sAddressNamePart;
    public string sCity;
    public string sState;
    public int nPostalCode;
  }
}
```

The complete AddressDataOnly **program can be found on the CD.**

The output from executing this program appears as follows:

```
123 My Street
Houston, TX 76001
Hit Enter to terminate...
```

This example is straightforward given what we know about classes and objects. The program starts by creating an object of class `Address` and assigning it to the variable `addr`. The example continues by assigning values to each of the members of `addr`. Finally, the program terminates after displaying each of the `Address` data members contained in `addr`.

The actual `Address` class is defined at the bottom of the program.

The class `Address` could have been defined before `Class1`. A class definition can appear anywhere after the line beginning with `using` and the final closing brace.

Distinguishing among objects

Builders can construct a number of houses using the same floor plan. Similarly, a program can create a number of objects of the same class:

```
Address addr1 = new Address();
Address addr2 = new Address();

addr1.nAddressNumberPart = 123;
addr1.sAddressNamePart = "My Street";

// the following has no affect on addr1
addr2.nAddressNumberPart = 456;
addr2.nAddressNamePart = "Your Street";
```

The variable `addr1.nAddressNumberPart` is assigned the value 123; however, this assignment has no effect on the separate variable `addr2.nAddressNumberPart` just as storing 123 in n1 has no effect on n2.

In part, the ability to distinguish among objects is the real power of the class construct. The object associated with "123 Main Street" can be created, manipulated, and dispensed with as a single entity, separate from other objects (including the object associated with "456 Your Street").

Object Reference

**10 Min.
To Go**

A reference to an object is like the name of a person. When my son was born, my wife and I assigned him the name "Ken." Why? This is such an obvious and common act that we don't often stop to think about why we assign people names.

A person's name is nothing more than a handle by which that person can be referred. I might say "There's Ken" when my son walks into the room. To use C# terms, I should have said, "There's the male referred to as Ken."

This is very similar to the situation when C# objects are "born":

```
class Person
{
  string sName;
  int    nID;
}
Person ken = new Person();
```

This statement creates an object of class `Person` and assigns it the name ken. By convention, object names begin with lowercase letters.

It isn't that I couldn't have said simply:

```
new Person();
```

This statement creates a `Person` object without assigning it a reference. Without a valid reference, the object is said to be *unreachable*, meaning that there is no way to access it. There is no way to uniquely identify a person who has no name.

Accessing an object

The comparison between human names and C# object references holds in other types of statements as well:

```
Person ken = new Person();
ken.sName = "Kenneth";
ken.nID = 1234;
```

The first statement creates a `Person` object and assigns it the reference ken. The second stores the string Kenneth in the field sName and 1234 in the `int` field nID of the `Person` object referenced by the variable ken. This is demonstrated in Figure 7-1. (Notice that assigning a name to the `Person` object is not the same thing as naming the person.)

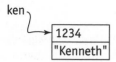

```
ken
     ┌→┌──────────┐
        │ 1234     │
        │"Kenneth" │
        └──────────┘
```

Nickname ──→ Null

Figure 7-1   *The variable* ken *now references a* Person *object with id of 1234 and name of "Kenneth"*

The preceding paragraph sounds very stilted, but these are the types of statements we must use when trying to be very specific — computers are nothing if not specific. In normal techie speech, we might resort to a bit of shorthand and say something like: "The first statement creates the `Person` object ken. The second assigns 1234 to the nID member of ken."

Shorthand is fine as long as you remember exactly what is being left out. You should be able to re-create the stilted first paragraph above from the more humanlike second paragraph.

Assigning one reference to another

A reference to an object can be assigned to another reference in the same way that a variable n1 can be assigned to n2.

```
// create a null reference
Person ken;

// assign the reference a value
ken = new Person();
ken.sName = "Kenneth";

// create a new reference and point it to the same object
// to which ken refers. In short, assign ken to nickname
Person nickname = ken;
```

The first line creates an object ken without assigning it a value. A reference that has not been initialized with a value is said to point to the *null object*. Any attempt to use an uninitialized reference generates an immediate error that terminates the program.

The C# compiler can catch most attempts to use an uninitialized reference and generate a warning at build time.

The second statement creates a Person object and assigns it to ken. The last statement in this code snippet assigns the reference ken to the reference nickname. This has the effect of causing nickname to refer to the same object that ken refers to. This is displayed graphically in Figure 7-2.

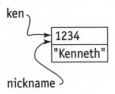

Figure 7-2 *Both variables reference the same object after executing the assignment nickname = ken.*

Once the assignment has been made, referencing nickname has the same effect as referencing ken:

```
// store of an id in the object referred to by ken
Person ken = new Person();
ken.nID = 1234;

// store of an id in the object referred to by nickname
Person nickname = ken;
nickname.nID = 1234;
```

Notice that nickname does not refer to the variable ken. Instead, nickname refers to the same object to which ken refers. This has the following somewhat unexpected result:

```
Person ken = new Person();
Person nickname = ken;
ken.nID = 1234;
nickname.nID = 5678;
```

The value of ken.nID is now 5678.

In addition, the reference nickname would still be valid even if the variable ken were somehow lost (went out of scope, for example).

 Refer to Session 4 for an explanation of scope.

```
Person ken = new Person();
Person nickname = ken;

// wipe out the ken reference
ken = null;

// the object is still accessible through the nickname reference
nickname.nID = 1234;
```

The object does not lose scope until both ken and nickname are set to a null value. Said another way: You can reach the object as long as it is referenced by either ken or nickname.

Done!

REVIEW

The object is the base type of all types in C#. An object describes the actions that can be carried out on a set of data. In this session we discovered how to create objects and how to access them. We also took a look at how to assign one object reference to another.

QUIZ YOURSELF

1. In what way is a class semantically similar to an array? What is the primary difference? (See the first paragraph in "Defining a Class.")
2. Define a class Pool containing an int element nDepth and a double element dArea. (See "Defining a Class.")
3. Declare a Pool object and assign it to the reference variable pool1. (See "Creating an Object.")
4. Set the depth of the Pool object to 2 and the surface area to 50. (Don't worry about the units of length or area.)
5. Create a second reference called pool2 that refers to the same Pool object as pool1.

The Function

Session Checklist

✔ Defining a C# function

✔ Passing arguments to a function

✔ Getting results

✔ Reviewing the WriteLine() function

**30 Min.
To Go**

he programmer can create a class such as Student to represent the abstract concept of a student. The data members of a class definition allow the class to mimic many of the properties of students. A Student class has data members like FirstName, LastName, and StudentID, for example. However, most real objects actually do things. Students enroll in classes, complete homework, and attend classes (sometimes). For this reason, C# allows classes to include active components along with data members called functions.

Defining and Using a Function

Consider the following class:

```
class Example
{
  int nInt;
  public void Function()
  {
    Console.WriteLine("this is a function");
  }
}
```

The element nInt is a data member such as those you've seen in Session 6, but the element Function() is new. Function() is known as a member function. A member function is a set of C# code that an application can execute by providing the function's name.

The following code snippet creates an Example object and assigns a value to its nInt data member:

```
Example example = new Example(); // create an object
example.nInt = 1;                // initialize the data member
```

The following snippet defines and accesses Function() in almost the same way:

```
Example example = new Example(); // create an object
example.Function();              // invoke the member function
                                 // with that object
```

The call to example.Function() passes control to the code contained within the function. Executing this code snippet generates the following output:

```
this is a function
```

Once the function has completed execution, it returns control to the point where it was called.

The C# code contained within Function() does nothing more than write a silly string to the console, but functions generally perform useful and sometimes complex operations like calculating the sine of something or concatenating two strings or looking up a student's records from a database.

Passing Arguments to a Function

A method such as Function() is of limited use. No data passes into or out of the function. Compare this with real-world functions. For example, the sine (a built-in mathematical function) operation requires an argument — you have to take the sine of something. Similarly, you can concatenate two strings — thus, the concatenate function requires at least two strings to concatenate. Most functions require some type of arguments.

You pass arguments to a function by listing them in the parentheses following the function name. Consider the small expansion of the earlier Example class:

```
class Example
{
  public void Function(string funcString)
  {
    Console.WriteLine("Function() was passed the argument: "
                  + funcString);
  }
}
```

This function is invoked with an argument as follows:

```
Example example = new Example();
example.Function("Hello");
```

Executing this code outputs the string:

```
Function() was passed the argument: Hello
```

Let's change the example in one minor way:

```
Example example = new Example();
string upperString = "Hello";
example.Function(upperString);
```

This code snippet assigns the variable upperString to reference the string Hello. Within Function(), however, that same object Hello is referenced by the variable funcString.

Passing multiple arguments to functions

A function can be defined with multiple arguments of varying types. Consider the following example function, AverageAndDisplay().

```
// PassingMultipleArguments - you pass arguments to a member
//                            function by listing them within
//                            the parentheses after the function
//                            name. You may list 0 to as many
//                            arguments as you like.
namespace PassingMultipleArguments
{
  using System;

  class Class1
  {
    public static int Main(string[] args)
    {
      // create the Example object
      Example example = new Example();

      // now access the member function
      example.AverageAndDisplay("grade 1", 3.5, "grade 2", 4.0);

      // wait for user to acknowledge the results
      Console.WriteLine("Hit Enter to terminate...");
      Console.Read();
      return 0;
    }
  }

  class Example
  {
    // AverageAndDisplay - average two numbers with their
    //                     labels and display the results
    public void AverageAndDisplay(string s1, double d1,
      string s2, double d2)
    {
```

```
        double dAverage = (d1 + d2) / 2;
        Console.WriteLine("The average of " + s1
            + " whose value is " + d1
            + " and " + s2
            + " whose value is " + d2
            + " is " + dAverage);
    }
  }
}
```

generates the following output:

```
The average of grade 1 whose value is 3.5 and grade 2 whose value is 4 is
3.75
```

The complete `CalculateInterestWithTest` **program can be found on the CD.**

Execution begins with the first statement after `Main()` as usual. This line creates an object example of class `Example`. The program continues by invoking `AverageAndDisplay()` and passing the two strings grade 1 and grade 2 and the two double values 3.5 and 4.0.

The function `AverageAndDisplay()` begins by calculating the average of the two double values passed it. (Notice that in `AverageAndDisplay()` there is no special significance to the names d1 and d2.)

`AverageAndDisplay()` continues by displaying the values contained in d1 and d2, their names contained in s1 and s2, and the calculated average stored in dAverage.

Null and empty references

A reference variable is assigned the default value `null` when created. However, a null reference is not the same thing as an empty reference. For example, the following two references are completely different:

```
class Example
{
  int nValue;
}

// create a null reference ref1
Example ref1;

// now create a reference to a zero object
Example ref2 = new Example();
ref2.nValue = 0;
```

The variable `ref1` points to the null object — that is to say, it points to no object. By comparison, `ref2` points to an object whose value is zero.

This difference is much less clear in the following example:

```
string s1;
string s2 = "";
```

This is essentially the same case: s1 points to the null object whereas s2 points to a string that is empty. The difference is significant, as is shown in the following function:

```
// NullVsEmptyStringTest - compare the difference between
//                         passing a null reference vs.
//                         a reference to a zero length
//                         string
namespace NullVsEmptyStringTest
{
  using System;

  public class Class1
  {
    public static int Main(string[] strings)
    {
      Console.WriteLine("This program exercises the " +
        "function TestString()");
      Console.WriteLine();
      Example exampleObject = new Example();

      Console.WriteLine("Pass a null object:");
      string s = null;
      exampleObject.TestString(s);
      Console.WriteLine();

      // now pass the function a null string
      Console.WriteLine("Pass an empty string:");
      exampleObject.TestString("");
      Console.WriteLine();

      // finally, pass a real string
      Console.WriteLine("Pass a real string:");
      exampleObject.TestString("test string");
      Console.WriteLine();

      // wait for user to acknowledge the results
      Console.WriteLine("Hit Enter to terminate...");
      Console.Read();
      return 0;
    }
  }

  class Example
  {
    public void TestString(string sTest)
    {
      // first test for a null string
```

```
      if (sTest == null)
      {
        Console.WriteLine("sTest is null");
        return;
      }

      // check to see if sTest points to a null string
      if (String.Compare(sTest, "") == 0)
      {
        Console.WriteLine("sTest references an empty string");
        return;
      }

      // OK, output the string
      Console.WriteLine("sTest refers to: '" + sTest + "'");
    }
  }
}
```

 The complete `NullVsEmptyStringTest` **program can be found on the CD.**

The function `TestString()` uses the comparison `sTest == null` to test for a null string. `TestString()` has to compare the `sTest` object with the `null` in order to detect a null string. (`Compare()` returns a zero if the two strings passed it are equal.)

The output from this program is as follows:

```
This program exercises the function TestString()

Pass a null object:
sTest is null

Pass an empty string:
sTest references an empty string

Pass a real string:
sTest refers to: 'test string'

Hit Enter to terminate...
```

Matching argument definitions with usage

20 Min. To Go

The types of each argument in the call must match the function definition in both type and order. The following, taken from the `AverageAndDisplay()` example in the section "Passing multiple arguments to functions," would be illegal and would generate a compile time error:

```
Example example = new Example();
example.AverageAndDisplay("grade 1", "grade 2",
                          dGrade1, dGrade2);
```

C# can't match the type of each argument in the call with the corresponding argument in the function definition. The string grade 1 matches the first string in the function definition; however, the function definition calls for a double as its second argument rather than the string's being passed. (It's clear that the programmer accidentally transposed the second and third arguments.)

Passing intrinsic arguments by reference

Unlike object references, *intrinsic* or value-type objects are normally *passed by value,* meaning that the value contained within the variable is passed, not the variable itself. This has the effect that changing the value of an intrinsic variable within a function does not change the value of that variable in the calling program:

```
namespace Example
{
  using System;

  class Test
  {
    public static void Update(int i, double d)
    {
      i = 10;
      d = 20.0;
    }

    public static int Main(string[] args)
    {
      int i = 1;
      double d = 2.0;

      Update(i, d);

      Console.WriteLine("i = " + i
                    + ", d = " + d);


      // wait for user to acknowledge the results
      Console.WriteLine("Hit Enter to terminate...");
      Console.Read();
      return 0;
    }
  }
}
```

Executing this program generates the following output:

```
i = 1, d = 2
```

The call to Update() passes the values 1 and 2.0, but not a reference to the variables i and d. Thus, changing their value within the function has no effect on the value of the variables back in the calling routine.

It is sometimes advantageous to provide the same *pass by reference* capability as that provided by class objects. C# allows the programmer this capability via the ref and out keywords. A slight modification to our example program snippet demonstrates the point:

```
namespace Example
{
  using System;

  class Test
  {

    public static void Update(ref int i, ref double d)
    {
      i = 10;
      d = 20.0;
    }

    public static int Main(string[] args)
    {
      int i = 1;
      double d = 2.0;

      Update(ref i, ref d);

      Console.WriteLine("i = " + i
                  + ", d = " + d);

      // wait for user to acknowledge the results
      Console.WriteLine("Hit Enter to terminate...");
      Console.Read();
      return 0;
    }
  }
}
```

The ref keyword indicates that the values of i and d should be imported into and then exported back out of the calling routine.

Executing the program generates the following output:

```
i = 10, d = 20
```

Output only arguments

Normally, C# insists that all of the arguments to a function have a specified value. Otherwise, the caller might pass some unknown, "garbage" value or a null reference, and the program might generate unpredictable results.

For example, the following code snippet is not legal C# (the compiler generates an error message when you try to compile it):

```
// the following does not compile properly
namespace Example
```

```
{
  using System;

  public class Test
  {
    public static int Main(string[] strings)
    {
      // declare but don't initialize the student variable
      Student student;

      // now try to pass it to a function
      Example example = new Example().
      example.ReturnStudent(student);


      // wait for user to acknowledge the results
      Console.WriteLine("Hit Enter to terminate...");
      Console.Read();
      return 0;
    }
  }

  class Example
  {
    public static void ReturnStudent(Student student)
    {
      Console.WriteLine(student);
    }

    public class Student
    {
      public string name;
    }
  }
}
```

The problem with this small program is that the object student has not been assigned a value at the time of the call to ReturnStudent(). This makes the call to WriteLine() nonsensical (not exactly nonsensical; it's just that we have no idea what the call to WriteLine() might do with this uninitialized value).

However, there are times when assigning an initial value to an argument makes no sense either. Consider the following minor change:

```
namespace Example
{
  using System;

  public class Test
  {
    public static int Main(string[] strings)
```

```
      {
        Student student = new Student();
        student.name = "Sarah";

        Example example = new Example();
        example.ReturnStudent(student);

        // wait for user to acknowledge the results
        Console.WriteLine("Hit Enter to terminate...");
        Console.Read();
        return 0;
      }
   }

   class Example
   {
      public static void Return(Student student)
      {
        student = new Student();
        student.name = "Jenny";
      }

      public class Student
      {
        public string name;
      }
   }
}
```

There is little point in creating the student object in Main() because the
ReturnStudent() function will immediately overwrite that object anyway. What we need is a
way to indicate to C# that the function doesn't care what the initial value of the argument is.

The following change to the function does this using the keyword out:

```
// ExamplePassingAnArgumentOut - the out descriptor allows
//                               a function a value in an argument
//                               (like the ref descriptor) without
//                               the need to initialize the argument
//                               to a meaningless value before the call
namespace PassingAnArgumentOut
{
   using System;

   public class Test
   {
      public static int Main(string[] strings)
      {
        // let the ReturnStudent() function create the
        // object for us
        Student student;
```

```
        Example example = new Example();
        example.ReturnStudent(out student);

        Console.WriteLine("Student is " + student.name);

        // wait for user to acknowledge the results
        Console.WriteLine("Hit Enter to terminate...");
        Console.Read();
        return 0;
    }
}

class Example
{
    public void ReturnStudent(out Student student)
    {
        student = new Student();
        student.name = "Jenny";
    }
}

public class Student
{
    public string name;
}
}
```

The program generates the following output:

```
Student is Jenny
Hit Enter to terminate...
```

The complete `PassingArgumentOut` **program can be found on the CD.**

An out **variable is automatically** ref.

Returning Values from a Function

**10 Min.
To Go**

Many real-world operations create values to return to the caller. For example, sine accepts an argument and returns the trigonometric sine.

A function returns a value to its caller as follows:

```
class Example
{
```

```
public double Average(double d1, double d2)
{
    double dAverage = (d1 + d2) / 2;
    return dAverage;
}
}
```

Notice first that function is declared `public double Average()` — the `double` here refers to the fact that the `Average()` function returns a double precision value to the caller. When the function execution encounters the statement `return dAverage`, the function returns the `double` value contained in dAverage.

People sometimes say that "the function returns dAverage." This is a careless but common shorthand — it makes no sense to say that dAverage or any other variable is passed or returned anywhere. In this case, it is the *value* contained within dAverage that is returned to the caller.

The call to the function `Average()` appears as follows:

```
Example example = new Example();
double v1 = 1.0;
double v2 = 3.0;
double dAverageValue = example.Average(v1, v2);
```

This call passes the values 1.0 and 3.0 to the function `Average` and stores the returned value in dAverageValue.

Defining a function that returns no value

The declaration

```
public double Average()
```

declares that the function `Average()` returns the average of its arguments as a `double`. The earlier example function `AverageAndDisplay()` displays its average, returning nothing to the caller. Rather than leave the return type blank, `AverageAndDisplay()` was declared:

```
public void AverageAndDisplay()
```

The term `void` corresponds to the *nontype*. That is, the declaration `void` indicates that the `AverageAndDisplay()` function returns no value to the caller.

A nonvoid function executes a `return` followed by a value to return to the caller. A `void` function exits when control reaches the closing brace; however, a `void` function can return at any point by executing a `return` control that does not include a value. Consider the following `DisplayRatio()` function:

```
class Example
{
    public void DisplayRatio(double dNumerator,
                             double dDenominator)
    {
```

```
        // if the denominator is zero...
        if (dDenominator == 0.0)
        {
          // ...output an error message and...
          Console.WriteLine(
                    "The denominator of a ratio cannot be 0");

          // ...return to the caller
          return;
        }

        // this is only executed if dDenominator is non-zero
        double dRatio = dNumerator / dDenominator;
        Console.WriteLine("The ratio of " + dNumerator
                      + " over " + dDenominator
                      + " is " + dRatio);
      }
   }
```

The DisplayRatio() function first checks to make sure that the dDenominator value is zero. If it is zero, the program displays an error message and returns to the caller without attempting to calculate a ratio, thereby dividing the numerator value by zero and causing a processor fault.

The WriteLine() function

You may have noticed by this time that the WriteLine() construct we've been using in our programs so far is nothing more than a function call that is invoked with something called a Console object:

```
Console.WriteLine("this is a method call");
```

WriteLine() is one of a large number of predefined functions that are provided by the C# system.

The argument to the simplest version of the WriteLine() function is a single string. This is the version we have been using in earlier sessions. A second form of WriteLine() provides a more flexible set of arguments:

```
Console.WriteLine("My name is {0} and my age is {1}.",
                  "Sarah", 3);
```

Here the string Sarah is inserted where the symbol {0} appears — zero refers to the first argument after the string itself. The integer 3 is inserted at the position marked by {1}. This is much more efficient than the semantically equivalent

```
Console.WriteLine("My name is " + "Sarah"
                  + " and my age is " + 3 + ".");
```

This second form of WriteLine() also provides for a number of controls on the output format. Refer to Session 13 for formatting string output.

Why bother with functions?

Functions serve a number of purposes. When Fortran introduced the function concept in the 1950s, the sole purpose was to avoid duplication of code by combining similar sections into a common element. Suppose we were to write a program that needed to calculate and display ratios in multiple places. Our program can call the `DisplayRatio()` function wherever needed and avoid duplication. The savings may not seem so important for a function as small as `DisplayRatio()`; however, functions can grow to be quite large and complex.

A second advantage of functions quickly became obvious. It is easier to code a single function correctly. The `DisplayRatio()` function includes a check to make sure that the denominator is not zero. If we repeated the calculation code throughout our program, it would be all too easy to forget this test occasionally — in some cases, we might remember to include the check and in other places forget.

Not so obvious is yet a third advantage to carefully crafted functions. A function can reduce the complexity of the program. To do this, a well-defined function should stand for some concept. You should be able to describe the purpose of the function without using the words *and* or *or*.

A function like `calculateSin()` is ideal. The programmer who has been tasked with coding some complex operation can invoke functions like `calculateSin()`, `calculateCosin()`, and `calculateSquareRoot()` without worrying about how this operation is performed internally. This greatly reduces the number of things she has to worry about.

Large programs such as word processors are built up from layers and layers of functions at ever-increasing levels of abstraction. For example, a `RedisplayDocument()` function would undoubtedly call a `Reparagraph()` function to redisplay the paragraphs within the document. `Reparagraph()` would need to invoke a `CalculateWordWrap()` function to decide where to word-wrap the lines that make up the paragraph. `CalculateWordWrap()` would have to call a `LookUpWordBreak()` function in order to decide where to break a word at the end of the line in order to make the sentences wrap more naturally. Each of these functions was described in a single, simple sentence.

Without the ability to abstract complex concepts, it would become essentially impossible to write programs of even moderate complexity, much less an operating system such as Microsoft Windows, a program such as WordPerfect, or a game such as StarFighter, to name a few examples.

Done!

REVIEW

Functions represent a collection of C# source code. C# programmers create functions for a number of reasons. Creating functions avoids duplicating sections of C# code. Even more important, the programmer can create a function to represent some action. For example, the class BankAccount represents the concept of a bank account. The data members nBalance and nAccountNumber represent static properties of the bank account. But member functions such as CalculatingInterest() and DepositCheck() represent the actions that can be performed either by or on bank accounts.

C# can pass data to a function in the form of arguments. In addition, functions can return results. For example, a function int square(int) might accept a number 10 as its argument and return the square of 10, the value 100.

Finally, you saw some of the controls that the ubiquitous WriteLine() function understands when outputting text to a console window.

QUIZ YOURSELF

1. Declare a function max() that takes no arguments and returns nothing. (See "Defining and Using a Function.")

2. Define a function max() that accepts two int variables as its arguments. (See "Passing multiple arguments to functions.")

3. Define a function max() that accepts two int variables as its arguments and that returns an int. (See "Returning Values from a Function.")

Object Methods

Session Checklist

✔ Referring to the current object

✔ Converting a member function into a method

✔ Expanding a method's full name

30 Min. To Go

A programmer defines a class to describe a real-world object. She defines data members within that class to describe the static properties of the object. However, objects can do things like wake up or sit down. Sometimes doing things causes them to change their state, just as waking up changes you from asleep to awake. The class structure uses a structure called a *member function* to describe what objects do and what effects these actions have on the object itself.

Passing Objects to Member Functions

Member functions are supposed to allow classes to more closely mimic real-world objects. However, even though a function DisplayRatio() might be defined in the class Example, it has little to do with any example object:

```
class Example
{
  public void DisplayRatio(double dNumerator,
                           double dDenominator)
  {
    Console.WriteLine("ratio = {0}", dNumerator/dDenominator);
  }
}
```

The Example class is simply a nice placeholder for the DisplayRatio() function.

By comparison, consider the following simple example:

```
namespace Example
{
  using System;

  class Student
  {
    public string sFirstName;
    public string sLastName;

    public void SetName(string sFName, string sLName)
    {
      sFirstName = sFName;
      sLastName  = sLName;
    }

    public string ToNameString()
    {
      string s = sFirstName + " " + sLastName;
      return s;
    }

    public static int Main()
    {
      Student student = new Student();

      student.SetName("Stephen", "Davis");

      Console.WriteLine("Student's name is "
                        + student.ToNameString());

      // wait for user to acknowledge the results
      Console.WriteLine("Hit Enter to terminate...");
      Console.Read();
      return 0;
    }
  }
}
```

The output from this program is the simple line:

```
Student's name is Stephen Davis
```

This program begins by creating a new Student object called student. The program then invokes the SetName() function, which stores the two strings Stephen and Davis in the data members sFirstName and sLastName. Finally, the program calls the member function ToNameString(), which returns the name of student by concatenating the two strings.

There are two differences between the SetName() function here and the earlier DisplayRatio() function. One is that SetName() is an action that can be performed on a student — you can assign a student a name. The second is that the SetName() function modifies the state of the Student object. Before the call, the student had no name; after the call, the student was assigned a name.

 For historical reasons that have nothing to do with C#, a member function that represents some property of the parent class is known as a *method*.

But which object did SetName() modify? Consider the following example to see the problem:

```
Student christa = new Student();
Student sarah = new Student();

christa.SetName("Christa", "Smith");
sarah.SetName("Sarah", "Jones");
```

The first time SetName() is called, it stores and updates the first and last name of the christa object. The second call updates the sarah object. Thus, we say that a method operates on the *current object*. In the first call, the current object was christa, in the second sarah.

Adding methods to the AddressWithMethods program

In this section we find out how to add methods to our AddressDataOnly program.

The following AddressWithMethods program represents an Address class complete with methods to set and get its data members:

```
// AddressWithMethods  - declare a class Address which contains
//                   the data members to describe a US address
//                   along with the member functions (methods)
//                   necessary to manipulate it
namespace AddressWithMethods
{
  using System;

  class Class1
  {
    public static int Main(string[] args)
    {
      // create an object of class Address
      Address addr = new Address();

      // store values into the various members
      addr.SetStreet(123, "My Street");
      addr.SetCity("Houston", "TX", 76001);

      // Output the address using the GetStreet
      // and GetCity methods
      Console.WriteLine("Output using string methods:");
      Console.WriteLine(addr.GetStreetString());
      Console.WriteLine(addr.GetCityString());
```

```
        // now let the object output itself
        Console.WriteLine();
        Console.WriteLine("Let the object output itself:");
        addr.Output();

        // wait for user to acknowledge the results
        Console.WriteLine("Hit Enter to terminate...");
        Console.Read();
        return 0;
    }
}

// Address - define a "floor plan" for a US address
class Address
{
    // street portion
    public int nAddressNumberPart;
    public string sAddressNamePart;

    // city portion
    public string sCity;
    public string sState;
    public int nPostalCode;

    // SetStreet - change the street address
    public void SetStreet(int nNumber, string sName)
    {
        nAddressNumberPart = nNumber;
        sAddressNamePart = sName;
    }

    // GetStreetString - return the street portion of an
    //                   address as a string
    public string GetStreetString()
    {
        string s = nAddressNumberPart + " " +
                   sAddressNamePart;
        return s;
    }

    // SetCity - change the city portion of
    //           an address
    public void SetCity(string sCityIn,
                        string sStateIn,
                        int nPostalCodeIn)
    {
        sCity = sCityIn;
        sState = sStateIn;
        nPostalCode = nPostalCodeIn;
    }
```

```
// GetCityString - return the city portion of an
//                  address as a string
public string GetCityString()
{
    string s = sCity + ", " + sState + " " + nPostalCode;
    return s;
}

//
// GetAddressString - return the entire address as
//                    a string
public string GetAddressString()
{
    string s = GetStreetString() + "\n" + GetCityString();
    return s;
}

// Output - output self to the console
public void Output()
{
    Console.WriteLine(GetAddressString());
}
    }
}
```

The size of this program makes it look formidable, but it's relatively simple when broken down into its pieces.

The complete AddressWithMethods **program can be found on the CD.**

A well-constructed C# program consists of a number of different methods, but each method is simple and easy to understand and performs a specific piece of functionality.

**20 Min.
To Go**

Let's jump ahead to the Address class. The function SetStreet() updates the nAddressNumberPart and sAddressNamePart data members of the current object. Similarly, SetCity() updates the city, state, and postal code parts of the address. The GetStreetString() and GetCityString() methods simply return the appropriate portions of the current object's address. The method GetAddressString() returns the entire address in string format. The Output() method writes the address of the current object out to the console.

Remember, the special character \n **represents a newline character.**

The Main() program creates an Address object addr. It then initializes the street and city using the corresponding set method. The program continues by displaying the address contained in the addr object, first by calling the individual get methods and then by invoking the single Output() method.

 A set method is a method whose only purpose is to store a value (or values) into a class. A get method retrieves a value (or values). Session 19 explains the advantages of get and set methods in detail.

Focusing on the Output() method

Look back at the Output() method of the Address class. Notice two things:

- Output() invokes the method GetAddressString(), which in turn invokes the methods GetStreetString() and GetCityString() without referring to the object directly. That's because Output() is using the current object. Thus, the call addr. Output() converts the call GetAddressString() into addr.GetAddressString(). (You'll see exactly how this is done later in this session.)
- Output() calls GetAddressString(). Output() has direct access to the data members of Address. Output() could easily convert the street and city data members into a string on its own. However, Output() provides for a clean division of labor. The GetStreetString() method is the function tasked with returning the street address. The GetAddressString() honors that fact by using GetStreetString() to return the street portion. Output() for its part honors the fact that GetAddressString() has the sole responsibility for converting an Address object into a string.

A well-defined class can end up with multiple methods, but each one is made as simple as possible by calling upon its siblings.

Why bother with methods?

Why bother with methods? Why aren't simple functions good enough? Methods serve two different but important functions.

- The SetStreet() and GetStreetString() methods hide the details of how streets are stored within the Address class. This is data that external functions should not have to deal with (similar to the way we use utensils such as microwave ovens — buttons with names like Start and Reset hide the internal circuitry of the oven).
- The second function of a method is to represent real properties of the class. An airplane can perform many actions, including accelerating, banking, taking off, and landing. A thorough Airplane class should have Accelerate(), Bank(), TakeOff(), and Land() methods, which mimic these properties. Matching a class representation to the real thing allows the programmer to think of her program in terms that are native to the problem and not of some artificial vocabulary dictated by the programming language.

Expanding a Function's Full Name

There has been a subtle but important problem with my description of method names thus far. To see the problem, consider the following example code snippet:

```
class Person
{
  public void Address()
  {
    Console.WriteLine("Hi");
  }
}

class Letter
{
  string sAddress;
  public void Address(string sNewAddress)
  {
    sAddress = sNewAddress;
  }
}
```

Any subsequent discussion of the Address() method is now ambiguous. The Address() method within Person has nothing to do with that in Letter. If my programmer friend tells me to access the Address() method, which Address() does she mean?

The problem lies not with the methods themselves but with my description. In fact, there is no Address() method, only a Person.Address() method and a Letter.Address() method. Attaching the class name onto the front of the method name makes it clear which method is intended.

This description is very similar to people's names. Within my family, I am known as Stephen. (Actually, within my family I am known by my middle name, but you get the point.) There are no other Stephens within my family (at least not within my close family). However, there are two other Stephens where I work.

If I am at lunch with a few of the guys and neither of the other two Stephens is present, the name Stephen clearly refers to me. Back in the trenches (or cubicles), yelling out "Stephen" is ambiguous because it could refer to any one of us. In that context, you'll need to yell out "Stephen Davis," as opposed to "Stephen Williams" or "Stephen Leija."

Thus, you can actually consider Address() to be the first name or nickname of a method.

The situation is actually worse than that:

```
class Person
{
  public void Address(int nNumber)
  {
    Console.WriteLine("Hello to all " + nNumber + " of you");
  }

  public void Address(string sName)
  {
```

```
      Console.WriteLine("Hi, " + sName);
   }

   public static int Main(string[] args)
   {
      Person person = new Person();

      person.Address(5);
      person.Address("Jenny");
      // wait for user to acknowledge the results
      Console.WriteLine("Hit Enter to terminate...");
      Console.Read();
      return 0;
   }
```

Here you can see that a single class can have two methods with the same nickname. There are two separate references to a `Person.Address()` method within `Main()`. Comparing the arguments provided within the call with those expected by the function makes it clear which method is intended with each call.

Once again, the problem lies not with the C# code but with my description. There are in fact two different, unrelated functions: `Person.Address(int)` and `Person.Address(string)`.

`Person.Address(string)` is called the fully qualified name of the method. Two different methods cannot have the same fully qualified name.

Done!

REVIEW

In this session you saw the fundamental difference between a member function and a method: A method is a member function that represents a property of the class. Thus, while `Example.DoubleArgument()` is probably a member function, `Airplane.TakeOff()` is probably a method.

Certain ambiguities can arise when referring to methods. For example, both `Car` and `Microwave` may have a method `Start()`. The ambiguity goes away when you realize that the full name for the methods are `Car.Start()` and `Microwave.Start()`. In fact, you even saw how method names could be overloaded within the same class so long as the arguments were sufficiently different that C# could tell them apart. (By "overloaded," I mean the ability to call a method of the same name with different parameters. For example, `AddNumber(int)` and `AddNumber(long)` are the same method name, but each is called with different parameters.)

QUIZ YOURSELF

1. What is a method?
2. Using the `Pool` class from the quiz in Session 7, how would a method `MaxDepth()`, which accepts another `Pool` object and returns the maximum depth, be declared?
3. What would be the full name of the `MaxDepth()` function? (See "Expanding a Function's Full Name.")

The this Pointer

Session Checklist

✔ Accessing the "current" object

✔ Using the this reference

✔ Accessing this explicitly

**30 Min.
To Go**

P rior sessions described the ways in which the members of a class are accessed through a class object as in the following:

```
class Student
{
  string sName;
  int nID;
};

class Class1
{
  public static int Main(string[] args)
  {
    Student s = new Student();
    s.sName = "U. R. Reeder";

    return 0;
  }
}
```

This session describes those situations in which the class object is implicit.

Accessing an Object with an Implicit Reference

Consider the following Address class and the way it is used:

```csharp
using System;

class Street
{
  public int nAddressNumberPart;
  public string sAddressNamePart;
  // SetStreet - change the street address
  public void SetStreet(int nNumber, string sName)
  {
    SetAddressNumber(nNumber);
    SetStreetName(sName);
  }
  // SetAddressNumber - set the numeric part of the address
  public void SetAddressNumber(int nNumber)
  {
    nAddressNumberPart = nNumber;
  }
  // SetStreetName - set the street name part of the address
  public void SetStreetName(string sName)
  {
    sAddressNamePart = sName;
  }
}
public class Class1
{
  public static int Main(string[] args)
  {
    Street addr1 = new Street();
    addr1.SetStreet(123, "MyStreet");
    Street addr2 = new Street();
    addr2.SetStreet(456, "UrStreet");

    // wait for user to acknowledge the results
    Console.WriteLine("Hit Enter to terminate...");
    Console.Read();
    return 0;
  }
}
```

Main() first creates an object addr1 of class Street. It uses this object in the call addr1. SetStreet(), which initializes the street address. The object of this call is specifically and clearly addr1. Things become less clear, however, as you follow the execution path.

SetStreet() invokes the methods SetAddressNumber() and SetStreetName(). It does so, however, without referring to any object. How does SetAddressNumber() know which object to initialize? The problem becomes more obvious when you consider the very next call in Main(): addr2.SetStreet(). Somehow, SetStreet() knows to use addr1 the first time it's called and addr2 the second time.

The answer is simple: The current object is passed as an *implicit argument* in the call to a method. Thus,

```
addr1.SetStreet(123, "Main");
```

is equivalent to

```
Address.SetStreet(addr1, 123, "Main"); // equivalent call
                                       // (but this won't
                                       // build properly)
```

It isn't that SetStreet() can be invoked in two different ways, it's just that the two calls are semantically equivalent — the object just to the left of the period (.) is passed to the function just as other arguments are.

What about the call to SetAddressNumber()? What about the reference to nAddressNumberPart? No object appears here, either in front of or after the reference to nAddressNumberPart. This problem is solved in exactly the same way:

```
SetStreet(addr1, 123, "Main")
```

calls SetAddressNumberPart() as if it had been written

```
SetAddressNumberPart(addr1, 123)
```

which uses this addr1 object to set the data member

```
addr1.nAddressNumberPart = 123;
```

The second sequence of calls works the same way:

```
    addr2.SetStreet(456, "UrStreet");
```

is treated as if it had been written

```
SetStreet(addr2, 456, "UrStreet")
```

which calls

```
SetAddressNumberPart(addr2, 456)
```

which makes the assignment

```
addr2.nAddressNumberPart = 456
```

The "hidden" argument to SetStreet() is sometimes referred to as the *current object*. (I'll give it a more specific name in the next section.) Thus, the current object within SetStreet() is addr1 the first time it is called and addr2 the second time. SetStreet() passes the current object to SetAddressNumberPart(). This method sets the nAddressNumberPart data member of the current objects. In general, an access to any member from within a method is assumed to be with respect to the current object. The current object continues to be passed along silently from one method call to the next. An access to a data member from within a method refers to the data member of the current object.

I can't stress enough that methods cannot be invoked with the object as the explicit first argument to an otherwise unspecified method. The call `object.MethodCall()` is semantically equivalent to its ungrammatical counterpart `MethodCall(object)`.

**20 Min.
To Go**

The this reference

Unlike most arguments, however, the current object does not appear in the function argument list, and so it is not assigned a name by the programmer. Instead, C# assigns this object the not-very-imaginative name `this`. Thus, a subset of the previous example could have been written as follows (I've included only a small part to save space):

```
// SetStreet - change the street address
public void SetStreet(int nNumber, string sName)
{
  this.SetAddressNumber(nNumber);
  this.SetStreetName(sName;
}
// SetAddressNumber - set the numeric part of the address
public void SetAddressNumber(int nNumber)
{
  this.nAddressNumberPart = nNumber;
}

// SetStreetName - set the street name part of the address
public void SetStreetName(string sName)
{
  this.sAddressNamePart = sName;
}
```

Notice the explicit addition of the keyword `this`. Adding `this` to the member references adds nothing because `this` is assumed anyway. However, now when `Main()` makes the following call,

```
Address address = new Address();
address.SetStreet(123, "Main");
```

it's clear that `this` refers to `address`. `SetStreet()` passes the same `this` object on when it later calls `SetStreetName()`.

Using this to avoid name hiding

The programmer doesn't normally need to refer to `this` explicitly because it is understood implicitly by the compiler. There are two common cases in which `this` appears explicitly. One is to avoid name collisions from within a method. Consider the following error-prone example:

```
class Person
{
  public string sName;
  public int nID;
```

```
public void SomeMethod(string sNewName)
{
  // define a local variable sName
  string sName = "Some other guy";

  //data member sName is now unreachable
  sName = sNewName;
}
}
```

The method SomeMethod() starts by defining a local variable sName. Unfortunately that is the same name as that used by one of the data members. This new declaration hides the data member for the remainder of the method. (This is a specific example of the scope rules described in Session 4.)

Avoiding this type of name hiding in this case is trivially easy — there are only two members to worry about. It may not be so easy in the case of a real-world class with a large number of data members.

A similar situation is avoided in a conventional function:

```
public void SomeFunction()
{
  string sName = "A.Name";

  Person person = new Person();
  person.sName = "A. Nother Name";
}
```

The reference to the local sName and the data member sName causes no confusion because the object reference sorts it all out.

Member hiding within a method is handled the same way: by making explicit reference to the object:

```
class Person
{
  public string sName;
  public int nID;

  public void SomeMethod(string sNewName)
  {
    // define a local variable sName
    string sName = "Some other guy";

    // sName now refers to the data member
    this.sName = sNewName;
  }
}
```

The reference to this.sName means the sName data member of the current object. This data member has nothing to do with the locally defined sName.

Using this when naming arguments to a function

Name hiding can be an advantage when naming arguments to a function. This is demonstrated in the function Init() in the following code segment:

```
class Person
{
  public string sName;
  public int nID;

  public void Init(string sName, int nID)
  {
    this.sName = sName;
    this.nID   = nID;
  }
}
```

The arguments to the Init() method are called sName and nID, which correspond with the names of the corresponding data members. This makes the function easier to read because the programmer knows by looking at the names of the arguments to the function which argument is to be stored where. This avoids the nuisance of giving the arguments names like sNewName and sNewID.

The addition of this makes it clear which sName is intended. Within Init() the name sName refers to the function argument, but this.sName refers to the data member.

Using this when referencing objects

The this keyword appears when our programs store the current object for use later or by some other function. Consider the following example program:

```
// ReferencingThisExplicitly - this program demonstrates
//             how to explicitly use the reference to this
using System;

namespace ReferencingThisExplicitly
{
  public class Class1
  {
    public static int Main(string[] strings)
    {
      // create a student
      Student student = new Student();
      student.Init("Stephen Davis", 1234);

      // now enroll the student in a course
      Console.WriteLine
        ("Enrolling Stephen Davis in Biology 101");
      student.Enroll("Biology 101");
```

```
        // display student course
        Console.WriteLine("Resulting student record:");
        student.DisplayCourse();

        // wait for user to acknowledge the results
        Console.WriteLine("Press Enter to terminate...");
        Console.Read();
        return 0;
    }
}

// Student - our class university student
public class Student
{
    // all students have a name and id
    public string sName;
    public int    nID;

    // the course in which the student is enrolled
    CourseInstance courseInstance;

    // Init - initialize the student object
    public void Init(string sInputName, int nInputID)
    {
        sName = sInputName;
        nID = nInputID;

        courseInstance = null;
    }

    // Enroll - enroll the current student in a course
    public void Enroll(string sCourseID)
    {
        courseInstance = new CourseInstance();

        // adding a course to myself via 'this'
        courseInstance.Init(this, sCourseID);
    }

    // Display the name of the student
    // and the course
    public void DisplayCourse()
    {
        Console.WriteLine(sName);
        courseInstance.Display();
    }
}
```

```
// CourseInstance - a combination of a student with
//university course
public class CourseInstance
{
  public Student student;
  public string sCourseID;

  // Init - tie the student to the course
  public void Init(Student inputStudent,
                   string sInputCourseID)
  {
    student = inputStudent;
    sCourseID = sInputCourseID;
  }

  // Display - output the name of the course
  public void Display()
  {
    Console.WriteLine(sCourseID);
  }
}
}
```

The entire version of the `ReferencingThisExplicitly` **program can be found on the CD.**

**10 Min.
To Go**

This program demonstrates how two objects can reference each other. The program enrolls a student "Stephen Davis" into the class "Biology 101" (if the truth be told, I never did take biology in school).

The Student object has room for a name, an id, and a single instance of a university course (not a very industrious student). Main() creates the student and then invokes Init() to initialize the Student object. At this point, the courseInstance reference is set to null because the student is not yet enrolled in a class.

The Enroll() method enrolls the student by creating a CourseInstance object. The arguments to CourseInstance.Init() are the name of the course and the student to enroll. Which student should we pass? Clearly, we need to pass the "Stephen Davis" student. This is the current student, the student referred to by this.

The explicit reference to this allows the Student to perform an operation on itself. In this case, Enroll() itself is in a new CourseInstance.

Done!

REVIEW

In this session, you saw how methods manipulate the current object, which is passed as a silent first argument in the method call. This object carries the keyword designation this. Normally C# applies the this reference when necessary for you; however, you saw a few cases in which the programmer must refer to this explicitly.

QUIZ YOURSELF

1. What is this? (See "The this reference.")
2. Consider the following two methods (see "The this reference"):

```
public class MyClass
{
  int nValue;

  public int RetValue1()
  {
    return nValue;
  }
  public int RetValue2()
  {
    return this.nValue;
  }
}
```

Is there any difference between the two methods?

PART

II

Saturday Morning Part Review

1. Write out the `while` loop equivalent of `for(int n = 0; n < 10; n++) { nSum = nSum + 1;}`.

2. Rewrite the following infinite loop program from Part I using the `break` so that it is no longer infinite.

```
void CountUntilOdd()
{
  double dValue = 0;
  while(IsEven(dValue))
  {
    Console.Write("x = " + dValue);
    dValue = dValue + 1.0;
    Console.WriteLine(" and then " + dValue);
    dValue = dValue + 1.0;
  }
}
```

3. Write a program that prompts the user for an integer value. If the user enters a 0, output the message "The value entered is 0." If the user enters a 1, 2, or 3, output the corresponding message. If the user enters any other value, output "The value entered is something else." Use the `switch` control.

4. Write a program `Reverse` that prompts the user for five integer values. The program outputs these values in the order in which they were entered and then in reverse order.

5. How would you go about changing the `Reverse` program so that the user could specify the number of values to enter rather than fix it?

6. Why does C# provide a `class` structure?

7. Write a small segment of code to create an object of the following class and initialize its members:

```
public class Person
{
  public string sFirstName;
  public string sLastName;
  public int nID;
}
```

8. What is the difference between the following static function and method?

```
public class SomeClass
{
  int nValue;
  public static void StaticFunc(SomeClass sc, int n)
  {
    sc.nValue = n;
  }
  public void Method(int n)
  {
    nValue = n;
  }
}
```

9. Rewrite your answer to Problem 7 so that the `Person` class provides an `InitPerson()` method that initializes the object with an application provided first and last names followed by an integer id.

10. How could the program write `InitPerson()` using the `this` keyword to make the method slightly more readable?

11. Write a small program that allocates two `Pool` objects. The program should then call a `DeeperPool()` method of the class `Pool` that returns a reference to the deeper of the two pools.

PART

III

Saturday Afternoon

Special Class Considerations

Session Checklist

✔ Declaring class or static members

✔ Investigating the limitations of a static member

✔ Declaring constants

Session 7 describes the concept of the C# function. Session 8 expands this concept into the C# object method. We need to wrap up a few special features of the class.

**30 Min.
To Go**

Class Members

Each of the methods you have seen so far must be invoked with an object of some type, even if it is a meaningless example object. This type of member function is called an *instance member* or an *object member* because it is a property of a single instance of a class.

On some occasions it seems somewhat arbitrary to create an object only for the purposes of invoking a method that doesn't modify the object in any way. For example, the output of this small program,

```
namespace Test
{
  using System;

  public class Class1
  {
    public static int Main(string[] strings)
    {
      // concatenate my first name with my last name:
      Holder holder = new Holder();
```

```
     Console.WriteLine("my name is {0}",
                holder.Concatenate("Stephen", "Davis"));

     // wait for user to acknowledge the results
     Console.WriteLine("Hit Enter to terminate...");
     Console.Read();
     return 0;
   }
 }

 class Holder
 {
   public string Concatenate(string s1, string s2)
   {
     return String.Format("{0} {1}", s1, s2);
   }
 }
}
```

is simply my name:

```
my name is Stephen Davis
Hit Enter to terminate...
```

The function Main() was forced to create an object of class Holder in order to invoke Concatenate() even though Concatenate() did not access any other member of Holder — in fact, there isn't even another member of Holder to access. What we need is a method that belongs to the class but not to any specific member of the class.

Creating a class member

A data member or member function that does not refer to any specific object is known as a *class member* or *static member*. It gets the latter name because it is declared with the descriptor static:

```
class Holder
{
  public static string Concatenate(string s1, string s2)
  {
    return String.Format("{0} {1}", s1, s2);
  }
}
```

A static method is invoked with the name of the class rather than with the name of any specific object:

```
// concatenate my first name with my last name:
Console.WriteLine("my name is {0}",
            Holder.Concatenate("Stephen", "Davis"));
```

The use of the keyword static **seems somewhat arbitrary. There's nothing about a class member that makes it any more or less static than an object member; however, that's the keyword used and so the name** *static member* **has stuck.**

Static methods have no this

Consider the following incorrect example program (this does not compile, by the way):

```
namespace Test
{
  using System;

  public class Class1
  {
    public static int Main(string[] strings)
    {
      // create a holder object to hold my favorite number
      Holder holderObject1 = new Holder();
      holderObject1.InitHolder(7);
      Holder holderObject2 = new Holder();
      holderObject2.InitHolder(8);

      // now convert that number to a string for output
      // to the console
      Console.WriteLine("My favorite number is {0}",
                    Holder.ConvertToString());

      // wait for user to acknowledge the results
      Console.WriteLine("Hit Enter to terminate...");
      Console.Read();
      return 0;
    }
  }

  class Holder
  {
    int nValue;

    // store off the value to be "held"
    public void InitHolder(int nValue)
    {
      this.nValue = nValue;
    }

    // ConvertToString - convert the current object into a string
    public string ConvertToString()
```

```
    {
        return String.Format("{0}", nValue);
    }
  }
}
```

The method `InitHolder()` initializes the value contained by the `Holder` class, `nValue`. The method `ConvertToString()` attempts to convert `nValue` into a string for display. Because `ConvertString()` is declared `static`, however, it is invoked with the class name `Holder` rather than with an object name such as `holderObject`. The question then becomes, which `nValue` is `ConvertString()` supposed to access? The value associated with `holderObject1`? `holderObject2`? some other object? There is no answer, because there is no reference pointer.

Because a static method is invoked with a class name rather than with an object name, a static method has no `this` pointer to point to the current object — there is no current object. Without a `this` pointer, a static method cannot directly access a nonstatic member (an object). Thus, the reference to `nValue` from within `ConvertToString()` is illegal.

**20 Min.
To Go**

Examining a more realistic example

Let's consider the example of a simple Student class:

```
class Student
{
  // the student's name
  public string sName;

  // the student's grade point average
  public double dGrade;

  // Init - initialize a new student object
  public void Init(string sName, double dGrade)
  {
    // save off the object's data
    this.sName = sName;
    this.dGrade = dGrade;
  }
}
```

This class defines a name and a grade property. These two members are clearly object members because each Student object has its own separate name and grade.

Suppose, however, we want to retain a reference to the best student along with her grade point average. There is only one best student — individual students don't have their own best student. The concept of a best student is a property of the class Student.

The following small program expands the Student class by adding the `bestStudent` and `dBestGrade` shared members.

```
// StaticFunctionExample - demonstrate the use of a static function
namespace StaticFunctionExample
```

```
{
  using System;

  class Class1
  {

    public static int Main(string[] args)
    {
      // accumulate the names and grades of a series of
      // of Springfield's best students
      string[] sN = {"Bart", "Homer", "Marge", "Lisa", "Maggie"};
      double[] sG = {    25,     0.5,      80,    100,        80};

      // create an array of students from these descriptions
      for(int index = 0; index < sN.Length; index++)
      {
        // notify user of next student
        Console.WriteLine("Creating student {0}, grade is {1}",
          sN[index], sG[index]);

        // now create a Student object with that data
        Student s = new Student();
        s.Init(sN[index], sG[index]);

        // display the best student to date
        Student bestStudent = Student.GetBestStudent();
        Console.WriteLine(
          "The best student to date is {0} ({1})",
          bestStudent.sName, bestStudent.dGrade);
        Console.WriteLine();
      }

      // wait for user to acknowledge the results
      Console.WriteLine("Hit Enter to terminate...");
      Console.Read();
      return 0;
    }
  }

  // Student - description of a student with name and grade
  class Student
  {
    public string sName;
    public double dGrade = 0.0;

    // the best student and her grade across all Student objects
    // (start with an initial student with a grade of zero)
    public static Student bestStudent = new Student();

    public static Student GetBestStudent()
```

```
    {
      return bestStudent;
    }

    // Init - initialize a new student object
    public void Init(string sName, double dGrade)
    {
      // save off the object's data
      this.sName = sName;
      this.dGrade = dGrade;

      // if our grade is greater than the grade of the best
      // student so far...
      if (dGrade > bestStudent.dGrade)
      {
        // ...then save off this student as the new best student
        bestStudent = this;
      }
    }
  }
}
```

 The complete `StaticFunctionExample` **program can be found on the CD.**

The sN and sG arrays at the beginning of the program define the names and corresponding grades of each member of the Simpson family. (I used the short names sN and sG to keep the declaration from wrapping on the page.) The two arrays are synched (that is, each grade in the double array is matched to the name in the string array) so that Bart gets the failing grade 25, Homer gets the expected lousy grade of 0.5, and Lisa makes her usually perfect 100.

The for loop converts each of these names and grades into a series of Student objects using the Init() method. After each Student is created, the for loop outputs the student with the best grade seen so far.

The Student class contains the expected data members sName and dGrade. In addition, the Student class includes a data member bestStudent flagged with the keyword static. The GetBestStudent() method is also marked static. The static keyword marks a variable or function as a shared member.

The Init() initialization method first stores the name and grade of the current student. Init() continues by comparing the current dGrade with the grade of the best student so far. If the current grade is better, it replaces the previous best student.

 bestStudent is initialized to point to an empty student with a grade of zero. The initialization of a static variable occurs when the program first starts. This initialization is needed because the first student initialized must have something with which to be compared.

*10 Min.
To Go*

The output from this program appears as follows:

```
Creating student Bart, grade is 25
The best student to date is Bart (25)

Creating student Homer, grade is 0.5
The best student to date is Bart (25)

Creating student Marge, grade is 80
The best student to date is Marge (80)

Creating student Lisa, grade is 100
The best student to date is Lisa (100)

Creating student Maggie, grade is 80
The best student to date is Lisa (100)
```

Of course, Lisa has the best grades of all of the Simpson family.

Notice how the program calls the static GetBestStudent() method in the earlier example: Student.GetBestStudent(). The argument of the method is the class name rather than the name of an object. This makes sense because the method is a property of the class; however, this has an interesting side effect. Without a this pointer, an expression like the following is impossible:

```
public static void GetBestStudent()
{
  Console.WriteLine(sName);
}
```

System and the static Main() method

The last two points to the standard program template are the using System at the beginning of the program and the static Main() declaration. Your C# program is bundled with a large number of helper functions. One set is the System functions. (There are others, as you'll see in later sessions.) The WriteLine() function you have been using to generate console displays is one of the System functions.

The C# library cannot perform any of the neat features you want by itself. When the C# compiler builds your program, it points the System library to your Main() function. When your program is executed, System performs a few background operations and then calls Main(). Calling Main() effectively passes control to your code. Returning from Main() hands control back to the System functions, which terminate the program.

Main() is declared static because none of your objects has yet been created when your program begins execution.

sName refers to the name of the current object, the object pointed to by this. But GetBestStudent() was not invoked with any object — there is no current object for a static method to access.

Defining special objects (defining read-only versus const data members)

C# provides a few other special type descriptors that can be used on data members. First, data members may be specially flagged to be read-only. In addition, arguments to functions can be flagged in a similar fashion.

One special type of static descriptor is the const data member. The value of a const variable must be established in the declaration — it may not be changed anywhere within the program:

```
class Class1
{
  // number of days in the year (including leap day)
  public const int nDaysInYear = 366;

  public static void Main(string[] args)
  {
    int[] nMaxTemperatures = new int[nDaysInYear];

    for(int index = 0; index < nDaysInYear; index++)
    {
      // ...accumulate the maximum temperature for each
      // day of the year...
    }
  }
}
```

The constant nDaysInYear can be used in place of the value 366 anywhere within your program. The const variable is useful because it can replace a meaningless constant such as 366 with the descriptive name nDaysInYear to enhance the readability of your program.

Done!

REVIEW

A data member or member function that does not refer to any specific object is known as a *class member* or *static member*. It gets the latter name because it is declared with the descriptor static.

QUIZ YOURSELF

1. What is the difference between an instance member and a class member? (See "Class Members.")
2. What keyword is used to declare a class member? (See "Creating a class member.")

The String Class

Session Checklist

✔ Examining properties of the string class

✔ Manipulating strings

✔ Parsing strings entered by the user at the console

**30 Min.
To Go**

I t's a close contest as to which variable type is more important, the int or the string. You can do an operation using only integers, but what is the user to think when the program spits out 3, for example? Or perhaps 366. What does that mean? It's only by adding an explanation in the form of a string that the output becomes "The first prime number is 3" or "The number of days in a leap year is 366".

This session examines many of the properties of the string variable type.

The String Class Type

In earlier sessions we spoke of string as an intrinsic variable type, like int or char; however, the string type is slightly different from other types in that it is synonymous with a class String. For example, the following is legal:

```
String s1 = "abcd"; // assign a string literal to a String obj
string s2 = s1;     // assign a String obj to a string variable
```

Notice that s1 is an object of type String class spelled with an uppercase *S*, whereas s2 is simply a string spelled with a lowercase *s*. Neither assignment would be legal unless the intrinsic string and the class String were of the same (or compatible) types.

You will see later in this session that all of the intrinsic types have corresponding class types; however, string is equivalent to its class type.

The String class is one of the many classes provided in the standard C# library. You have seen the addition operator used on strings a number of times:

```
string sName = "Randy";
Console.WriteLine("His name is " + sName);
```

This is a special operator provided by the String class. However, the String class provides a series of other methods with which to manipulate text strings.

Operating on a String

Many of the String functions are used to create a new string that is somehow a modification of the original. For example, converting a string with incorrect capitalization into sentence capitalization format (*sentence capitalization* means using uppercase for the first letter of a sentence and lowercase for all other letters except for proper nouns).

A string is immutable

One thing you should know right away is that you cannot change a string object itself once it has been created. Even though I might speak of modifying a string, no C# operation modifies the actual string object. Plenty of operations manipulate the logical string, but they always return the modified string as a new object.

For example, the operation "His name is" + "Randy" changes neither of the two strings but generates a third string "His name is Randy." One result of this immutability of strings is that it is not actually necessary to make copies of string members when copying the members of a class.

Consider the following simplistic example, which makes a copy of a Student object:

```
namespace Example
{
  using System;

  class Class1
  {
    public static void Main(string[] args)
    {
      // create a student object
      Student s1 = new Student();
      s1.sName = "Jenny";

      // now make a copy by copying each member
      Student s2 = new Student();
      s2.sName = s1.sName;
      s2.nID = s1.nID

      // there are no possible problems since the string
      // referenced by s2 cannot be changed by an C# function
```

```
      s1.sName.ToUpper();    // convert string to upper case
    }

    class Student
    {
      public String sName;
      public int    nID;
    }
  }
}
```

Technically s2 is not a completely independent copy of s1, because s1.sName and s2.sName point to the same string; however, there is no chance of s1.sName's being modified by references to s2 because the string pointed to by sName cannot be changed. The call to ToUpper() in this simple example returns a new string with every letter in sName converted to uppercase; however, it doesn't modify the string itself. Most classes contain some type of string data members — the immutability of strings greatly reduces the need to construct cumbersome deep copy methods.

The immutability of strings is important for another reason: string **constants. A string such as "this is a string" is a form of string constant just as 1 is an** int **constant. A compiler might choose to "combine" all accesses to the single constant "this is a string." Reusing** string **constants can reduce the footprint of the resulting program.**

Reusing string **constants would be impossible if a string could be modified.**

Manipulating a string as an object

A number of operations treat the entire string as a single object. A good example is the Compare() method. Compare() compares two strings as if they were numbers:

- If the left string is greater than the right string, Compare() returns a 1.
- If the left string is less than the right string, Compare() returns a -1.
- If the two strings are equal, Compare() returns a 0.

The algorithm works as follows when written in *notional C#* (C# without all the details):

```
compare(string s1, string s2)
{
  // loop through each character of the strings until
  // a character in one string is greater than the
  // corresponding character in the other string
  foreach character in the shorter string
    if (s1's character > s2's character when treated as a number)
      return 1
    if (s2's character < s1's character)
      return -1
```

```
      // OK, every letter matches, but if the string s1 is longer
      // then it's greater
      if s1 has more characters left
        return 1

      // if s2 is longer, it's greater
      if s2 has more characters left
        return -1

      // if every character matches and the two strings are the same
      // length, then they are "equal"
      return 0
    }
```

Thus, abcd is greater than abbd, and abcde is greater than abcd. Very often we don't care whether one string is greater than another but only whether the two strings are equal.

The following test program demonstrates this principle. BuildASentence prompts the user to enter lines of text. Each line is concatenated to the previous line to build a single sentence. The program exits if the user enters the words EXIT, exit, QUIT, or quit:

```
// BuildASentence - the following program constructs
//                  sentences by concatenating user
//                  input until the user enters
//                  one of the termination characters
namespace BuildASentence
{
  using System;

  public class Class1
  {
    public static int Main(string[] args)
    {
      Console.WriteLine("Each line you entered will be "
                  + "added to a sentence until you "
                  + "enter EXIT or QUIT");

      // ask the user for input; continue concatenating
      // the phrases input until the user enters exit or
      // quit (start with a null sentence)
      string sSentence = "";
      for(;;)
      {
        // get the next line
        Console.WriteLine("Enter a string");
        string sLine = Console.ReadLine();

        // exit the loop if it's a terminator
        if (IsTerminateString(sLine))
        {
          break;
        }
```

```
        // otherwise, add it to the sentence
        sSentence = String.Concat(sSentence, sLine);

        // let the user know how she's doing
        Console.WriteLine("\nYou've entered: {0}", sSentence);
    }

    Console.WriteLine("\nTotal sentence:\n{0}", sSentence);


    // wait for user to acknowledge the results
    Console.WriteLine("Hit Enter to terminate...");
    Console.Read();
    return 0;
}

// return a true if the source string is equal
// to any of the termination characters
public static bool IsTerminateString(string source) {

    string[] sTerms = {"EXIT",
                       "exit",
                       "QUIT",
                       "quit"};

    // compare the string entered to each of the
    // legal exit commands
    foreach(string sTerm in sTerms)
    {
        // return a true if we have a match
        if (String.Compare(source, sTerm) == 0)
        {
            return true;
        }
    }
    return false;
}
}
}
```

The complete BuildASentence **program can be found on the CD.**

After prompting the user as to what is expected of him, the program creates an empty initial sentence string sSentence. From there the program enters an infinite loop. (It is a convention that the control for(;;) loops forever.)

20 Min.
To Go

BuildASentence then prompts the user to enter a line of text, which it reads using the ReadLine() method. Having read the line, the program checks to see if it is a terminator using the locally created IsTerminateString(). The function returns a true if sLine is one of the terminator phrases and a false otherwise.

It is a firm convention that the name of a function that checks a property and returns a `true` or `false` must start with `Is`. In this case, the name of the function implies the question "Is `sLine` a Terminate String?" Of course, this is a human convention only — C# doesn't care.

If `sLine` is not one of the terminate strings, then it is concatenated to the end of the sentence using the `String.Concat()` function. The program outputs the immediate result so that the user can see what's going on.

The `IsTerminateString()` method defines an array of strings `sTerms`. Each member of this array is one of the strings that will cause the program to terminate. Notice that the program must include both `EXIT` and `exit` because `Compare()` considers the two strings differently by default. (Given the way the program is written, these are the only two choices. The words `Exit`, `eXit`, and so forth would not be recognized as terminators.)

The `IsTerminateString()` function loops through each of the strings in the array. If `Compare()` reports a match to any one of the terminate phrases, the function returns a `true`. If the function reaches the end of the loop without a match, the function returns a `false`.

The following shows an example run of the `BuildASentence` program:

```
Each line you entered will be added to a
sentence until you enter EXIT or QUIT
Enter a string
Programming with

You've entered: Programming with
Enter a string
 C# is fun

You've entered: Programming with C# is fun
Enter a string
 (more or less)

You've entered: Programming with C# is fun (more or less)
Enter a string
EXIT

Total sentence:
Programming with C# is fun (more or less)
Press any key to continue
```

I have highlighted my input in bold to make it easier to read. Notice that I started each phrase with a space to divide one phrase from another in the output.

Avoiding case

The `IsTerminateString()` considered `EXIT` and `exit` to be different terminators because by default the `Compare()` doesn't account for changes in case. However, it is possible to instruct Compare() to consider lower- and uppercase letters as equivalent. Thus, we could have written IsTerminateString() as follows:

```
public static bool IsTerminateString(string source)
{
  // indicate true if passed either exit or quit,
  // irrespective of case
  return (String.Compare("exit", source, true) == 0) ||
         (String.Compare("quit", source, true) == 0);
}
```

The Compare() function is overloaded with a second version that includes a third argument. This argument indicates whether the comparison should ignore the letter case (in other words, do we compare on case sensitivity). The true indicates "ignore."

This version of IsTerminateString() is made much simpler than the previous looping version. Not only does the function not need to worry about case, but it can use a single conditional expression because there are now only two options to worry about.

 Notice that this function does not use an if statement. The function simply returns the bool expression that it calculates.

Parsing Numeric Input

The ReadLine() function used for reading from the console returns a string object. A program must convert this string itself if it is expecting numeric input.

Each of the intrinsic variable types has a corresponding class. For example, the int type is tied to the Int32 class. These classes offer a number of functions, one of which is Parse(String), which converts a string into its numeric equivalent. Thus, the following code segment reads a number from the keyboard and stores it in an int variable:

```
string s = Console.ReadLine();
int n = Int32.Parse(s);
```

Similar Parse() methods exist for the other variable types, such as Double.Parse() and Boolean.Parse().

If s in the expression Int32.Parse(s) cannot be converted into an integer, the Parse() function *throws an exception*. We won't study exceptions until Session 16, but suffice it to say that such errors are easily handled. Unfortunately, an unhandled exception terminates the program. Until your program is prepared to handle exceptions, you need to do your best to make sure that the input is, in fact, an integer before calling the Parse() function.

The following function returns a true if the string passed to it consists of only digits. (The assumption is that a sequence of nothing but digits is probably a legal number.)

```
// IsAllDigits - return a true if all of the characters
//               in the string are digits
public static bool IsAllDigits(string sRaw)
```

```
{
  // first get rid of any benign characters
  // at either end; if there's nothing left
  // then we don't have a number
  string s = sRaw.Trim();   // ignore whitespace on either side
  if (s.Length == 0)
  {
    return false;
  }

  // loop through the string
  for(int index = 0; index < s.Length; index++)
  {
    // a non-digit indicate that the string
    // is probably not a number
    if (Char.IsDigit(s[index]) == false)
    {
      return false;
    }
  }

  // no non-digits found; it's probably OK
  return true;
}
```

The function IsAllDigits() first removes any harmless whitespace at either end of the string — if nothing is left, then the string was blank and could not have been an integer. The function then loops through each character in the string. If any of these characters turns out to be a nondigit, the function decides that the string is most likely not a number. If this function returns a true, the probability is very high that the string can be successfully converted into an integer. (Note that to simplify the example, I've ignored floating point numbers like 1.2 and 1e3 and hexadecimal numbers like 0x3F.)

The following code sample inputs a number from the keyboard and prints it back out to the console. (The IsAllDigits() function has been left out of the listing to save space.)

```
namespace Example
{
  using System;

  class Class1
  {
    public static int Main(string[] args)
    {
      // input a string from the keyboard
      Console.WriteLine("Enter an integer number");
      string s = Console.ReadLine();

      // first check to see if this could be a number
      if (!IsAllDigits(s))
      {
        Console.WriteLine("Heh! That isn't a number");
```

```
        }
        else
        {
          // convert the string into an integer
          int n = Int32.Parse(s);

          // now write out the number times 2
          Console.WriteLine("2 * {0} = {1}", n, 2 * n);
        }
        // wait for user to acknowledge the results
        Console.WriteLine("Hit Enter to terminate...");
        Console.Read();
        return 0;
      }
    }
  }
```

The program reads a line of input from the console keyboard. If IsAllDigits() returns a false, the program criticizes the user. If not, the program converts the string into a number using the Int32.Parse() call. Finally, the program outputs the number plus two times the number — the latter to prove that the program did, in fact, convert the string as advertised.

The output from a sample run of the program appears as follows:

```
Enter an integer number
4
2 * 4 = 8
Hit Enter to terminate...
```

Handling a Series of Numbers

10 Min.
To Go

Often a program receives a series of numbers in a single line from the keyboard. This can be easily handled using the String.Split() method. This function chops up a single string into an array of smaller strings. For example, if you tell Split() to divide a string using a comma as the delimiter, then 1,2,3 becomes the three strings 1, 2, and 3.

The following program uses the Split() method to input a sequence of numbers to be summed:

```
// ParseSequenceWithSplit - input a series of numbers
//                 separated by commas, parse them into
//                 integers and output the sum
namespace ParseSequenceWithSplit
{
  using System;

  class Class1
  {
    public static int Main(string[] args)
    {
```

```csharp
    // prompt the user to input a sequence of numbers
    Console.WriteLine(
        "Input a series of numbers separated by commas:"
                    );

    // read a line of text
    string input = Console.ReadLine();
    Console.WriteLine();

    // now convert the line into individual segments
    // based upon either commas or spaces
    char[] cDividers = {',', ' '};
    string[] segments = input.Split(cDividers);

    // convert each segment into a number
    int nSum = 0;
    foreach(string s in segments)
    {
      // (skip any empty segments)
      if (s.Length > 0)
      {
        // skip strings that aren't numbers
        if (IsAllDigits(s))
        {
          // convert the string into a 32-bit int
          int num = Int32.Parse(s);
          Console.WriteLine("Next number = {0}", num);

          // add this number into the sum
          nSum += num;
        }
      }
    }

    // output the sum
    Console.WriteLine("Sum = {0}", nSum);

    // wait for user to acknowledge the results
    Console.WriteLine("Hit Enter to terminate...");
    Console.Read();
    return 0;
}

// IsAllDigits - return a true if all of the characters
//               in the string are digits
public static bool IsAllDigits(string sRaw)
{
    // first get rid of any benign characters
    // at either end; if there's nothing left
```

```
      // then we don't have a number
      string s = sRaw.Trim();
      if (s.Length == 0)
      {
        return false;
      }

      // loop through the string
      for(int index = 0; index < s.Length; index++)
      {
        // a non-digit indicates that the string
        // is probably not a number
        if (Char.IsDigit(s[index]) == false)
        {
          return false;
        }
      }

      // no non-digit found; it's probably OK
      return true;
    }
  }
}
```

The complete ParseSequenceWithSplit **program can be found on the CD.**

The ParseSequenceWithSplit program begins by reading a string from the keyboard. The cDividers array containing a comma and a space is passed to the Split() method to indicate that these are the characters used to divide between individual numbers.

The program iterates through each of the smaller subarrays created by Split() using the foreach control. If the subarray is of zero length (this would result from two dividers in a row), the function returns false. The program next checks to make sure that the string actually contains a number by using the IsAllDigits() method. Valid numbers are converted into integers and then added to an accumulator nSum. Invalid numbers are ignored. (I chose not to generate an error message.)

The following demonstrates the output of a typical run:

```
Input a series of numbers separated by commas:
1, 2, a, 3, 4

Next number = 1
Next number = 2
Next number = 3
Next number = 4
Sum = 10
Hit Enter to terminate...
```

Done!

REVIEW

In this session, you saw how the `string` type is another representation of the `String` class. The `String` class provides a number of methods for manipulating the contents of the string object. The most common is the `Compare()` method, which compares two strings.

The `String` class also provides a number of methods for converting a string value such as `1,2,3` into the corresponding numeric `int` value. However, the user must be very careful to ensure that the string being converted is, in fact, a number.

The `String` class uses the split method to break a single string containing multiple values into their subparts.

The `String` class presents a number of other useful methods. The methods used for output are discussed in Session 13.

QUIZ YOURSELF

1. What is the class type of my name? (See "The String Class Type.")
2. How do I change the string my name to your name? (See "Operating on a String.")
3. What would the call `String.Compare("mystring", "mystring")` return? (See "Manipulating a string as an object.")

Controlling String Output

Session Checklist

✔ Formatting string output manually

✔ Using the String.Format() method to format output

**30 Min.
To Go**

Controlling the output from programs is a very important aspect of string manipulation. Face it — the output from the program is what the user sees. No matter how elegant the internal logic of the program might be, the user will not likely be impressed if the output is shabby in appearance.

Controlling Output Manually

The String class provides the program with help in directly formatting string data for output. This session examines the Trim(), Pad(), PadRight(), PadLeft(), Substring(), and Concat() methods.

Using the Trim() and Pad() methods

The Trim() method can be used to remove unwanted characters from either end of a string. This is most commonly used to remove spaces so that output strings line up correctly.

The Pad() methods, on the other hand, add characters to either end of a string to bring the string up to some predetermined length. For example, the programmer might add spaces to the left or right of a string in order to left- or right-justify it or add * characters to the left of a currency number.

The following small AlignOutput program uses both of these methods to trim up and justify a series of names:

```
// AlignOutput - left justify and align a set of strings
//               to improve the appearance of program output
```

```
namespace AlignOutput
{
  using System;

  class Class1
  {
    public static int Main(string[] args)
    {
      string[] names = {"Christa   ",
                        "  Sarah",
                        "Jonathan",
                        "Sam",
                        " Schmekowitz "};

      // first we output the names as they start out
      // (keep track of the longest string while we're at it)
      Console.WriteLine("The following names are of "
                        + "different lengths");

      foreach(string s in names)
      {
        Console.WriteLine("This is the name '{0}' before", s);
      }
      Console.WriteLine();

      // this time we fix the strings so that they are
      // left justified and all the same length
      string[] sAlignedNames = TrimAndPad(names);

      // finally output the resulting padded,
      // justified strings
      Console.WriteLine("The following are the same names "
                        + "rationalized to the same length");
      foreach(string s in sAlignedNames)
      {
        Console.WriteLine(
                    "This is the name '{0}' afterwards", s);
      }

    // wait for user to acknowledge the results
    Console.WriteLine("Hit Enter to terminate...");
    Console.Read();
      return 0;
    }

    // TrimAndPad - given an array of strings, trim
    //              whitespace from both ends and then
    //              repad the strings to align them
    //              with the longest member
    public static string[] TrimAndPad(string[] strings)
    {
      // copy the source array into an array that we can
```

```
            // manipulate
            string[] stringsToAlign = new String[strings.Length];

            // first remove any unnecessary spaces from either
            // end of the names
            for(int i = 0; i < stringsToAlign.Length; i++)
            {
                stringsToAlign[i] = strings[i].Trim();
            }

            // now find the length of the longest string so that
            // all other strings line up with that string
            int nMaxLength = 0;
            foreach(string s in stringsToAlign)
            {
                if (s.Length > nMaxLength)
                {
                    nMaxLength = s.Length;
                }
            }

            // finally justify all of the strings to the length
            // of the maximum string
            for(int i = 0; i < stringsToAlign.Length; i++)
            {
                stringsToAlign[i] =
                        stringsToAlign[i].PadRight(nMaxLength + 1);
            }

            // return the result to the caller
            return stringsToAlign;
        }
    }
}
```

The complete AlignOutput **program can be found on the CD.**

AlignOutput defines an array of names of uneven alignment and length. (These names could just as easily been read from the console or from a file.) The Main() method first displays the names as is.

Main() then aligns the names using the TrimAndPad() method before redisplaying the resulting trimmed-up strings:

```
The following names are of different lengths
This is the name 'Christa  ' before
This is the name '  Sarah' before
This is the name 'Jonathan' before
This is the name 'Sam' before
This is the name ' Schmekowitz ' before
```

```
The following are the same names rationalized to the same length
This is the name 'Christa    ' afterwards
This is the name 'Sarah      ' afterwards
This is the name 'Jonathan   ' afterwards
This is the name 'Sam        ' afterwards
This is the name 'Schmekowitz ' afterwards
```

The `TrimAndPad()` method begins by making a copy of the input `strings` array. In general, a method that operates on arrays should return a new, modified array rather than modify the arrays it is passed.

`TrimAndPad()` first loops through the array, calling `Trim()` on each element to remove unneeded whitespace on either end. The method loops again through the array to find the longest member. The method loops one final time, calling `PadRight()` to expand each array to match the length of the longest member in the array.

`PadRight(10)` expands an array to be at least 10 characters long. `PadRight(10)` would add 4 spaces to the right of a 6-character string.

`TrimAndPad()` returns the array of trimmed and padded strings.

Using the concatenate method

The programmer is often faced with the problem of breaking up a string or inserting some substring into the middle of another. Replacing one character with another is most easily handled with the `Replace()` method. For example,

```
string s = "Danger NoSmoking";
a.Replace(s, ' ', ',')
```

converts the string into "Danger NoSmoking."

Replacing all appearances of one character (in this case space) with another (exclamation mark) is especially useful when generating comma-separated strings for easier parsing. However, the more common and more difficult case involves breaking a single string into substrings, manipulating them separately, and then recombining them into a single modified string.

For example, consider the following `RemoveWhiteSpace` program. It uses the `RemoveSpecialChars()` method, which removes all of a set of special characters from a given string. The `RemoveWhiteSpace` program uses this method to remove whitespace (space, tab, and newline) from a string.

```
// RemoveSpecialChars - define a RemoveSpecialChars() method
// 	          which can remove any of a set of chars
// 	          from a given string.
namespace RemoveWhiteSpace
{
  using System;
  public class Class1
  {
    public static int Main(string[] strings)
    {
      // define the special characters
      char[] cSpecialChars = {'\n', ',', '_'};
```

```
      // start with a string embedded with whitespace
      string s = "_This is, a str\ning";
      Console.WriteLine("Starting string:" + s);
      Console.WriteLine
        ("\nRemoving newlines, commas and underscores\n");
      // output the string with the whitespace missing
      Console.WriteLine("Resulting string:" +
        RemoveSpecialChars(s, cSpecialChars));
      // wait for user to acknowledge the results
      Console.WriteLine("Hit Enter to terminate...");
      Console.Read();
      return 0;
    }
    // RemoveSpecialChars - remove every occurrence of
    //                      the specified character from
    //                      the string
    public static string RemoveSpecialChars(string sInput,
      char[] cTargets)
    {
      string sOutput = sInput;
      foreach(char c in cTargets)
      {
        for (;;)
        {
          // find the offset of the character; exit the loop
          // if there are no more
          int nOffset = sOutput.IndexOf(c);
          if (nOffset == -1)
          {
            break;
          }
          // break the string into the part prior to the
          // character and the part after the character
          string sBefore = sOutput.Substring(0, nOffset);
          string sAfter  = sOutput.Substring(nOffset + 1);
          // now put the two substrings back together with the
          // character in the middle missing
          sOutput = String.Concat(sBefore, sAfter);
        }
      }
      return sOutput;
    }
  }
}
```

The key to this program is the RemoveSpecialChars() method. This method returns a string consisting of the input string sInput with every one of a set of characters contained in the array cTargets removed. To better understand this method, assume that the string was ab,cd,e and that the array of special characters was the single character , (comma).

The RemoveSpecialChars() method enters a loop from which it will not return until every comma has been removed. The IndexOf() method returns the index within the array of the first comma that it can find. A return value of -1 indicates that no comma was found.

After the first call, IndexOf() returns a 2 (a is 0, b is 1, and , is 2). The next two methods break the string apart at the index. Substring(0, 2) creates a substring consisting of two characters starting with offset 0 — that is, ab. The second call to Substring(3) creates a string consisting of the characters starting at offset 3 and continuing to the end of the string — that is, cd,e. (It's the +1 that skips over the comma.) The Concat() method puts the two substrings back together to create abcd,e.

Control passes back up to the top of the loop. During the next iteration the comma is found to be at offset 4. The concatenated string is abcde. Because there is no comma left, the index returned on the final passes is -1.

20 Min. To Go

The RemoveWhiteSpace program prints out a string containing several forms of whitespace. The program then uses the RemoveSpecialChars() method to strip out the special characters. The output from this program appears as follows:

```
Starting string:_This is, a str
ing

Removing newlines, commas and underscores

Resulting string:This is a string
Hit Enter to terminate...
```

 Study this particular method carefully. You will find it necessary to use the IndexOf(), Substring(), and Concat() methods often in the manipulation of strings for output, both to the console and to files.

String.Format() Controls

The String class also provides the Format() method for formatting output, especially the output of numbers.

 Console.Write() **and** WriteLine() **use the** String.Format() **method to format output.**

In its simplest form, Format() provides for the insertion of string, numeric, or Boolean input in the middle of a control string. For example, look at the following call:

```
String.Format("{0} times {1} equals {2}", 2, 3, 2*3);
```

The first argument to Format() is known as the control string. The {*n*} in the middle of the control string indicates that the *n*th argument following the control string is to be inserted at that point. 0 refers to the first argument, in this case 2, 1 to the next, 3, and so forth.

The resulting string is:

```
"2 times 3 equals 6"
```

Unless otherwise directed, Format() uses a default output format for each argument type. Format() allows the user to affect the output format by including modifiers in the place holders. See Table 13-1 for a listing of some of these controls. For example, {0:E6} says to output the number in exponential form using six spaces for the mantissa.

Table 13-1 *Format Controls Using String.Format()*

Control	Example	Result	Description
C — Currency	{0:C} of 123.456	$123.45	The currency sign depends upon the localization setting.
	{0:C} of -123.456	($123.45)	
D — Decimal	{0:D5} of 123	00123	Integers only.
E — Exponential	{0:E} of 123.45	1.2345E+02	This is also known as scientific notation.
F — Fixed	{0:F2} of 123.4567	123.45	The number after the F indicates the number of digits after the decimal point.
N — Number	{0:N} 123456.789	123,456.79	Adds commas plus rounds off to near 100th.
	{0:N1} 123456.789	123,456.8	Controls the number of digits after the decimal points.
	{0:N0} 123456.789	123,457	
X — Hexadecimal	X	255	Outputs hexadecimal digit.
	{0:000.00} 12.3	012.30	Forces a 0 if a digit is not already present.
	{0:###.##} 12.3	12.3	Forces the space to be left blank; no other field can encroach on the 3 digits to the left and 2 digits after the decimal point (good for maintaining decimal point alignment).
	{0:##0.0#} 0	0.0	Combining the # and 0s forces the space to be allocated by the #s and forces at least one digit to appear, even if the number is 0.
	{0:#00.#%} 0.1234	12.3%	The % displays the number as a percentage (multiplies by 100 and adds the percent sign).
	{0:#00.#%} 0.0123	01.2%	Same as above, except insert leading zero. Notice that the ".#" control leaves one digit after the decimal point

These format controls can seem a bit bewildering. (I haven't even mentioned the detailed currency and date controls.) To help you wade through these options, the following `OutputFormatControls` program allows you to enter a floating point number followed by a control sequence. The program then displays the number using the specified `Format()` control.

```
// OutputFormatControls - allow the user to reformat input
//                        numbers using a variety of format
//                        controls input at run time
namespace OutputFormatControls
{
  using System;

  public class Class1
  {
    public static int Main(string[] args)
    {
      // keep looping - inputing numbers until
      // the user enters a blank line rather than
      // a number
      for(;;)
      {
        // first input a number -
        // terminate when the user inputs nothing
        //   but a blank line
        Console.WriteLine("Enter a double number");
        string sNumber = Console.ReadLine();
        if (sNumber.Length == 0)
        {
          break;
        }
        double dNumber = Double.Parse(sNumber);

        // now input the control codes; split them
        // using spaces as dividers
        Console.WriteLine("Enter the control codes"
                    + " separated by a blank");
        char[] separator = {' '};
        string sFormatString = Console.ReadLine();
        string[] sFormats =
                    sFormatString.Split(separator);

        // loop through the individual format controls
        foreach(string s in sFormats)
        {
          if (s.Length != 0)
          {
            // create a complete format control
            // from the control letters entered earlier
            string sFormatCommand = "{0:" + s + "}";

            // output the number entered using the
```

```
            // reconstructed format control
            Console.Write(
                "The format control {0} results in ",
                sFormatCommand);
            Console.WriteLine(sFormatCommand, dNumber);
            Console.WriteLine();
          }
        }
      }

      // wait for user to acknowledge
      Console.WriteLine("Hit Enter to terminate...");
      Console.Read();
      return 0;
    }
  }
}
```

The complete OutputFormatControls **program can be found on the CD.**

**10 Min.
To Go**

The OutputFormatControls program continues to read floating point numbers into a variable dNumber until the user enters a blank line. (Notice that the program does not include any tests to determine whether the input is a legal floating point number.)

The program then reads a series of control strings separated by spaces. Each control is combined with a {0} string into the variable sFormatCommand. For example, if you entered N4, the program would store the control {0:N4} into sFormatCommand. The statement

```
Console.WriteLine(sFormatCommand, dNumber);
```

writes out the number dNumber using the newly constructed sFormatCommand.

Typical output from the program appears as follows (my input is in boldface):

```
Enter a double number
12345.6789
Enter the control codes separated by a blank
C E F1 N0 0000000.00000
The format control {0:C} results in $12,345.68

The format control {0:E} results in 1.234568E+004

The format control {0:F1} results in 12345.7

The format control {0:N0} results in 12,346

The format control {0:0000000.00000} results in 0012345.67890

Enter a double number
.12345
```

```
Enter the control codes separated by a blank
00.0%
The format control {0:00.0%} results in 12.3%
Enter a double number

Hit Enter to terminate...
```

For example, when applied to the number 12345.6789, the control N0 added commas in the proper place (the N part) and lopped off everything after the decimal point (the 0 portion) to render 12,346 (remember the last digit was rounded off, not truncated).

Similarly, when applied to 0.12345, the control 00.0% outputs 12.3%. The percent sign in the control multiplied the number by 100 and added the percent sign to the result. The 00.0 indicated that the output should include at least two digits to the left of the decimal point and only one digit after the decimal point.

The number 0.01 is displayed as 01.0% using the same 00.0% control. Try it using the OutputFormatControls.

Done!

REVIEW

This session reviewed a number of ways of manipulating string output for purposes of display. The C# library provides a number of String methods that help in making output more pleasing. Some of the methods, such as Trim() to remove leading characters and the Pad() method to add characters, are useful in aligning characters in columns.

In addition, the C# library provides methods to perform simple manipulation, such as character replacement. However, sophisticated manipulation generally involves dividing strings into substrings — often using the IndexOf() method — manipulating the substrings, and putting them back together using the Concat() method.

Thankfully, C# provides a much easier approach to formatting numeric output in the String.Format() method. Special controls can be added within the Format() call to control display features such as the number of significant digits, the aligning of decimal points, and the alignment of numbers within columns.

QUIZ YOURSELF

1. What are the Trim() and Pad() methods used for? (See "Using the Trim and Pad methods.")
2. What are the concatenate methods used for? (See "Using the concatenate methods.")
3. What are the String.Format() controls used for? (See "String.Format Controls.")

Arrays

Session Checklist

✔ Declaring arrays of object

✔ Passing an array to a function

✔ Passing an array to a program

✔ Creating multidimensional arrays

✔ Calling a function with an unspecified number of functions

**30 Min.
To Go**

The array construct extends beyond just arrays of integers or doubles. The array class can also contain arrays of objects. This session examines the classlike properties of the array.

Review of Simple Arrays

Earlier sessions (7 and 13) demonstrate how to use arrays of the intrinsic, value-type types (int, double, and so on) as in the following examples:

```
// declare an array of 10 integers and allocate the
// space off of the "heap"
int[] nArray = new int[10];

// store a 5 into the first element of the array
nArray[0] = 5;

// store a 6 into the last element of the array
nArray[9] = 6;
```

```
// notice that the following would be illegal
// since there is no element 10 elements beyond
// the first element
// nArray[10] = 7;

// assign a value to each member of the array
for(int index = 0; index < nArray.Length; index++)
{
  nArray[index] = 2 * index;
}

// the foreach flow control can also be used
// to access different elements of the array
foreach(int nElement in nArray)
{
  Console.WriteLine("next element = {0}", nElement);
}
```

This code snippet declares an array nArray of ten ints. The memory for nArray is allocated from a block of memory known as the *heap*. It then stores a 5 in the first element of the array nArray[0] and a 6 in the last element of the array nArray[9]. Notice that, because the index starts counting from zero, nArray[10] is invalid.

The for loop stores a different value in each element of the array while the foreach loop reads each element back out. The value of .Length is the number of elements in an array.

You have also seen how an array can be declared and initialized at the same time:

```
int[] nArray = {1, 2, 3};
```

When to for and when to foreach

You will see that I sometimes use the for control for iterating through the elements of an array and sometimes the foreach. I do this to familiarize you with both controls. In general the two controls are interchangeable when used for arrays. There are, however, two differences between the for and foreach controls when used with arrays. The first is that the foreach (referenced in Session 5) cannot be used to change the value of a array. In this example,

```
foreach(int n in nArray)
{
  n = 10;
}
```

n is a variable in its own right and does not refer directly to a position within the array. The assignment n = 10; within the foreach changes the value of n only — it has no effect on nArray.

The second difference is less critical: The foreach does not have the index variable provided by the for control. It is this index variable that allows loops like

```
for(int index = 0; index < nArray.Length; index++)
{
    Console.WriteLine("line {0} is {1}", index, nArray[index]);
}
```

to display both the value of an array element and its location within the collection. However, the index can be simulated with the foreach as follows:

```
int index = 0;
foreach(int n in nArray)
{
    Console.WriteLine("line {0} is {1}", index, nArray[index]);
    index++;
}
```

The index variable keeps track of the number of times the program has iterated through the loop. Again, this technique will prove more important with different types of collections.

Passing an Array to a Function

An array can be passed to a function as follows:

```
// PassingArrays - demonstrate how an array can be
//                 passed to a function
namespace PassingArrays
{
    using System;

  public class Test
  {
    public static int Main(string[] strings)
    {
      // create an array of ints...
      int[] nMyArray = new int[5];

      // ...pass them to a function...
      InitArray(nMyArray);

      // ...and display the results
      for(int index = 0; index < nMyArray.Length; index++)
```

```
        {
            Console.WriteLine("square of {0} = {1}",
                                index, nMyArray[index]);
        }

        // wait for user to acknowledge the results
        Console.WriteLine("Hit Enter to terminate...");
        Console.Read();
        return 0;
    }

    public static void InitArray(int[] nArray)
    {
        for(int index = 0; index < nArray.Length; index++)
        {
            nArray[index] = index * index;
        }
    }
  }
}
```

The complete PassingArrays **program can be found on the CD.**

This Main() function creates an array nMyArray of length 5. Main() passes this array to the function InitArray().

The InitArray() function loops through the array provided, storing the square of the offset of each element in the array.

Main() finishes by displaying the value of the array after InitArray() has completed. The output from this program appears as follows:

```
square of 0 = 0
square of 1 = 1
square of 2 = 4
square of 3 = 9
square of 4 = 16
Hit Enter to terminate...
```

In Session 10 you were introduced to the fact that the string **was really just another name for the** String **class contained in the standard C# library. In a similar fashion, every array is described by the standard** Array **class. Creating an array creates an object of class** Array **to describe the array. The** Array **class contains a number of members and methods to describe the resulting array. The most commonly used member is** Length, **which describes the number of elements in the array.**

Passing Arguments to a Program

Other types of arrays may be passed to functions as well. For example, our old standby
Main(string[] args) receives as its argument an array of string values. What are these
strings?

When executing a program from the command line, the user has the option of adding
arguments after the program name. You see this all the time in commands like copy myfile
C:\myDirectory, which copies the file myfile into the mydirectory folder in the root
directory of the C: drive.

The array of string values passed to Main() are the arguments to the current program.
This is demonstrated in the following DisplayArguments example:

```
// DisplayArguments - display the arguments passed to the
//                          program
namespace DisplayArguments
{
  using System;

  public class DisplayArguments
  {
    public static int Main(string[] args)
    {
      // count the number of arguments
      Console.WriteLine("There are {0} program arguments",
                     args.Length);

      // the arguments are:
      int nCount = 0;
      foreach(string arg in args)
      {
        Console.WriteLine("Argument {0} is {1}",
                       nCount++, arg);
      }

      // wait for user to acknowledge the results
      Console.WriteLine("Hit Enter to terminate...");
      Console.Read();
      return 0;
    }
  }
}
```

The complete DisplayArguments **program can be found on the CD.**

This program begins by displaying the length of the args array. This corresponds to the
number of arguments passed to the function. The program then loops through the elements
of args, outputting each element to the console.

An example execution of this program generated the following results:

```
DisplayArguments /c arg1 arg2
There are 3 program arguments
Argument 0 is /c
Argument 1 is arg1
Argument 2 is arg2
Hit Enter to terminate...
```

You can see that the name of the program itself does not appear in the argument list. (There is another function by which the program can find out its own name dynamically.) In addition, the switch /c is not handled differently from other arguments — it is left up to the program itself to handle the parsing of arguments to the program.

Most command line programs allow for switches that control the output of the display.

**20 Min.
To Go**

Executing a command line program from a command prompt window

A program like DisplayArguments can also be executed from the Windows interface by double-clicking on the name of the program either within a window or from Windows Explorer.

● Double clicking on DisplayArguments in the window shown in Figure 14-1 executes the program with no arguments:

```
There are 0 program arguments
Hit Enter to terminate...
```

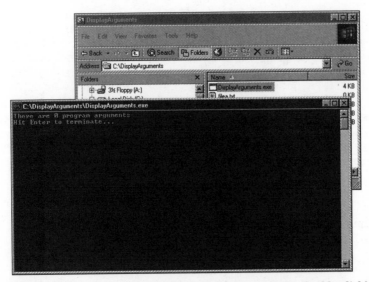

Figure 14-1 *You can execute the console program by double-clicking on its name within a Windows window.*

- Dragging and dropping a file, filea.txt, onto DisplayArguments executes the command DisplayArguments filea.txt. This is shown graphically in Figure 14-2.

  ```
  There are 1 program arguments
  Argument 0 is C:\C#Programs\DisplayArguments\filea.txt
  Hit Enter to terminate...
  ```

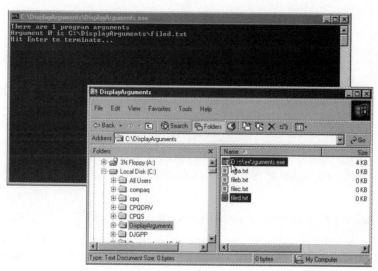

Figure 14-2   *Dropping a console program executes the program with the file name as its argument.*

- Dragging and dropping the files filea.txt, fileb.txt, filec.txt, and filed.txt onto DisplayArguments simultaneously executes the program with multiple arguments as shown in Figure 14-3. (To do this, select filea.txt in the list, hold the Shift key down, and then select filed.txt. All four files should appear selected. Now click and drag the set of files over to and drop it on DisplayArguments .)

  ```
  There are 4 program arguments
  Argument 0 is C:\C#Programs\filec.txt
  Argument 1 is C:\C#Programs\fileb.txt
  Argument 2 is C:\C#Programs\filea.txt
  Argument 3 is C:\C#Programs\filed.txt
  Hit Enter to terminate...
  ```

Notice that Windows passes the files to DisplayArguments in no particular order.

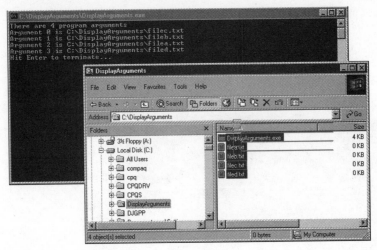

Figure 14-3 *Dropping a number of files on the console program executes the program with the entire list of file names as its argument.*

Executing a command line program within Visual Studio .NET

By default, Visual Studio .NET provides no arguments when executing the program from within the editor. You can tell Visual Studio to provide arguments to the program as follows:

1. Open the Solution Explorer. The Solution Explorer window provides a description of the projects that make up your "solution" — that is, your task — and the files that make up each project. Right-click on DisplayArguments as shown in Figure 14-4.

2. Select Properties from the drop-down menu that appears. (This should be the bottom-most option in the list.) Open the Configuration Properties folder. Click on the Debug option. Now enter whatever arguments you prefer in the Command Line Arguments field as shown in Figure 14-5.

3. Select OK and execute the program normally. The output from executing the program with the arguments /c arg1 arg2 appears as:

```
There are 3 program arguments
Argument 0 is /c
Argument 1 is arg1
Argument 2 is arg2
Hit Enter to terminate...
```

The only difference between the output from executing the program from Visual Studio .NET and that from the command line is the absence of the program name in the display.

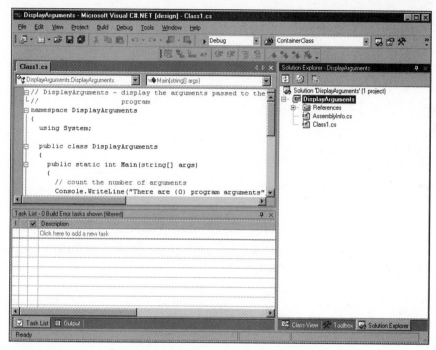

Figure 14-4 *A drop-down menu of project-related options appears when you right-click on the project name.*

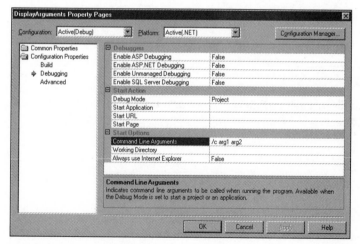

Figure 14-5 *The project debug properties allows the user to enter program arguments to be used when executing the program from the debugger.*

Initializing an object array

The same rules that govern the declaration of arrays of intrinsic variable types apply to arrays of strings and arrays of user-defined objects:

```
// declare an empty array of strings
string[] strings_a = new String[2];

// now populate the string
strings_a[0] = "first string";
strings_a[1] = "second string";
```

However, the following is also allowed:

```
string[] strings_b = {"first string",
                      "second string"};
```

In fact, the cardinality (number of elements) of the array can be declared explicitly as well as derived from the number of items in the initialization list.

```
string[] strings_c = new string[2] {"first string",
                                     "second string"};
```

By comparison with the `string` and `int` cases, the following is also legal:

```
Student students_a = {new Student(), new Student()};
```

or

```
Student students_b = new Student[2] {new Student(),
                                     new Student()};
```

Multidimensional Arrays

C# also supports a multidimensional array, also known as a matrix. C# supports two types of matrices: the *simple matrix* and the *jagged matrix*.

The simple matrix

A matrix is declared as follows:

```
int[,] nMatrix = new int[2, 3];
```

This declares a two-dimensional matrix of two column/rows and three column/rows. (The number of dimensions is also known as the *rank* of the matrix.)

I am often asked: Is it two columns and three rows or two rows and three columns? I view this as a largely nonsensical question. It is whichever you prefer. *Row* and *column* are human inventions designed to give the matrix a physical representation. The programmer does not and should not know how the matrix is represented in memory.

The size and rank of a matrix can also be determined by its initialization:

```
int [,] nMatrix = {{1, 2},
                   {3, 4},
                   {5, 6}};
```

The individual elements of the matrix are accessed as follows:

```
for (int indexX = 0; indexX < 2; indexX++)
{
  for (int indexY = 0; indexY < 3; indexY++)
  {
    nMatrix[indexX, indexY] = indexX * indexY;
  }
}
```

The jagged matrix

A more convenient construct is the *jagged* matrix. A jagged matrix is truly nothing more than an array of arrays. Jagged arrays are less efficient and are more difficult to construct, but they much more flexible than simple arrays.

Consider the following problem: I would like to store in a single matrix the names of each family along a row and the names of each member of the family along the columns. Assume that there are three families.

A simple matrix representation might appear as follows:

```
string[,] m = {{"Brown", "Jon", "Marcie", "Ben", "Leigh"},
               {"Davis", "Jenny", "Kinsey", "", ""},
               {"Stephens", "Logan", "", "", ""}};
```

A total of five elements are required for the Brown family: one for the last name and a separate element for each of the members of the family. The Davis family has only two members, however. This second row must be padded with two blank slots because all rows in a simple matrix must have the same number of columns. This is true even of the Stephens family with its single, lonely member, Logan.

This situation is not too bad because the largest family, the Browns, still has only four members. Things get much worse when the extremes are larger. Consider the number of students attending universities. Some universities have tens of thousands of students whereas some have only a few hundred. Padding the smaller university with ten thousand null strings seems (and is) ridiculous.

The jagged matrix solves the problem in the following way:

```
string[][] jm = new string[3][];
jm[0] = new string[5]{"Brown", "Jon", "Marcie", "Ben", "Leigh"};
jm[1] = new string[3]{"Davis", "Jenny", "Kinsey"};
jm[2] = new string[2]{"Stephens", "Logan"};
```

The `string[][]` declaration defines `jm` to be an array of arrays. `new string[3][]` specifies that there are three elements in `jm`. `jm[0]` consists of an array of five strings, whereas `jm[1]` consists of an array of three strings, and so forth.

Figure 14-9 demonstrates the difference between the simple and the jagged arrays graphically. The following simple program outputs all of the names in a jagged matrix:

```
public static int Main(string[] args)
{
  string[][] jm = new string[3][];
  jm[0] = new string[5]{"Brown", "Jon", "Marcie",
                                  "Ben", "Leigh"};
  jm[1] = new string[3]{"Davis", "Jenny", "Kinsey"};
  jm[2] = new string[2]{"Stephens", "Logan"};

  for(int i = 0; i < jm.Length; i++)
  {
    for (int j = 0; j < jm[i].Length; j++)
    {
      Console.Write("{0} ", jm[i][j]);
    }
    Console.WriteLine();
  }

  // wait for user to acknowledge the results
  Console.WriteLine("Hit Enter to terminate...");
  Console.Read();
  return 0;
}
```

Notice that the array `jm` has a length of 3, which is accessible through the `Length` member because `jm` contains references to three arrays. Each of these arrays in turn has its own length, each of which differs from the other arrays in the jagged matrix. The output of this program appears as follows:

```
Brown Jon Marcie Ben Leigh
Davis Jenny Kinsey
Stephens Logan
Hit Enter to terminate...
```

From this discussion you might conclude that the jagged matrix always uses the least amount of memory because it allocates only the exact number of elements required. However, this may not be the case because the overhead for creating and storing a separate array for each column may outweigh the benefits. In addition, a simple matrix is almost certainly faster to access than a jagged array. However, for most applications the jagged array is a smaller, more flexible construct with only a slight performance penalty.

Functions with an Unspecified Number of Arguments

10 Min. To Go

C# allows the programmer to declare a function with an unspecified number of arguments.

Creating such functions is generally a bad idea because doing so deprives C# of comparing the usage against the declaration. However, there are times when the advantages outweigh the danger — for instance, if the number of elements is unknown at runtime.

You declare the known arguments to the function first but follow up with the keyword params followed by an array name. C# populates this array with the remaining arguments at the time of the call.

Consider, for example, the following program containing the function Sum(). Sum() accepts any number of int arguments and returns their sum:

```
// UnspecifiedParamsProgram - this program demonstrates
//                             how to use the params feature
//                             to write functions which
//                             accept a variable number
//                             of arguments
namespace UnspecifiedParamsProgram.cs
{
  using System;

  public class Class1
  {
    public static int Main(string[] args)
    {
      // sum a series of numbers using the SumArgs
      // function
      int nSum;
      Console.WriteLine("{0}",
                        SumArgs(out nSum, 1, 2, 3));

      // invoke the SumArgs function passing the array
      // directly
      int[] nArray = {4, 5, 6};
      Console.WriteLine("{0}",
                        SumArgs(out nSum, nArray));
```

```
      // wait for user to acknowledge the results
      Console.WriteLine("Hit Enter to terminate...");
      Console.Read();
      return 0;
    }

    // SumArgs - add the arguments passed to the
    //           function; the function accepts
    //           any number of integer arguments
    public static int SumArgs(out int nSum,
                              params int[] list)
    {
      // iterate through the parameters passed
      // to the function
      nSum = 0;
      foreach(int n in list)
      {
        // add each one to the accumulator variable
        nSum += n;
      }
      return nSum;
    }
  }
}
```

The complete `UnspecifiedParamsProgram` **program can be found on the CD.**

The first argument to SumArgs() is an out variable nSum, which will be the sum of the remaining arguments. The same value is returned from the function directly.

I added the out nSum **argument primarily to demonstrate how a** params **argument list and a "normal" argument can be mixed in the same declaration.**

The second argument is declared as if it were an array of integers; however, the params keyword indicates that the array is to be constructed by C# automatically during the call.

For example, the first call to SumArgs() within Main() appears as follows:

```
Console.WriteLine("{0}", SumArgs(out nSum, 1, 2, 3));
```

C# turns the 1, 2, 3 sequence into an array list, which it passes on to the Sum(). The Sum() function itself iterates through the list argument as it would any other array.

```
foreach(int n in list)
{
  // add each one to the accumulator variable
  nSum += n;
}
```

In fact, the second call within Main() creates the array on its own, which it then passes to Sum():

```
int[] nArray = {4, 5, 6};
Console.WriteLine("{0}",
                  SumArgs(out nSum, nArray));
```

The Sum() **function wasn't very difficult because all of the remaining arguments were expected to be** ints. **A function like** Console.WriteLine() **is more complicated because it accepts arguments of different types. This problem is handled via a process known as** *reflection*. **Suffice it to say here that you can query an object for its type. Using this information, you can perform different operations depending upon the type of argument you encounter.**

Done!

REVIEW

Arrays of class objects are created in the same way as arrays of simple intrinsics such as int or double; however, the semantics are slightly different. Creating an array of objects makes room for references to objects but not the objects themselves. Fortunately, manipulating arrays of objects is no different from manipulating arrays of intrinsics, once they've been created.

The arguments to a program are passed to the Main() function as an array of strings (string[]).

Finally, it is possible to pass a variable number of arguments to a single function. The most common example of this is WriteLine(). The receiving function sees these variable arguments as an array.

QUIZ YOURSELF

1. What is the purpose of the Length property? (See "Review of Simple Arrays.")
2. What is the type of an array of int objects? (See the function InitArray() in the "Passing an Array to a Function" section.)
3. What is the purpose of the array of strings passed to Main()? (See "Passing an Array to a Function.")
4. How can a DOS program be executed under Windows? (See "Executing a command line program from a command prompt window.")
5. What is a jagged matrix? (See "The jagged matrix.")

Classes in the Real World

Session Checklist

✔ Making nachos

✔ Overview of object-oriented programming

✔ Introduction to abstraction and classification

✔ Examining the object-oriented properties of a C# class

This session serves as an introduction to object-oriented programming, an important concept that every C# programmer must master.

**30 Min.
To Go**

What, exactly, is object-oriented programming? Object-oriented programming, or OOP as those in the know prefer to call it, relies on two principles you learned as a child: abstraction and classification. Let me use an analogy.

Abstraction and Microwave Ovens

Sometimes when my son and I are watching football, I whip up a terribly unhealthy batch of nachos. I dump some chips on a plate, throw on some beans, cheese, and lots of jalapeños, and cook the mixture in the microwave oven for five minutes.

To use my microwave, I open the door, throw the stuff in, and punch a few buttons on the front. After a few minutes, the nachos are done. Think for a minute about all the things I don't do to use my microwave:

- I don't rewire or change anything inside the microwave to get it to work. The microwave has an interface — the front panel with all the buttons and the little time display — that lets me do everything I need.

- I don't have to reprogram the software used to drive the little processor inside my microwave, even if I cooked a different dish the last time I used the microwave.

- I don't look inside the case of my microwave.
- Even if I were a microwave designer and knew all about the inner workings of a microwave oven, including its software, I could still use it to heat my nachos without thinking about all that stuff.

These are not profound observations. You can handle only so much stress in your life. To reduce the number of things that you deal with, you work at a certain level of detail. In object-oriented (OO) terminology, the level of detail at which you are working is called the level of abstraction. I abstract away the details of the microwave's workings.

When I'm working on nachos, I view my microwave oven as a box. I can't worry about the insides of my appliance while I'm trying to feed a hungry son. This is a very important point. My first microwave oven came with an instruction manual. Unlike most consumers, I read the manual. Having done so, I realized why most users don't bother to read the manual: It told me very little that I couldn't have figured out by reading the labels of the buttons and having a basic understanding of how ovens and other electronic contraptions work.

Just as critical is the fact that as long as I use the microwave only through its interface (the keypad), there should be nothing I can do to cause the microwave to enter an inconsistent state and crash or, worse, turn my nachos into a blackened, flaming mass.

Functional nachos

Suppose I were to ask my son to write an algorithm for how Dad makes nachos. After he understood what I wanted, he would probably write, "Open a can of beans, grate some cheese, cut the jalapeños," and so on. When it came to the part about microwaving the mixture, he would write something like "Cook in the microwave for five minutes."

That description is straightforward and complete. But it's not the way a functional programmer would code a program to make nachos.

Here, I am using the term functional programmer to mean programmers who have the knowledge equivalent to that contained in Parts I and II of this book. These programmers know how to declare variables, how to perform operations, and how to pass arguments into and out of functions — all of the operations you need to write a program.

Functional programmers live in a world devoid of objects such as microwave ovens and other appliances. They tend to worry about flow charts with their myriad functional paths. In a functional solution to the nachos problem, the flow of control would pass through my finger to the front panel and then to the internals of the microwave. Pretty soon, flow would be coursing through the complex logic paths of the software inside the oven with instructions about how long to turn on the microwave tube and whether to sound the come-and-get-it tone.

The situation may be a little better than described: A functional programmer would write functions to perform certain operations. The users of these functions could read the documentation to determine what the function does and how to use it. However, the fact remains that it would be difficult to use any but the simplest functions without peeking inside to see how the function works and what other effects the function might have.

It is possible to write large and potentially complex pieces of code using a functional approach. Consider some very large functional projects that were completed successfully:

- The operating systems for mainframe computers
- Complex controls programs upon which almost all business is dependent
- The software that put men on the moon

These are just a very few of many.

In the functional world, it's difficult to think in terms of levels of abstraction. There are no objects, no abstractions behind which to hide inherent complexity. Beyond a certain point, the cost to develop these functional programs rises rapidly with size.

Object-oriented nachos

Let's contrast the functional methodology with the object-oriented approach to making nachos.

1. I describe the "the nacho problem" in human terms without regard to what the final software solution might be. From this human description I can identify the types of objects that are important to the problem: chips, beans, cheese, and an oven.

2. Now, I start modeling these objects. For example, what are the salient properties of an oven? You have to be able to insert the object to be cooked into the oven, make the oven start cooking, make it stop cooking, and remove the object. There may be other properties that you would like to add to your oven — timers, self-cleaners, and so forth — but those four properties are all we need to implement the nachos solution. I would repeat this operation for all of the objects identified in Step 1.

Notice that I didn't say "Insert the chips and beans into the oven" in my description of the microwave. This was on purpose. I should concentrate on how the oven works and not specifically on how it will be used.

3. I should run a quick check to make sure that the properties I have described for the chips, beans, cheese, and oven are sufficient to solve the problem. I may have omitted some important feature that is critical in making nachos. For example, although it's extremely unlikely, I may have forgotten to mention that the nachos must be hot enough to make my eyes water. I might also be on the lookout for features that are not needed. An oven timer would be useful, but I definitely do not need a defrost mode. There is a tendency to add unnecessary features (a property called "featuritis").

4. Finally, I write the software to model each of these objects. For example, the microwave software would need to provide the four operations identified in Step 3. I can then use these objects to solve the original problem of making nachos.

Each of these steps represents a level of abstraction. Step 1 describes the problem using human terms and concepts. This is said to be the problem domain. Each step burrows closer and closer until we reach Step 4, known as the software domain.

Classification and Microwave Ovens

Critical to the concept of abstraction is that of classification. If I were to ask my son, "What's a microwave?" he would probably say, "It's an oven that...." If I then asked, "What's an oven?" he might reply, "It's a kitchen appliance that...." (If I then asked, "What's a kitchen appliance?" he would probably say, "Why are you asking so many stupid questions?")

The answers my son gave here are actually quite insightful. His answers stem from his understanding of our particular microwave as an example of the type of things called microwave ovens. In addition, my son sees microwave ovens as just a special type of oven, which itself is just a special type of kitchen appliance.

My son does not need to go into all of the detail of the fact that the microwave is used in the kitchen to make things hot so that certain chemical reactions can occur to make our food both safe and tasty. My son merely describes those few properties that distinguish a microwave oven from every other type of oven. The listener adds that bit of knowledge to her understanding of an oven to arrive at the meaning of a microwave oven.

In object-oriented computerese, my microwave is an instance of the class microwave. The class microwave is a subclass of the class oven, and the class oven is a subclass of the class kitchen appliances.

Humans classify. Everything about our world is ordered into taxonomies. We do this to reduce the number of things we have to remember. Take, for example, the first time you saw an SUV. The advertisement probably called the SUV "revolutionary, the likes of which have never been seen." But you and I know that that just isn't true. I like the looks of some SUVs (others need to go back to take another crack at it), but an SUV is a car. As such, it shares all (or at least most) of the properties of other cars. It has a steering wheel, seats, a motor, brakes, and so on. I bet I could even drive one without reading the user's manual first.

I don't have to clutter my limited storage with all the things that an SUV has in common with other cars. All I have to remember is "an SUV is a car that..." and tack on those few things that are unique to an SUV (like the price tag). I can go further. Cars are a subclass of wheeled vehicles along with other members, such as trucks and motorcycles. Maybe wheeled vehicles are a subclass of vehicles, which include boats and planes. And on and on and on.

Just as an aside, it is this human taxonomy that can make learning a new language difficult. As one of my German instructors once told me, "It isn't what the other person says, it's what he doesn't say that makes it difficult to understand." In any conversation, the speaker and the listener assume much about the other's knowledge base in order to reduce the number of words and, thereby, shorten sentences.

Why Classify Objects in Software?

Why do we classify? It sounds like a lot of trouble. Besides, people have been using the functional approach for so long, so why change now?

It may seem easier to design and build a microwave oven specifically for a single purpose rather than build a separate, more generic oven object. Suppose, for example, that I want to build a microwave to cook nachos and nachos only. There would be no need to put a front panel on it, other than a START button. I always cook nachos the same amount of time. I could dispense with all that DEFROST and TEMP COOK nonsense. The oven would need to hold only one flat little plate. Three cubic feet of space would be wasted on nachos.

For that matter, I can dispense with the concept of microwave oven altogether. All I really need is the guts of the oven. Then, in the recipe, I put the instructions to make it work: "Put nachos in the box. Connect the red wire to the black wire. Bring the microwave tube up to about 3,000 volts. Notice a slight hum. Try not to stand too close if you intend to have children." Stuff like that.

But the functional approach has some problems:

- *Too complex:* I don't want the details of oven building mixed into the details of nacho making. If I can't define the objects and pull them out of the morass of details to deal with separately, I must deal with all the complexities of the problem at the same time.

- *Not flexible:* Someday I may need to replace the microwave oven with some other type of oven. I should be able to do so as long as its interface is the same. Without being clearly delineated and developed separately, it becomes impossible to cleanly remove an object type and replace it with another.

- *Not reusable:* Ovens are used to make lots of different dishes. I don't want to create a new oven every time I encounter a new recipe. Having solved a problem once, I would like to be able to reuse the solution in future programs. (To be fair, the reusability aspect is often overstated; however, classes are often reusable within an application or between similar applications.)

What Are the Properties of an Object-Oriented Class?

Object-oriented programming reduces detail by classifying the objects necessary to solve the software problem at hand and describing their relationship to the problem.

The C# class represents the type of object. Thus, the class MicrowaveOven would contain the properties of such an oven. A variable represents a particular instance. Thus, in the following snippet, myOven is the microwave that is bolted into my kitchen right over the stove top:

```
MicrowaveOven myOven = new MicrowaveOven();
```

A class member represents a property of the class. Thus, the method MicrowaveOven.Start() probably represents the ability of the microwave to start cooking. However, you can start only a given microwave oven:

```
// start cooking
myOven.Start();
```

The terminology here is important. People often say something to the effect that "The microwave object has the property Defrost()." This is not strictly true. The MicrowaveOven class has the property Defrost(). You invoke that method on a given object in order to defrost that object.

A class MicrowaveOvent must have four properties — external interface, controlled access, specialization, and polymorphism — if it is to represent a real-world thing in an object-oriented programming way.

**10 Min.
To Go**

Provide an interface to the user

A class must be able to project an external interface that is sufficient but as simple as possible.

People complain constantly that their VCRs are too complex (this is less of a problem with today's onscreen controls). There are too many buttons with too many different functions. Often the same button has a different function depending upon the state of the machine. In addition, no two VCRs seem to have the same interface. For whatever reason, the VCR projects an interface that is too difficult and too nonstandard for many people to use.

Compare this with an automobile. It would be difficult to argue that a car is less complicated than a VCR. However, there are at least three significant differences.

- Automobiles tend to offer the same controls in more or less the same place. My sister once had a car with the turn signal on the right of the steering column and the light control on the left. I never learned to turn left in that car at night without turning the lights off.

- Any differences that do exist are clearly documented with more or less internationally accepted symbology. The air conditioner control in my car differs in some details from that of my wife's car, but I have no trouble understanding how to operator the controls in either car.

- Well-designed autos do not use the same control to perform more than one operation depending upon the state of the car. (I can think of one exception to this rule: Some of the buttons on most cruise controls are overloaded with multiple functions.)

Controlled access

A class must be able to control access to its internal members.

A microwave oven must be built so that no combination of keystrokes I can enter on the keypad will cause the oven to hurt me. There are certainly combinations that don't do anything and there might even be keystroke combinations that damage the device. A manufacturer that built such a device would (and should) be rapidly run out of business through lawsuits.

Almost all kitchen devices of any complexity, including microwave ovens, have a small seal to keep consumers from reaching inside the device. If that seal is broken, indicating that the top of the device has been removed, the manufacturer no longer bears any responsibility. If I modify the internals of the oven, then it is my responsibility if it subsequently sets the house on fire.

Similarly, a class must be able to control access to its data members. No sequence of calls to class members should cause my program to crash. The class cannot possibly ensure this if "external elements" have access to the internal state of the class. The class must be able to keep critical data members inaccessible to the outside world.

Specialization

A class must be able to specialize by inheriting the properties of more general classes.

My son was able to describe a microwave oven so succinctly because it inherits so many properties from its parent class, the oven. The microwave may have properties that the base oven does not share; however, the reverse is not true.

 A more common term for the parent class is the base class. Thus, Oven is the base class, and MicrowaveOven is the subclass.

Similarly, a convection oven inherits properties from the base class oven. The microwave oven and convection oven share no obvious relationship — a microwave oven likely performs operations that a convection oven does not, and vice versa.

Polymorphism

A class must be able to redefine implementation details in a seamless fashion. This property is an extension of the specialization property.

 Don't ask me who came up with the obscure term polymorphism (probably the same guy to used the term method to describe a member function), but it seems to have stuck. The word comes from poly meaning multiple and morph meaning form.

Both a microwave oven and a conventional oven might cook, but they do so in entirely different ways. Thus, the method Oven.Cook() and MicrowaveOven.Cook() might be completely different in detail. As a user of the two classes, I shouldn't have to care as long as they both cook food.

Done!

REVIEW

In an abstract way of explaining classes, this session covered why object-oriented programming is important in developing programs. This session covered the fundamentals of OO programming and the importance of using methods and properties. This session also covered how to control access to your classes. We also touched on the specialization and polymorphism of classes.

Quiz Yourself

1. Describe the difference between the way in which the object-oriented programmer and the functional programmer see the world. (See "Functional nachos.")

2. Why use the object-oriented programming technique? (See "Why Classify Objects in Software?")

Inheritance

30 Min.
To Go

When I say that a jet is a type of airplane, I mean that a jet shares the properties of an airplane (most important of which is the fact that like an airplane, a jet can fly). This ability to define one concept in terms of a more general concept is called inheritance. The jet inherits the properties of an airplane.

The ability of one class to inherit the properties of another is a hallmark of object-oriented languages, including C#.

Defining the BankAccount Class

Bank accounts at my simplistic bank are described in the class BankAccount as follows:

```
// BankAccount - simulate a bank account each of which
//               carries an account id (which is assigned
//               upon creation) and a balance
using System;

public class BankAccount
{
```

```
// bank accounts start at 1000 and increase sequentially
// from there
public static int nNextAccountNumber = 1000;

// maintain the account number and balance for each object
public int nAccountNumber;
public double dBalance;

// Init - initialize a bank account with the next
//        account id and a balance of 0
public void InitBankAccount()
{
  nAccountNumber = ++nNextAccountNumber;
  dBalance = 0.0;
}

// Deposit - any positive deposit is allowed
public void Deposit(double dAmount)
{
  if (dAmount > 0.0)
  {
    dBalance += dAmount;
  }
}

// Withdraw - you can withdraw any amount up to the
//            balance; return the amount withdrawn
public double Withdraw(double dWithdrawal)
{
  if (dBalance <= dWithdrawal)
  {
    dWithdrawal = dBalance;
  }

  dBalance -= dWithdrawal;
  return dWithdrawal;
}
}
```

 The BankAccount **class is contained within the** SimpleInheritance **example program on the CD-ROM.**

The class BankAccount maintains a counter (the static int nNextAccountNumber) from which the account number of each subsequent object is taken. The InitBankAccount() method creates a new bank account with the next account number and a balance of zero. The Deposit() method allows the user to add money to the account (negative deposits are ignored). The Withdraw() method allows amounts up to the current balance to be withdrawn.

Maintaining a counter of the number of objects created is one of the more common uses for a static class member.

Inheriting from the BankAccount Class

My bank also maintains a number of different types of bank accounts. One type, the savings account, has all the properties of a simple bank account plus the ability to accumulate interest. I implemented the corresponding SavingsAccount class as follows:

```
// SavingsAccount - a bank account that draws interest
public class SavingsAccount : BankAccount
{
   public double dInterestRate;

   // InitSavingsAccount - input the rate expressed as a
   //                      rate between 0 and 100
   public void InitSavingsAccount(double dInterestRate)
   {
     InitBankAccount();
     this.dInterestRate = dInterestRate / 100;
   }

   // AccumulateInterest - invoke once per period
   public void AccumulateInterest()
   {
     dBalance = dBalance + (dBalance * dInterestRate);
   }
}
```

The SavingsAccount **class is contained within the** SimpleInheritance **example program on the CD-ROM.**

The SavingsAccount class defines a data member dInterestRate, which is intended to retain the interest rate of the current account. Each time the method AccumulateInterest() is invoked, the balance is increased by the balance times the interest rate.

The declaration public class SavingsAccount : BankAccount indicates that the class SavingsAccount inherits the members of the base class BankAccount.

We say that SavingsAccount **inherits from or extends** BankAccount. BankAccount **is called the base class and** SavingsAccount **the subclass.**

Notice that the InitSavingsAccount() method invokes InitBankAccount(). This initializes the data members specific to the bank account. The InitSavingsAccount() method could have initialized these members directly; however, it is better practice to allow BankAccount to initialize its own members.

The following code segment demonstrates the use of the `SavingsAccount` class:

```
// create a new savings account
SavingsAccount sa = new SavingsAccount();
sa.InitSavingsAccount(5);

// and deposit 100 dollars into it
sa.Deposit(100);

// now accumulate interest
sa.AccumulateInterest();
```

This code segment first creates a `SavingsAccount` object and initializes it to an interest rate of 5 percent. The `InitSavingsAccount()` method invokes `InitBankAccount()` internally in order to assign an account number and zero initial balance. The code segment then makes a deposit of 100 dollars. Finally, the example accumulates the interest of one period.

Notice that the application code invokes `Deposit()` using the `SavingsAccount` object `sa` directly. Even though `Deposit()` is actually defined within the subclass `BankAccount`, it is a part of the `SavingAccount` object.

In fact, any future additions to the `BankAccount` class become a part of the `SavingsAccount` class automatically. (There are limitations to this rule, as we'll see later in this session.)

The IS_A relationship

The relationship between a class and its base class is so fundamental that it is written IS_A, as in `SavingsAccount IS_A BankAccount`. Programmers also say that the `SavingsAccount` and `BankAccount` classes have the IS_A relationship.

 The IS_A relationship is fundamental to object-oriented programming. If my recipe says "heat the bread in an oven," then I am free to use either a conventional oven or a microwave oven — a microwave oven IS_A oven (forget about the grammar). The IS_A relationship is fundamental to the way we think and, therefore, to object-oriented programming.

The IS_A between `SavingsAccount` and `BankAccount` carries over into a number of areas:

```
// DirectDeposit - deposit my paycheck automatically
void DirectDeposit(BankAccount ba, int nPay)
{
  ba.Deposit(nPay);
}

void SomeFunction()
{
  // first pass a BankAccount object to DirectDeposit
  BankAccount ba = new BankAccount();
  DirectDeposit(ba, 100);
```

```
  // now do the same with a SavingsAccount
  SavingsAccount sa = new SavingsAccount();
  DirectDeposit(sa, 100);

  // ...continue...
}
```

SomeFunction() first creates a BankAccount object and passes it to DirectDeposit() in line with the declaration DirectDeposit(BankAccount, int). SomeFunction() continues by creating a SavingsAccount object and passing it to DirectDeposit().

The second call is allowed even though the latter is defined to accept a BankAccount object because a SavingsAccount IS_A BankAccount. As such, a SavingsAccount object can be used anywhere a BankAccount object is required.

Gaining Access to BankAccount through Containment

**20 Min.
To Go**

The class SavingsAccount could have gained access to the members of BankAccount in a different way:

```
// SavingsAccount_ - a bank account that draws interest
public class SavingsAccount
{
  public BankAccount bankAccount;
  public double dInterestRate;

  // InitSavingsAccount - input the rate expressed as a
  //                      rate between 0 and 100
  public void InitSavingsAccount(BankAccount bankAccount,
                                 double dInterestRate)
  {
    this.bankAccount = bankAccount;
    this.dInterestRate = dInterestRate / 100;
  }

  // AccumulateInterest - invoke once per period
  public void AccumulateInterest()
  {
    bankAccount.dBalance = bankAccount.dBalance
                  + (bankAccount.dBalance * dInterestRate);
  }

  // Deposit - any positive deposit is allowed
  public void Deposit(double dAmount)
  {
    bankAccount.Deposit(dAmount);
  }
```

```
// Withdraw - you can withdraw any amount up to the
//            balance; return the amount withdrawn
public double Withdraw(double dWithdrawal)
{
   return bankAccount.Withdraw(dWithdrawal);
}
}
```

In this case, the class SavingsAccount contains a data member bankAccount (as opposed to inheriting from BankAccount). The bankAccount object contains the balance and account number information needed by the savings account. In this case, we say that the SavingsAccount HAS_A BankAccount.

The HAS_A relationship

The HAS_A relationship is fundamentally different from the IS_A relationship. This difference isn't immediately obvious from the example application code segment:

```
// create a new savings account
BankAccount ba = new BankAccount()
SavingsAccount_ sa = new SavingsAccount();
sa.InitSavingsAccount(ba, 5);

// and deposit 100 dollars into it
sa.Deposit(100);

// now accumulate interest
sa.AccumulateInterest();
```

The differences become clear within the SavingsAccount class itself.

The method AccumulateInterest can reference dBalance only through the data member bankAccount. In addition, the SavingsAccount class must repeat each of the properties of the BankAccount with a do-nothing method that forwards the request to the corresponding BankAccount method.

However, as much as it might try, this version of SavingsAccount is not a BankingAccount. Additions to the BankAccount class are not automatically passed down to SavingsAccount. If my bank adds an Audit() method, the bank programmer must remember to implement a new vestigial SavingsAccount_.Audit() method.

In addition, a SavingsAccount cannot be used as a BankAccount. For example, the following code example fails:

```
// DirectDeposit - deposit my paycheck automatically
void DirectDeposit(BankAccount ba, int nPay)
{
   ba.Deposit(nPay);
}
```

```
void SomeFunction()
{
  // the following example fails
  SavingsAccount_ sa = new SavingsAccount_();
  DirectDeposit(sa, 100);

  // ...continue...
}
```

There is no obvious relationship between BankAccount and SavingsAccount as far as C# is concerned.

When to IS_A and When to HAS_A

The distinction between the IS_A and HAS_A relationships is more than just a matter of software convenience. This relationship has a corollary in the real world.

For example, a Ford Explorer IS_A car. An Explorer HAS_A motor. If my friend says, "Come on over in your car" and I show up in an Explorer, he has no grounds for complaint (okay, he has grounds for complaint, but not because an Explorer isn't a car). He may have something to say if I show up carrying the engine out of my Explorer, however.

The class Explorer should extend the class Car both to give Explorer access to the methods of a Car but also to express the fundamental relationship between the two.

Unfortunately, it isn't uncommon for the beginning programmer to have Car inherit from Motor. This gives the Car class access to the members of Motor that the Car needs to operate. For example, Car can inherit the method Motor.Start(). However, this example highlights one of the problems with this approach. Even though humans get sloppy in their speech, starting a car is not the same thing as starting the motor. For one thing, the car performs a number of electrical operations during the start operation that have nothing to do with the motor. In addition, Car.Start() might mean "Make the car go" as in start the motor, put it in gear, let off the brake, and so on.

Perhaps, even more than that, inheriting from Motor misstates the facts. A car is not a type of motor.

C# Support for Inheritance

C# implements a set of features designed to support inheritance.

Changing class

A program can change the class of an object. In fact, you have already seen this in one example. SomeFunction() was able to pass a SavingsAccount object to a method that was expecting a BankAccount object.

This conversion may be made more explicit:

```
BankAccount ba;
SavingsAccount sa = new SavingsAccout();

                        // OK:
ba = sa;                // an implicit down conversion is allowed
ba = (BankAccount)sa;   // the explicit cast is preferred

                        // No!
sa = ba;                // implicit up conversion not allowed

                        // this is OK since ba truly is a SavingsAccount
sa = (SavingsAccount)ba;
```

The first line stores a SavingsAccount object in a BankAccount variable. C# converts the object for you. The second line uses the cast operator to explicitly convert the object.

The final two lines convert the BankAccount object back into a SavingsAccount.

The IS_A property is not *reflexive*. That is, even though an Explorer is a car, a car is not necessarily an Explorer. Similarly, a BankAccount is not necessarily a SavingsAccount, and so the implicit conversion is not allowed. The final line is allowed only because the programmer has indicated her willingness to chance it, casting the ba object to an SavingsAccount object.

Invalid casts at runtime

Casting an object from BankAccount to SavingsAccount is generally a dangerous operation. Consider the following example:

```
public static void ProcessAmount(BankAccount bankAccount)
{
  // deposit a large sum to the account
  bankAccount.Deposit(10000.00);

  // if the object is a SavingsAccount
  // then collect interest now
  SavingsAccount savingsAccount = (SavingsAccount)bankAccount;
  savingsAccount.AccumulateInterest();
}

public static void TestCast()
{
  SavingsAccount sa = new SavingsAccount();
  ProcessAmount(sa);

  BankAccount ba = new BankAccount();
  ProcessAmount(ba);
}
```

The ProcessAmount() method performs a few operations, including the invoking of the AccumulateInterest() method. The cast of ba to a SavingsAccount is necessary because ba is declared to be a BankAccount. The program compiles properly because all type conversions are via explicit cast.

All goes well with the first call to ProcessAmount() from within Test(). The SavingsAccount object sa is passed to the ProcessAmount() method. The cast from BankAccount to SavingsAccount causes no problem because the object was originally a SavingsAccount anyway.

The second call to ProcessAmount() is not so lucky, however. The cast to SavingsAccount cannot be allowed. The BankAccount object passed to the function does not have an AccumulateInterest() method (this isn't the only difference). This conversion generates an error during the execution of the program (a so-called runtime error).

 Runtime errors are much more difficult to find and fix than compile time errors because you don't find out about them until the program happens to come upon the error during execution.

10 Min.
To Go

Avoiding invalid conversions using the is keyword

The ProcessAmount() function would be okay if it could check before performing the conversion to make sure that the object passed to it is actually a SavingsAccount object. C# provides the is keyword for this purpose.

The is operator accepts an object on the left and a type on the right. is returns a true if the runtime type of the object on the left is compatible with the type on the right.

The previous example can be modified to avoid the runtime error by using the is keyword:

```
public static void ProcessAmount(BankAccount bankAccount)
{
  // deposit a large sum to the account
  bankAccount.Deposit(10000.00);

  // if the object is a SavingsAccount...
  if (bankAccount is SavingsAccount)
  {
    // ...then collect interest now
    SavingsAccount savingsAccount = (SavingsAccount)bankAccount;
    savingsAccount.AccumulateInterest();
  }
}

public static void TestCast()
{
  SavingsAccount sa = new SavingsAccount();
  ProcessAmount(sa);
```

```
BankAccount ba = new BankAccount();
ProcessAmount(ba);
}
```

The object class

Consider the following three related classes:

```
public class MyBaseClass {}
public class MySubClass1 : MyBaseClass {}

public class MySubClass2 : MyBaseClass {}
```

The relationship between the three classes allows the programmer to make the following runtime test:

```
public class Test
{
  public static void GenericFunction(MyBaseClass mc)
  {
    // any MyBaseClass operation can be performed here

    // but if the object is truly a MySubClass1...
    if (mc is MySubClass1)
    {
      // ...then handle as a subclass
      MySubClass1 msc1 = (MySubClass1)mc;

      // ...cont...
    }
  }
}
```

GenericFunction() has no trouble differentiating between an object of class MyBaseClass and MySubClass1. However, it is also not confused if passed an object of a different subclass of MyBaseClass such as MySubClass2.

Is is possible to invoke a function with some completely generic class declaration? If so, can you differentiate between seemingly unrelated classes using the same is operator? The answer to both questions is yes. C# extends all classes from the common base class object. That is, any class that does not specifically inherit from another class inherits from the class object. Thus, the following two declarations are identical:

```
class MyClass1 : object {}
class MyClass2 {}
```

Thus, MyClass1 and MyClass2 share a common base class of object. This allows the following generic function:

```
public class Test
{
  public static void GenericFunction(object o)
  {
    if (o is MyClass1)
    {
      MyClass1 mc1 = (MyClass1)o;
      // ...
    }
  }
}
```

GenericFunction() can be invoked with any type of object.

The added if statement checks the BankAccount object to assure that it's actually of class SavingsAccount. The is operator returns a true when ProcessAmount() is called the first time. When passed a BankAccount object in the second call, however, the is operator returns a false. This avoids the illegal cast. This version of the program does not generate a runtime error.

On the one hand, I strongly recommend that all upcasts be protected with the is operator to avoid the possibility of a runtime error. On the other hand, upcasts should be avoided altogether, if possible.

Done!

REVIEW

The IS_A relationship is what allows the C# programmer to define one class in terms of another. We say that a savings account IS_A form of bank account. In C# terms, the subclass SavingsAccount inherits from the base class BankAccount.

The IS_A relationship differs fundamentally from the HAS_A relationship. We use the HAS_A term when a class A has a data member of class B. This gives A easy access to the methods of B without making them its own.

QUIZ YOURSELF

1. Why do I say that `SavingsAccount` is a type of `BankAccount`? (See "The IS_A relationship.")

2. What is the relationship between a TV and a picture tube? (See "When to IS_A and When to HAS_A.")

3. What is the `is` command for? (See "Avoiding invalid conversions using the `is` keyword.")

PART

III

Saturday Afternoon Part Review

1. Why can a static function not access the data members of the current object?

2. Write a program `SeeingSpots` that reads a string from the console and then writes that string back out with every occurrence of space replaced with a period. Use the function `Replace(c1, c2)` to replace the character `c1` with `c2` in the current string.

3. Rewrite `SeeingSpots` without using `Replace()`.

4. What `String.Format()` control outputs the `double` 123.456 as "123.4"?

5. What is the difference between the following three variables:
   ```
   char[] cName = {'S', 't', 'e', 'p', 'h', 'e', 'n'};
   string sName = "Stephen";
   string[] sNames = new String[] {"Stephen"};
   ```

6. What is the variable name `args` in the following declaration suggestive of its purpose?
   ```
   public static int Main(string[] args)
   ```

7. Name three of the four properties a C# class provides that allow one to say that C# is an object-oriented language.

PART

IV

Saturday Evening

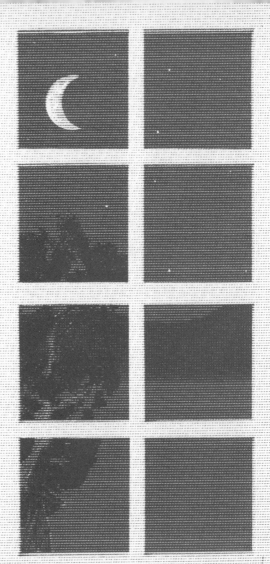

SESSION

17

Polymorphism

Session Checklist

✔ Hiding base class methods

✔ Avoiding accidentally hiding a method

✔ Overriding a base class method

30 Min. To Go

I t's all very nice to use C# inheritance to define the class SavingsAccount defined in Session 16 as a special case of the more generic class BankAccount. Not only does this save typing, but also it expresses an important relationship. However, this definition of inheritance is not sufficient to mimic the real world.

Let's return to our microwave oven example from Session 15. A microwave oven performs the same base functions as a conventional oven. Specifically, when I say "Start cooking," I want the oven to turn itself on and start the cooking process irrespective of the type of oven. The steps that a conventional oven performs internally are completely different from those that a microwave oven might take (and these are different yet in the convection oven).

The power of inheritance lies in the fact that I don't have to tell the specific type of oven how to start — I leave it up to the oven to decide based on its design. The ability of a program to decide which method to call on its own based upon the real-time type of the object is called *polymorphism,* which is the subject of this session.

Hiding Base Class Methods in the Subclass

Suppose that my bank adopted a policy toward savings account withdrawals different from other withdrawals at my bank. Suppose, for example, that the second withdrawal from a savings account during any given period cost the customer $1.50. This transaction could be implemented as follows:

```
// SavingsAccount - a bank account that draws interest
public class SavingsAccount : BankAccount
{
  public double dInterestRate;
  public int    nNumberOfWithdrawalsThisPeriod;

  // InitSavingsAccount - input the rate expressed as a
  //                      rate between 0 and 100
  public void InitSavingsAccount(double dInterestRate)
  {
    InitBankAccount();
    this.dInterestRate = dInterestRate / 100;
    nNumberOfWithdrawalsThisPeriod = 0;
  }

  // AccumulateInterest - invoke once per period
  public void AccumulateInterest()
  {
    dBalance = dBalance + (dBalance * dInterestRate);
    nNumberOfWithdrawalsThisPeriod = 0;
  }

  // Withdraw - you can withdraw any amount up to the
  //            balance; return the amount withdrawn
  public double Withdraw(double dWithdrawal)
  {
    double dAmountWithdrawn = base.Withdraw(dWithdrawal);
    if (++nNumberOfWithdrawalsThisPeriod > 1)
    {
      dAmountWithdrawn += base.Withdraw(1.5);
    }
    return dAmountWithdrawn;
  }
}
```

This version of the SavingsAccount class adds the descriptively named data member nNumberOfWithdrawalsThisPeriod. This variable is set to zero when the object is created. It is also set to zero every time the AccumulateInterest() method is invoked because this indicates the end of a period.

SavingsAccount implements its own version of Withdraw(), which is much like the original but takes into consideration the number of withdrawals. This new method starts by invoking the base method BankAccount.Withdraw() to perform the actual withdrawal.

The SavingsAccount **class could have duplicated the code found in** BankAccount.Withdraw() **and avoided the call; however, it is always best to rely on the base class to perform operations that affect only the base class.**

The SavingsAccount.Withdraw() method goes on to withdraw the $1.50 starting with the second withdrawal per period. The local variable dAmountWithdrawn is used to accumulate the amount actually withdrawn during the operation (including the $1.50). This amount is then returned to the caller to alert her as to how much her account was debited.

Avoiding accidentally hiding a method

C# generates an ominous-looking warning when it compiles the example program. The text of the warning message is long, but this is the important part:

```
'SavingsAccount.Withdraw(double)' hides inherited member 'BankAccount.Withdraw(double)'.
```

C# is trying to tell you that you have written a method in a subclass that has the same name as a method in the base class.

> **Actually, method hiding requires the same name and *signature*. The signature is the complete name including any arguments but not including the return type. A method** `SavingsAccount.Withdraw(int)` **would not hide** `BankAccount.Withdraw()`.

This new method can cause the type of confusion that I will describe in the next section of this session. C# is asking you to make sure that you really intended to hide the base class method. If not, you'll need to rename the method in the subclass.

Of course, you can ignore the warning. Warnings don't cause your program to work improperly. Ignoring compiler warnings is a really bad idea, however — not only might the message be warning you of a real mistake, but the warning message easily obscures real error messages lurking in the warning text.

You can tell C# that you really intended to hide the base class method by adding the descriptor new to the subclass method as follows:

```
new public double Withdraw(double dWithdrawal)
{
  // ...no change internally...
}
```

> **This keyword** new **here differs entirely from the keyword** new **used to create an object.**

The addition of the keyword new assures the C# compiler that you meant to give the two methods the same name, and the warning vanishes.

> **This hiding of a base class method is also known as *overloading* the base class method.**

Accessing a hidden method from within the class

Return to the `SavingsAccount.Withdraw()` method in the earlier example under "Avoiding accidentally hiding a method." The call to `BankAccount.Withdraw()` from within this new method includes the keyword base.

The following version of the function without the new keyword does not work:

```
new public double Withdraw(double dWithdrawal)
{
  double dAmountWithdrawn = Withdraw(dWithdrawal);
  if (++nNumberOfWithdrawalsThisPeriod > 1)
  {
    dAmountWithdrawn += Withdraw(1.5);
  }
  return dAmountWithdrawn;
}
```

The problem with this call is the same as that in the following:

```
void fn()
{
  fn(); // call yourself
}
```

The call to `fn()` from within `fn()` ends up calling itself over and over. Similarly, a call to `Withdraw()` from within the function calls itself in a loop, chasing its tail until the program eventually crashes.

Somehow you need to indicate to C# that the call from within `SavingsAccount` is meant to invoke the base class `BankAccount.Withdraw()` method. One approach is to cast the `this` pointer into an object of class `BankAccount` before making the following call:

```
new public double Withdraw(double dWithdrawal)
{
  // cast the reference to the current object
  // into an object of class BankAccount
  BankAccount ba = (BankAccount)this;

  // invoking the Withdraw() using this BankAccount object
  // calls the function BankAccount.Withdraw()
  double dAmountWithdrawn = ba.Withdraw(dWithdrawal);
  if (++nNumberOfWithdrawalsThisPeriod > 1)
  {
    dAmountWithdrawn += ba.Withdraw(1.5);
  }
  return dAmountWithdrawn;
}
```

This solution does work: The call `ba.Withdraw()` now invokes the `BankAccount` method just as we intended.

The problem with this approach is the explicit reference to `BankAccount`. A future change to the program might rearrange that inheritance hierarchy so that `SavingsAccount` no longer inherits directly from BankAccount. Such a rearrangement breaks this function in a way that might be very difficult for the future programmer to find.

We would prefer to tell C# to call the Withdraw() function from "the class immediately above us" in the hierarchy without naming it explicitly. This would be the class that SavingsAccount extends.

The C# keyword base is the same thing as this but recasts to the base class no matter what that class might be, as shown here:

```
// Withdraw - you can withdraw any amount up to the
//            balance; return the amount withdrawn
new public double Withdraw(double dWithdrawal)
{
  double dAmountWithdrawn = base.Withdraw(dWithdrawal);
  if (++nNumberOfWithdrawalsThisPeriod > 1)
  {
    dAmountWithdrawn += base.Withdraw(1.5);
  }
  return dAmountWithdrawn;
}
```

The call base.Withdraw() now invokes the BankAccount.Withdraw() method, thereby avoiding the "invoking itself" problem. In addition, this function will not break if the inheritance hierarchy is changed.

Accessing a hidden method from another class

20 Min. To Go

Confusion can arise when Withdraw() is invoked from methods that are part of outside classes as well.

Consider the following simple code snippet:

```
// invoke BankAccount.Withdraw()
BankAccount ba = new BankAccount();
ba.Withdraw(100);

// now invoke SavingsAccount.Withdraw()
SavingsAccount sa = new SavingsAccount();
sa.Withdraw(100)
```

Because ba is of class BankAccount, the call ba.Withdraw() goes to the method BankAccount.Withdraw(). Similarly, the call sa.Withdraw() invokes the SavingsAccount.Withdraw() method.

What happens if the SavingsAccount object sa is recast to be a BankAccount? Here's the answer:

```
SavingsAccount sa = new SavingsAccount();
BankAccount castsa = (BankAccount)sa;

// now invokes BankAccount.Withdraw()
castsa.Withdraw(100)
```

An argument could be made in either direction. The declared type of `castsa` is `BankAccount`, but we know that the *actual type* (also known as the *runtime type*) is `SavingsAccount`. It turns out that the nod goes to `BankAccount` — the call `castsa.Withdraw()` jumps to `BankAccount.Withdraw()`.

This situation doesn't typically arise in straight line-code like this; however, it is common when objects are passed as arguments to functions. Consider the following function:

```
public class Class1
{

   public static int Main(string[] strings)
   {
      // call Test with a BankAccount object
      BankAccount ba = new BankAccount();
      ba.InitBankAccount();
      ba.Deposit(500);
      Test(ba);

      // now repeat the experiment with a SavingsAccount
      // call Test with a BankAccount object
      SavingsAccount sa = new SavingsAccount();
      sa.InitSavingsAccount(7.5);
      sa.Deposit(500);
      Test(sa);

      return 0;
   }

   // Test - invoke Withdraw via an argument
   public static void Test(BankAccount baArgument)
   {
      baArgument.Withdraw(100);
   }
}
```

In this case, `Main()` calls `Test()` first with an object of type `BankAccount` and then with an object of type `SavingsAccount`. `Test()` calls `Withdraw()` with the object passed it. Both calls go to `BankAccount.Withdraw()` because of the declared type of `baArgument`.

Accessing an Overloaded Method Dynamically

Invoking a function based solely on the declared type of an object runs counter to human nature. For example, if I ask the mechanic to fix my heater I don't want him to forget to unplug it from the wall just because I forgot to call it an electric heater. Some things are obvious.

In many cases, we want the proper function to be called based on the runtime type. Thus, when I ask my knowledgeable mechanic to fix my heater, he knows to disconnect the gas line or the electricity or the oil line depending upon the type of heater it is.

One approach is for the program to determine the runtime type of the object using the `is` operator. The argument type might say `BankAccount`, but what type is it really?

```
// ManualPolymorphism - choose between two overloaded methods at
//                      run-time using the 'is' keyword
namespace ManualPolymorphism
{
  using System;

  // define a very simplistic BankAccount and SavingsAccount class
  public class BankAccount
  {
    virtual public void Withdraw()
    {
      Console.WriteLine("Call to BankAccount.Withdraw()");
    }
  }

  public class SavingsAccount : BankAccount
  {
    override public void Withdraw()
    {
      Console.WriteLine("Call to SavingsAccount.Withdraw()");
    }
  }

  public class Class1
  {

    public static int Main(string[] strings)
    {
      // call Test with a BankAccount object
      Console.WriteLine
        ("Calling Test with a BankObject");
      BankAccount ba = new BankAccount();
      Test(ba);

      // now repeat the experiment with a SavingsAccount
      // call Test with a BankAccount object
      Console.WriteLine();
      Console.WriteLine
        ("Calling Test with a SavingsAccount object");
      SavingsAccount sa = new SavingsAccount();
      Test(sa);

      // wait for user to acknowledge the results
      Console.WriteLine("Hit Enter to terminate...");
      Console.Read();
      return 0;
    }

    // Test - invoke Withdraw via an argument - determine
    //        which version to call based upon the runtime
    //        type of the object as determined by the is
    //        operator
```

```
public static void Test(BankAccount baArgument)
{
    // manual polymorphism - don't do this
    if (baArgument is SavingsAccount)
    {
        SavingsAccount saArgument = (SavingsAccount)baArgument;
        saArgument.Withdraw();
    }
    else
    {
        baArgument.Withdraw();
    }
}
}
}
```

The complete `ManualPolymorphism` **program can be found on the CD.**

`Main()` works exactly as before, passing first a BankAccount object and then a SavingsAccount object to the Test() function. Rather than just calling Withdraw() blindly, Test() first checks its argument. If the argument is actually of type SavingsAccount, Test() recasts the object before attempting the method call. The Withdraw() methods in this case do nothing but output a message to make clear which method is being invoked.

The programmer could have performed the cast and the call in a single line:

`((SavingsAccount)ba).Withdraw(100);`

I mention this only because you often see this in other programs.

This approach actually works: The first call passes to BankAccount.Withdraw() while the second is routed to SavingsAccount.Withdraw() as shown by the program output:

```
Calling Test with a BankObject
Call to BankAccount.Withdraw()

Calling Test with a SavingsAccount object
Call to SavingsAccount.Withdraw()
Hit Enter to terminate...
```

However, selecting between overloaded methods using the is keyword is a very bad idea.

The problem is that the method Test() has to know all of the different types of things that baArgument can be. This puts too much faith and too much responsibility in the hands of functions outside of the BankAccount class hierarchy. Right now there are only two types of bank accounts, but suppose my boss asks me to implement a new account type CheckingAccount? My program won't work properly if I don't search out and find every function that checks the runtime type of its argument. This would be the equivalent of my telling the mechanic, "Oh, by the way, this is an electric heater." I've told the mechanic that it's an electric heater, so he knows to unplug it before starting work. Were I to forget to mention it, however, he would blindly venture into the heater without disconnecting the electricity. The mechanic is putting a *lot* of faith in me to tell him the exact type of heater. I don't want to be responsible for the mechanic's life. I want him to make the decision as to whether or not it is necessary to disconnect the electric power before taking my heater apart.

Similarly, I shouldn't have to tell BankAccount which version of Withdraw() to call. This decision should be a function of the class. This ability of a class to decide on its own which overridden method to invoke is known as polymorphism. I tell C# to invoke Withdraw() polymorphically by marking the base class function with the keyword virtual and each subclass with the keyword override.

The following is the ManualInheritance program rewritten using the keyword virtual to achieve true polymorphism. This program has the same output statements in the Withdraw() methods to prove that the proper methods are indeed being invoked.

```
// VirtualInheritance - demonstrate polymorphism by
//                      implementing the Withdraw() method
//                      as a virtual method
namespace VirtualInheritance
{
  using System;

  public class Class1
  {

    public static int Main(string[] strings)
    {
      // call Test with a BankAccount object
      Console.WriteLine
        ("Calling Test with a BankObject");
      BankAccount ba = new BankAccount();
      Test(ba);

      // now repeat the experiment with a SavingsAccount
      // call Test with a BankAccount object
      Console.WriteLine();
      Console.WriteLine
        ("Calling Test with a SavingsAccount object");
      SavingsAccount sa = new SavingsAccount();
      Test(sa);

      // wait for user to acknowledge the results
      Console.WriteLine("Hit Enter to terminate...");
      Console.Read();
      return 0;
    }

    // Test - invoke Withdraw via an argument
    public static void Test(BankAccount ba)
```

```
      {
        ba.Withdraw();
      }
   }

   public class BankAccount
   {
      virtual public void Withdraw()
      {
        Console.WriteLine("Call to BankAccount.Withdraw()");
      }
   }

   public class SavingsAccount : BankAccount
   {
      override public void Withdraw()
      {
        Console.WriteLine("Call to SavingsAccount.Withdraw()");
      }
   }
}
```

 The full VirtualInheritance **program is available on the CD-ROM.**

The output from executing this program is as follows:

```
Calling Test with a BankObject
Call to BankAccount.Withdraw()

Calling Test with a SavingsAccount object
Call to SavingsAccount.Withdraw()
Press any key to continue
```

The Withdraw() method is flagged as virtual in the base class BankAccount while the Withdraw() method in the subclass is flagged with the keyword override. The Test() function makes no checks but simply passes along to Withdraw() the BankAccount object it receives.

The Main() function first passes a BankAccount object to the function Test(). This call is directed to the function BankAccount.Withdraw(), as you can see from the output. When Main() then passes a SavingsAccount object, the same call is sent to the SavingsAccount method.   •

 Recall that hiding a method without polymorphism is called overloading; hiding a method with a polymorphic, virtual method is called *overriding*. **The C# programmer says that the** Withdraw() **method in the** SavingsAccount **class overrides the** Withdraw() **method in the** Account **class.**

Notice that the method SavingsAccount.Withdraw() is no longer flagged as new. The override keyword tells C# that you are aware that the base class method of the same name exists.

Done!

REVIEW

A subclass may declare a method with the same name and arguments as a method in the base class. Normally C# generates a warning at compile time to indicate the potential error; however, the programmer can adorn the subclass method with the new keyword to indicate that the dual names are intentional.

Simple base class overloading is seldom what you want. More often than not you want C# to decide which class methods to invoke based upon the runtime type of the object. Thus, you want C# to decide whether to invoke Heater.Start() or ElectricHeater.Start() based upon whether the heater object provided is a heater or an electric heater. This is the property known as polymorphism.

QUIZ YOURSELF

1. What is polymorphism? (See the introduction to this session.)

2. How do you hide a base class member? (See "Hiding Base Class Methods in the Subclass.")

3. How do you access a hidden member from within the class? (See "Accessing a hidden method from within the class.")

4. How do you access a hidden member from another class? (See "Accessing a hidden method from another class.")

Abstract Classes

Session Checklist

✔ Examining abstract classes in the real world

✔ Declaring a method and the class containing it to be abstract

✔ Starting a new hierarchy on top of an existing hierarchy

✔ Sealing a class from being subclassed

**30 Min.
To Go**

The relationship between a savings account and a base account is a little more complicated than the discussion in Session 17 implies. In actual fact, an account is probably nothing more than a concept.

There is nothing called a heater that isn't either an electric heater, a gas heater, an oil heater, or one of a number of other types of heaters. The concept of a heater exists, but there is no concrete example of "heater." We say that the term *heater* is *abstract*, meaning that it is a concept with no actual instance.

Abstract terms abound in our world. There is no such thing as a bird that isn't some type of bird, a dog that isn't some breed of dog, and so on. However, whereas the class Dog may be abstract, the class GermanShepherd is not. My dog Trude is an instance of the class GermanShepherd.

The Abstract BankAccount

There is no such thing as a simple bank account — all bank accounts are, in fact, a savings or a checking account (or one of a number of other types of accounts that I don't need to discuss here). If I ask my bank manager for the policies of a bank account, her first question will be "What type of account?"

Suppose that the methods of all types of bank accounts were the same except for the Withdrawal() method. (We'll even accept that all accounts have a common Deposit() method, though in practice this is unlikely.)

The method BankAccount.Withdrawal() is abstract, which means that it has no implementation. That is to say, the different types of bank accounts all handle the withdrawal operation slightly differently.

The class BankAccount is also abstract because it contains one or more abstract methods.

The following code snippet demonstrates the C# version of this statement:

```
// (reduced version...)
// AbstractInheritance - the BankAccount class is actually
//                       abstract since there is no single
//                       implementation for Withdrawal
namespace AbstractInheritance
{
  using System;

  public class Class1
  {
    public static int Main(string[] strings)
    {
      //
      // You can't create a BankAccount object since it's
      // abstract
      //
      // BankAccount ba = new BankAccount();

      // now repeat the experiment with a SavingsAccount
      // call Test with a BankAccount object
      Console.WriteLine
        ("\nCreating a SavingsAccount object");
      SavingsAccount sa = new SavingsAccount();
      Test(sa);

      // and finally a CheckingAccount object

      Console.WriteLine
        ("\nCreating a CheckingAccount object");
      CheckingAccount ca = new CheckingAccount();
      Test(ca);

      // wait for user to acknowledge the results
      Console.WriteLine("Hit Enter to terminate...");
      Console.Read();
      return 0;
    }

    public static void Test(BankAccount ba)
    {

      Console.WriteLine("Calling ba.Withdrawal() from within Test");
```

```
      ba.Withdrawal(100);
    }
}


// BankAccount - simulate a bank account each of which
//                carries an account id (which is assigned
//                upon creation) and a balance
abstract public class BankAccount
{
  // Withdrawal - you can withdraw any amount up to the
  //              balance; return the amount withdrawn
  abstract public void Withdrawal(double dWithdrawal);
}


// SavingsAccount - a bank account that draws interest
public class SavingsAccount : BankAccount
{
  override public void Withdrawal(double dWithdrawal)
  {
    Console.WriteLine("Call to SavingsAccount.Withdrawal()");
  }
}

// CheckingAccount - a bank account that does not draw
//                   interest but charges a small fee for
//                   withdrawal
public class CheckingAccount : BankAccount
{
  override public void Withdrawal(double dWithdrawal)
  {
    Console.WriteLine("Call to CheckingAccount.Withdrawal()");
  }
}
}
```

I have stripped the classes down to the single `Withdrawal()` **method to highlight the points of interest. The** `Withdrawal()` **methods here do nothing more than generate output to the display. The full version of the program can be found on the CD-ROM with the name** `AbstractInheritance`.

The method BankAccount.Withdrawal() is flagged as abstract. In addition, the method has no body because no single implementation is true of all bank accounts. The BankAccount class is flagged with the keyword abstract. A class that contains any abstract methods is itself abstract.

The SavingsAccount class extends the BankAccount class by overriding the abstract Withdrawal() method with a *nonabstract* (also called *concrete*) version of the method. The SavingsAccount class is now concrete because it has no remaining abstract methods.

The CheckingAccount class extends BankAccount with its own concrete version of Withdrawal(). The Main() function passes a SavingsAccount object and a CheckingAccount object to the unchanged Test() method.

Executing the program generates the following output:

```
Creating a SavingsAccount object
Calling ba.Withdrawal() from within Test
Call to SavingsAccount.Withdrawal

Creating a CheckingAccount object
Calling ba.Withdrawal() from within Test
Call to CheckingAccount.Withdrawal
Hit Enter to terminate...
```

Notice that Main() cannot create a BankAccount object — the line that does so has been commented out. Removing the comment generates the following compile time error message:

```
Cannot create an instance of the abstract class
or interface 'AbstractInheritance.BankAccount'
```

You can't create a BankAccount that isn't either a CheckingAccount or a SavingsAccount any more than you can create a heater that isn't an electric, gas, oil, steam, or some other type of heater.

Restarting a Class Hierarchy

**20 Min.
To Go**

The virtual keyword can also be used to start a new inheritance hierarchy. Consider the class hierarchy demonstrated in the following InheritanceTest program:

```
// InheritanceTest - examine the way that the virtual
//                   keyword can be used to start a
//                   new inheritance ladder
namespace InheritanceTest
{
  using System;

  public class Class1
  {
    public static int Main(string[] strings)
    {
      Console.WriteLine("\nPassing a BankAccount");
      BankAccount ba = new BankAccount();
      Test1(ba);

      Console.WriteLine("\nPassing a SavingsAccount");
      SavingsAccount sa = new SavingsAccount();
      Test1(sa);
      Test2(sa);

      Console.WriteLine("\nPassing a SpecialSaleAccount");
      SpecialSaleAccount ssa = new SpecialSaleAccount();
      Test1(ssa);
      Test2(ssa);
      Test3(ssa);
```

```
      Console.WriteLine("\nPassing a SaleSpecialCustomer");
      SaleSpecialCustomer ssc = new SaleSpecialCustomer();
      Test1(ssc);
      Test2(ssc);
      Test3(ssc);
      Test4(ssc);

      // wait for user to acknowledge the results
      Console.WriteLine("Hit Enter to terminate...");
      Console.Read();

      return 0;
    }

    public static void Test1(BankAccount account)
    {
      Console.Write("to Test(BankAccount)");
      account.Withdrawal(100);
    }

    public static void Test2(SavingsAccount account)
    {
      Console.Write("to Test(SavingsAccount)");
      account.Withdrawal(100);
    }

    public static void Test3(SpecialSaleAccount account)
    {
      Console.Write("to Test(SpecialSaleAccount)");
      account.Withdrawal(100);
    }

    public static void Test4(SaleSpecialCustomer account)
    {
      Console.Write("to Test(SaleSpecialCustomer)");
      account.Withdrawal(100);
    }
}

// BankAccount - simulate a bank account each of which
//               carries an account id (which is assigned
//               upon creation) and a balance
public class BankAccount
{
  // Withdrawal - you can withdraw any amount up to the
  //              balance; return the amount withdrawn
  virtual public void Withdrawal(double dWithdrawal)
  {
    Console.WriteLine(" invokes BankAccount.Withdrawal()");
  }

}
```

```
// SavingsAccount - a bank account that draws interest
public class SavingsAccount : BankAccount
{
  override public void Withdrawal(double dWithdrawal)
  {
    Console.WriteLine(" invokes SavingsAccount.Withdrawal()");
  }
}

// SpecialSaleAccount - account used only during a sale
public class SpecialSaleAccount : SavingsAccount
{
  new virtual public void Withdrawal(double dWithdrawal)
  {
    Console.WriteLine(" invokes SpecialSaleAccount.Withdrawal()");
  }
}

// SaleSpecialCustomer - account used for special customers
//                       during the sale period
public class SaleSpecialCustomer : SpecialSaleAccount
{
  override public void Withdrawal(double dWithdrawal)
  {
    Console.WriteLine
      (" invokes SaleSpecialCustomer.Withdrawal()");
  }
}
}
```

The complete InheritanceTest **program can be found on the CD.**

Each of these classes extends the class above it. Notice, however, that the SpecialSaleAccount.Withdrawal() method has been flagged as virtual. This effectively breaks the inheritance ladder at that point. When viewed from the perspective of BankAccount, the SpecialSaleAccount and SaleSpecialCustomer classes look exactly like a SavingsAccount. It is only when viewed from the perspective of a SpecialSaleAccount that the new versions of Withdrawal() become available.

The function Main() invokes a series of Test() methods, each designed to accept a different subclass. Each of these versions of Test() calls Withdrawal() from the perspective of a different class of object.

The output from this program is as follows:

Creating a new hierarchy

Why does C# support creating a new inheritance hierarchy? Isn't polymorphism complicated enough already?

C# was created to be a *netable* language in the sense that classes which a program executes, even subclasses, may be distributed across the Internet. That is, a program that I am writing can directly utilize classes from standard repositories located on other computers via the Internet.

I am allowed to extend a class that I load over the Internet. However, overriding the methods of a standard, tested hierarchy of classes may have unintended effects. Establishing a new hierarchy of classes allows my program to enjoy the benefits of polymorphism without any danger of breaking the existing code.

```
Passing a BankAccount
  to Test(BankAccount) invokes BankAccount.Withdrawal()

Passing a SavingsAccount
  to Test(BankAccount) invokes SavingsAccount.Withdrawal()
  to Test(SavingsAccount) invokes SavingsAccount.Withdrawal()

Passing a SpecialSaleAccount
  to Test(BankAccount) invokes SavingsAccount.Withdrawal()
  to Test(SavingsAccount) invokes SavingsAccount.Withdrawal()
  to Test(SpecialSaleAccount) invokes
                          SpecialSaleAccount.Withdrawal()

Passing a SaleSpecialCustomer
  to Test(BankAccount) invokes SavingsAccount.Withdrawal()
  to Test(SavingsAccount) invokes SavingsAccount.Withdrawal()
  to Test(SpecialSaleAccount) invokes
                          SaleSpecialCustomer.Withdrawal()
  to Test(SaleSpecialCustomer) invokes
                          SaleSpecialCustomer.Withdrawal()
Hit Enter to terminate...
```

I have highlighted in bold the calls of special interest. The BankAccount and SavingsAccount classes operate exactly as we would expect. However, when calling Test(SavingsAccount) both the SpecialSaleAccount and SaleSpecialCustomer pass themselves off as a SavingsAccount. It's only when looking at the next lower level that the new hierarchy, a SaleSpecialCustomer, can be used in lieu of a SpecialSaleAccount. This is demonstrated graphically in Figure 18-1.

BankAccount
↑
SavingsAccount
↑
SpecialSaleAccount
↑
SaleSpecialCustomer

Figure 18-1 *The SpecialSaleAccount starts a new class hierarchy.*

Sealing a Class

**10 Min.
To Go**

If the programmer decides that she doesn't want future generations of programmers to be able to extend a particular class, she can lock the class using the keyword sealed. A sealed class cannot be used as the base class for any other class.

The following code snippet

```
using System;

public class BankAccount
{
  // Withdrawal - you can withdraw any amount up to the
  //              balance; return the amount withdrawn
  virtual public void Withdrawal(double dWithdraw)
  {
    Console.WriteLine("invokes BankAccount.Withdrawal()");
  }

}

public sealed class SavingsAccount : BankAccount
{
  override public void Withdrawal(double dWithdrawal)
  {
    Console.WriteLine("invokes SavingsAccount.Withdrawal()");
  }
}

public class SpecialSaleAccount : SavingsAccount
{
  override public void Withdrawal(double dWithdrawal)
  {
    Console.WriteLine("invokes SpecialSaleAccount.Withdrawal()");
  }
}
```

generates the following compiler error:

```
'SpecialSaleAccount' : cannot inherit from sealed class 'SavingsAccount'
```

The sealed keyword allows a programmer to protect her class from the prying methods of some subclass. For example, allowing a class that implements system security to be extended would allow the programmer to create a security back door. This opens up the program to malicious intrusion.

> **Sealing a class makes it impossible for a program in another program, possibly on the Internet somewhere, to use a modified version of your class. The remote program can use the class as it is or not, but it can't inherit bits and pieces of your class while overriding the rest.**

Done!

REVIEW

Many times the base class of a set of related subclasses represents a concept rather than a real thing. In these cases, there are often methods that have no meaning in the base class. For example, in this session a Withdrawal() from within BankAccount was performed. The different types of bank accounts have different rules governing withdrawals. In this case, the programmer should declare both the Withdrawal() method and the BankAccount class to be abstract. The subclasses don't become concrete until all of the abstract methods have been overridden.

In addition, this session demonstrated how you can create new inheritance hierarchies within an existing hierarchy and how you can seal a class to keep other classes from extending yours.

QUIZ YOURSELF

1. What is the purpose of the abstract keyword? (See "The Abstract BankAccount.")
2. What is the overriding property of an abstract class? (See "The Abstract BankAccount.")

Access Control Methods

Session Checklist

✔ Minimizing access to the internal members of a class

✔ Declaring class members private

✔ Providing accessor methods

**30 Min.
To Go**

essions 16, 17, and 18 demonstrate how a C# class emulates real-world classes by providing for inheritance and polymorphism. For example, my minivan is a type of car (inheritance). My car shares the same basic operations of other cars viewed from the driver's standpoint even if my car implements these operations differently (polymorphism).

One of the important features of a real-world object is this notion of the inside of the object versus the outside. The internal workings of my car are completely masked by a façade through which I manipulate the car.

There are features that I can modify, such as the accelerator position, the transmission setting, the windshield wiper speed, and so on. There are fields that I can monitor such as the gasoline level, the oil pressure, speed, and so on without the ability to directly influence them — these are known as read-only fields. The majority of internal properties are not accessible at all.

There are at least two good reasons for this level of access control. One is liability: The automobile manufacturer cannot make a reliable product if it has to depend upon the driver to work the critical internal mechanisms of the motor and transmission. Another is ease of use: An automobile presents a well-defined, reasonably simple user interface. Not too many drivers could (or would bother to) learn how to operate a car in which the user had to manipulate critical internal parts directly.

Similarly, a reliable class should be able to control access to its internal members to protect itself. Access control also allows the designer of the class to provide application software with a simple interface that other programmers can more easily learn and use.

Controlling Access to the Data Members of a Class

In all of the example programs you have seen in prior sessions, both the data members and member functions of the classes have been flagged as `public`, which is also the case in the following example:

```
public class BankAccount
{
   // bank accounts start at 1000 and increase sequentially
   // from there
   public static int nNextAccountNumber = 1000;

   // maintain the account number and balance for each object
   public int nAccountNumber;
   public double dBalance;

   // the implementation of these methods is shown in
   // the example programs in Chapter 13
   public void InitBankAccount()
   {
     // ...
   }

   public double Deposit(double dAmount)
   {
     // ...
   }

   public double Withdrawal(double dWithdrawal)
   {
     // ...
   }
}
```

Marking a member `public` makes that member available to any other code within your program.

The BankAccount class provides a method to initialize the members of the class, a Deposit() class to handle deposits, and a Withdrawal() method to perform withdrawals. The Deposit() and Withdrawal() methods even provide some rudimentary rules like "You can't deposit a negative number" and "You can't withdraw more than you have in your account." However, everyone's on the honor system as long as dBalance is accessible to external functions. (*External* here means external to the class but within the same program.)

Declaring a data member `private` makes it inaccessible to a function of any other class, as shown here:

```
public class Test
{
   public static int Main(string[] args)
   {
```

```
        BankAccount ba = new BankAccount();
        ba.InitBankAccount();

        // accessing the balance via the Deposit()
        // method is OK - Deposit() has access to all
        // of the data members
        ba.Deposit(10);

        // accessing the data member directly is a compile
        // time error
        ba.dBalance += 10;

        return 0;
    }

public class BankAccount
{
    // bank accounts start at 1000 and increase sequentially
    // from there
    private static int nNextAccountNumber = 1000;

    // maintain the account number and balance for each object
    private int nAccountNumber;
    private double dBalance;

    // the implementation of these methods is shown in
    // the example programs in Chapter 13
    public void InitBankAccount()
    {
      // ...
    }

    public double Deposit(double dAmount)
    {
      // ...
    }

    public double Withdrawal(double dWithdrawal)
    {
      // ...
    }
}
```

The three data members of the BankAccount class have all been flagged as private. These members are still accessible from methods such as InitBankAccount(), Deposit(), and Withdrawal() — these methods are unchanged.

In addition, the call to Deposit() within Main() is still legal because Deposit() is declared public. However, the second statement, ba.dBalance += 10;, is now illegal because dBalance is not accessible to Main().

Thus, the methods of the Test class can modify the balance of the object only via the public Deposit() and Withdrawal() methods.

The default access type is `private`. Failing to declare a member `public` (or one of the other access types described below) is the same as declaring it `private`. However, it is always best to include the `private` keyword anyway to remove any doubt.

Why worry about access control?

Declaring the internal members of a class public is a bad idea for several reasons. Making data members public makes it very difficult to determine when and how data members are getting modified. Why bother building checks into the `Deposit()` and `Withdrawal()` methods? Why bother with these methods at all? If other functions can access these data members, it's almost a sure bet that they will. Any method of any class can modify these elements at any time. Declaring the variables private ensures that control passes through the `Deposit()` and `Withdrawal()` methods, where safeguards to avoid overdraft are in place. (One could imagine a large set of checks that such public methods might include.)

Imagine that my program has been executing for an hour or so before I notice that the balance of one of the accounts is negative. The `Withdrawal()` method would have made sure that this didn't happen. Obviously some other function accessed the balance without going through `Withdrawal()`. Figuring out which function is responsible and under what conditions is very difficult.

Exposing all of the data members of the class makes the interface too complicated. As a programmer using the `BankAccount` class, I don't want to know about the internals of the class. All I need to know is that I can deposit and withdraw funds.

Exposing internal elements leads to a distribution of the class rules. For example, my `BankAccount` class will not allow the balance to go negative under any circumstances. That's a business rule that should be isolated within the `Withdrawal()` method. Otherwise, I'll have to add this check everywhere the balance is updated.

What happens when the bank decides to change the rules so that "valued customers" are allowed to carry a slightly negative balance for a short period in order to avoid unintended overdrafts? I now have to search through the program to update every section of code that accesses the balance.

Finally, making data members public tends to defeat polymorphism. In Session 17 I extended the `BankAccount` class into a special `SavingsAccount` class with its own rules. Through the magic of polymorphism, I was able to access bank accounts from other functions without worrying about whether they were `BankAccount` or `SavingsAccount` objects. I couldn't do this if the data members were left accessible through functions other than the virtual members of the bank account methods.

An example of minimizing the interface

I want to take you through an example of why minimizing the class interface is important.

20 Min. To Go

The program `DoubleBankAccount` on your CD-ROM contains a version of the following `BankAccount`, which is similar to that found in Session 16 except that this version carefully hides its internal data members by declaring them `private`.

```
// DoubleBankAccount - create a bank account using a double
//                     variable to store the account balance;
//                     (keep the balance in a private variable
//                     to hide its implementation from the
//                     outside world)
namespace Test
{
  using System;

  public class Class1
  {

    public static int Main(string[] strings)
    {
      // open a bank account
      Console.WriteLine("Create a bank account object");
      BankAccount ba = new BankAccount();
      ba.InitBankAccount();

      // make a deposit
      double dDeposit = 123.454;
      Console.WriteLine("Depositing {0:C}", dDeposit);
      ba.Deposit(dDeposit);

      // account balance
      Console.WriteLine("Account = {0}",
                         ba.GetString());

      // here's the problem
      double dAddition = 0.002;
      Console.WriteLine("Adding {0:C}", dAddition);
      ba.Deposit(dAddition);

      // resulting balance
      Console.WriteLine("Resulting account = {0}",
                         ba.GetString());


      // wait for user to acknowledge the results
      Console.WriteLine("Hit Enter to terminate...");
      Console.Read();
      return 0;
    }
  }

  // BankAccount
  public class BankAccount
  {
    private static int nNextAccountNumber = 1000;
    private int nAccountNumber;

    // maintain the balance as a single double variable
```

```
   private double dBalance;

   // GetBalance - return the current balance
   public double GetBalance()
   {
      return dBalance;
   }

   // AccountNumber
   public int GetAccountNumber()
   {
      return nAccountNumber;
   }
   public void SetAccountNumber(int nAccountNumber)
   {
      this.nAccountNumber = nAccountNumber;
   }

   // the following three methods are unchanged compared
   // to the BankAccount class in Chapter 12
   public void InitBankAccount()
   {
      // ...
   }

   public void Deposit(double dAmount)
   {
      // ...
   }

   public double Withdrawal(double dWithdrawal)
   {
      // ...
   }

   // GetString - return the account data as a string
   public string GetString()
   {
      string s = String.Format("#{0} = {1:C}",
                               GetAccountNumber(),
                               GetBalance());
      return s;
   }
  }
 }
```

The data members of this version of BankAccount have been marked private, which makes them inaccessible to application programs. However, there may be very good reasons why an application might need access to the balance of a particular account. The GetBalance() method has been added to allow other classes to read dBalance. In addition, the methods GetAccountNumber() and SetAccountNumber() allow external functions to both read and modify the data member nAccountNumber.

There is no particular significance to the names of these methods, but GetX() and SetX() are the conventional names for the read and modify methods for the property X.

Accessor methods

You may wonder why I would bother to declare the dBalance data member private but provide a method GetBalance() to return its value. There are actually two reasons. First, GetBalance() does not provide a means for modifying dBalance — it merely returns its value. This makes the balance read-only.

Second, GetBalance() hides the internal format of the class from external methods. It's entirely possible that GetBalance() goes through an extensive calculation regarding the reading of receipts, the addition of account charges, and whatever else my bank might want to subtract from my balance. External functions don't know and don't care.

A problem (rounding) with our DoubleBankAccount program

The Main() function creates a bank account and then deposits $123.454, an amount that contains a fractional number of cents. Main() then deposits a small fraction of a cent to the balance and displays the resulting balance.

Values that are calculated, such as interest on a principal, often have a fractional number of cents.

The output from this program appears as follows:

```
Create a bank account object
Depositing $123.45
Account = #1001 = $123.45
Adding $0.00
Resulting account = #1001 = $123.46
Hit Enter to terminate...
```

The program seems to have a bug. The output indicates that $123.45 plus zero is $123.46. Obviously, the problem lies in the fact that monetary values in this program are retained in a double variable that can retain very small fractions of a cent. However, monetary values are displayed to the nearest cent. Rounding down 123.454 yields 123.45, whereas the 123.456 resulting from the addition rounds up to 123.46.

10 Min.
To Go

Fixing the problem

Seeing the rounding off problem inherent in using double variables to contain numeric values, my bank decides to change the way the balance is stored. Rather than use a single double, my bank decides to use an integer to store the dollar amount and a second integer to represent the number of cents. Any rounding is done as part of the Deposit() method.

I realize that using a `decimal` variable type would have been a better solution. A version of the program called `DecimalBankAccount` does exactly that by declaring the balance to be a `decimal` value. This program is available on the CD-ROM. However, using two integers makes the point here more obvious. The demonstration `IntegerBankAccount` program shown here can also be found on the CD-ROM.

This modified version of the BankAccount class is part of the IntegerBankAccount program:

```
// BankAccount - simulate a bank account each of which
//               carries an account id (which is assigned
//               upon creation) and a balance
public class BankAccount
{
  // maintain the balance as a decimal with two significant
  // places
  private int nCents;
  private int nDollars;

  public void InitBankAccount()
  {
    nAccountNumber = ++nNextAccountNumber;

    // use the private accessor internally to hide the
    // format details from internal methods
    SetBalance(0.0);
  }

  // Balance - making the GetBalance() method public and
  //           SetBalance() private renders balance read-only
  public double GetBalance()
  {
    double dBalance = (double)nDollars
                    + ((double)nCents / 100.0);
    return dBalance;
  }
  private void SetBalance(double dBalance)
  {
    nDollars = (int)dBalance;

    // peel off the hundreths
    dBalance = dBalance - nDollars;
    nCents = (int)(100.0 * dBalance + 0.5);
  }

  // ...the remainder of the class is unchanged...
}
```

A private method SetBalance() has been added to convert the double formatted balance into two int variables, nDollars and nCents. The bank account balance is still hidden from the outside world for security reasons — external classes do not have access to the private SetBalance() method. The GetBalance() method reverses the conversion, turning the two ints into a single double.

The method InitBankAccount() demonstrates that the SetBalance() method is used throughout the BankAccount class — even methods internal to the class need not be bothered with details of how a balance is stored.

No other changes have been made to the BankAccount class. Even more important, no changes have been made to the Main() method at all. Executing the program now generates the desired results:

```
Create a bank account object
Depositing $123.45
Account = #1001 = $123.45
Adding $0.00
Resulting account = #1001 = $123.45
Hit Enter to terminate...
```

Solving the problem with the BankAccount class would not have been possible if other methods in other classes had accessed the balance directly. Exposing the dBalance data member freezes the way the balance is stored. If it is exposed as a double, for example, then a double it must remain whether that's the best solution or not. Declaring dBalance private hides the way the bank balance is stored from external, prying methods. In C# terms, we say that declaring dBalance private removes it from the class's public interface.

Other Levels of Security

C# provides other levels of security besides just *public* and *private*. A *protected* member is accessible to members of the class plus any subclass. An *internal* member is accessible to any class within the current namespace (essentially, within the same module). *Internal protected* is a combination of the two.

Keeping a member hidden from the public view by not declaring it public reduces the amount of information one class knows about the other (this is called *coupling*). However, in many cases the subclass is already coupled tightly to the base class. The programmer often has to have intimate knowledge of the base class in order to write the subclass. There may be little point in hiding the base class data.

Declaring a data member protected is often a nice compromise. A protected data member is kept away from the prying eyes of external classes but left accessible to subclasses that really need it.

Done!

REVIEW

A class should not expose its internal workings to outside classes lest they depend on internal details that are subject to change. Only members that are declared public are available to the world for use. Declaring a method private makes it unavailable to other classes. Declaring a method protected makes it available to methods within the class and to any subclass of that class.

Normally, data members should be made available to outside classes via accessor methods only: methods that read and write that data member.

C# provides for the declaration of class properties that provide a simplified means of accessing data members without specifically calling out the `get` and `set` accessor methods.

QUIZ YOURSELF

1. Why is it advantageous to declare data members `private`? (See the introduction to this session.)
2. What is the meaning of the `public` keyword? `private`? (See "Controlling Access to the Data Members of a Class.")
3. What does it mean to minimize a class interface? (See "Why worry about access control?")

Properties

Session Checklist

✔ Defining properties for a class

✔ Static properties

✔ Virtual properties

**30 Min.
To Go**

The GetX() and SetX() methods demonstrated in the IntegerBankAccount program are called access functions or simply accessors. Though good programming habit in theory, using access functions can get clumsy in practice. The following code is necessary to increase nAccountNumber by one:

```
SetAccountNumber(GetAccountNumber() + 1);
```

C# defines a construct called a *property* that makes using access functions much easier. The following code snippet defines a read-write property AccountNumber:

```
public int AccountNumber
{
  get{return nAccountNumber;}
  set{nAccountNumber = value;}
}
```

The get section is called whenever the property is read, whereas the set section is invoked whenever the property is written to.

In use, these properties appear as follows:

```
BankAccount ba = new BankAccount();

// write the account number property
ba.AccountNumber = 1001;
```

```
// read both properties
Console.WriteLine("#{0} = {1:C}",
                  ba.AccountNumber, ba.Balance);
```

The properties AccountNumber and Balance look very much like public data members, both in appearance and in use. However, properties allow the class to protect internal members — Balance is a read-only property — and hide their implementation.

By convention, the names of properties begin with a capital letter.

The C# library uses properties throughout. The following sections discuss three specific types of properties:

- Static properties
- Read-only properties
- Virtual properties

Static properties

A static (class) data member may be exposed through a static property as shown in the following simple example:

```
public class BankAccount
{
  private static int nNextAccountNumber = 1000;
  public static int NextAccountNumber
  {
    get{return nNextAccountNumber;}
  }

  // ...
}
```

The NextAccountNumber property is accessed through the class because it is not a property of any single object:

```
// read the account number property
int nValue = BankAccount.NextAccountNumber;
```

A get operation can perform extra work other than simply retrieving the associated property:

```
public static int NextAccountNumber
{
  // retrieve the property and set it up for the
  // next retrieval
  get{return ++nNextAccountNumber;}
}
```

This is probably not a good idea, however, because it isn't obvious to the user of the property that anything other than the actual reading of the property is happening.

**20 Min.
To Go**

Read-only properties

The following Balance property is read-only because there is no set section — only the get section is defined:

```
public double Balance
{
  get
  {
    double dCents = (double)nCents;
    return (double)nDollars + dCents / 100.0;
  }
}
```

Virtual properties

Like any nonstatic method, a property can be virtual. The following VirtualAccessor program uses virtual properties to convert monetary values from one currency to another.

This program defines a Currency class, which is the base of all currency types. Currency uses the euro as its base currency. In this particular example, only the subclasses DeutschMark (German mark) and Dollar are defined. The virtual property CurrencyAmount returns the value of the Currency object expressed in the units of the current object.

```
// VirtualAccessor - use the example of various currencies
//                   based on a common currency standard
//                   as an example of the use of virtual
//                   accessors
namespace VirtualAccessor
{
  using System;

  public class Class1
  {

    public static int Main(string[] strings)
    {
      // create an object of class DM with 2.50 Marks
      Console.WriteLine("Create a DeutschMark object 'dm'");
      Console.WriteLine("The rate of 1.96DM per Euro is fixed");
      DeutschMark dm = new DeutschMark();
      Console.WriteLine("Deposit 2.5 DM into 'dm'");
      dm.CurrencyValue = 2.50M;
      Console.WriteLine("Value in DeutschMark = {0:N}DM\n",
                        dm.CurrencyValue);

      // create a dollar with a conversion rate of
      // 1.2 Dollars per Euro
```

```
        Console.WriteLine("Create a dollar object 'dollar'");
        Dollar dollar = new Dollar();
        Console.WriteLine
                ("The current rate is $1.20 per 1 Euro");
        dollar.InitDollar(1.2M);

        // how many dollars does it take to have the
        // same value as the DeutschMark object
        Console.WriteLine("Store the value of the 'dm' object"
                    + " into the 'dollar' object");
        dollar.EuroValue = dm.EuroValue;
        Console.WriteLine("Value in dollars = ${0:N}\n",
                    dollar.CurrencyValue);

        // double the Dollar amount
        dollar.CurrencyValue = 2 * dollar.CurrencyValue;
        Console.WriteLine("Double the 'dollar' object\n");

        // convert the result back into DM
        Console.WriteLine("Convert the results back into DM");
        dm.EuroValue = dollar.EuroValue;
        Console.WriteLine("Resulting value in DM = {0:N}DM\n",
                    dm.CurrencyValue);

        // wait for user to acknowledge the results
        Console.WriteLine("Hit Enter to terminate...");
        Console.Read();
        return 0;
    }
}

// Currency - the base class of all currency types
abstract public class Currency
{
    private decimal mEuroValue = 0M; // [Euro]

    // the "EuroValue" is the value of the currency
    // object when expressed in Euros;
    // "CurrencyValue" is the value expressed in the
    // current currency
    public abstract decimal CurrencyValue{get; set;}
    public decimal EuroValue
    {
        get
        {
            return mEuroValue;
        }
        set
        {
            mEuroValue = value;
        }
    }
```

```
    }

    // DeutschMark
    public class DeutschMark : Currency
    {
      // conversion between DM and Euro
      private static decimal mDMtoEuro = 1.96M;

      // CurrencyValue - convert the number of DMarks to/from
      //              Euros (this is a fixed ratio)
      public override decimal CurrencyValue
      {
        get{return EuroValue * mDMtoEuro;}
        set{EuroValue = value / mDMtoEuro;}
      }
    }

    // Dollar - $12.34
    public class Dollar : Currency
    {
      // conversion factor
      public decimal mDollartoEuroConversion;

      public void InitDollar(decimal mDollartoEuro)
      {
        // first save off the conversion the factor
        mDollartoEuroConversion = mDollartoEuro;
      }

      // CurrencyValue - convert the number of Dollars
      //              to/from Euro's
      public override decimal CurrencyValue
      {
        get{return EuroValue * mDollartoEuroConversion;}
        set{EuroValue = value / mDollartoEuroConversion;}
      }
    }
  }
```

The complete VirtualAccessor **program can be found on the CD.**

The abstract class Currency defines a data member mEuroValue, which is the value of the object expressed in units of euros. (I could just as well have used dollars, yen, or gold bullion.) The property EuroValue provides access to this base value.

10 Min. To Go

The property CurrencyValue returns the value of the object converted to the currency units defined in subclass. The Currency class is abstract because every subclass has its own units.

The subclass DeutschMark is particularly simple because the conversion rate from DM to euro is fixed at 1.9558 or, roughly, 1.96. Multiply the value in euros by 1.96 to return the value expressed in deutsche marks.

The subclass Dollar is only slightly more complicated. The conversion rate of the dollar to the euro floats. Therefore, the application program must provide the conversion rate at the time of the call. The CurrencyValue method converts the base currency in euros to the local currency.

The Main() function starts out by creating a DeutschMark object dm, which is set to a value of 2.50DM. It then displays the value of dm to make sure the value was set properly.

The program then creates a dollar object. The program sets the value of the dollar object to that of the dm object by assigning the value in a common currency using the EuroValue property. It then displays the value of the dollar object.

Main() continues by multiplying the dollar object by two and storing the results back in the dm object as a way of proving that the conversions in both directions are being handled correctly.

The output from the program is as follows:

```
Create a DeutschMark object 'dm'
The rate of 1.96DM per Euro is fixed
Deposit 2.5 DM into 'dm'
Value in DeutschMark = 2.50DM

Create a dollar object 'dollar'
The current rate is $1.20 per 1 Euro
Store the value of the 'dm' object into the 'dollar' object
Value in dollars = $1.53

Double the 'dollar' object

Convert the results back into DM
Resulting value in DM = 5.00DM

Hit Enter to terminate...
```

Done!

REVIEW

A class should not expose its internal workings to outside classes, because the implementation details of the class are subject to change. Only members that are declared public are available to the world for use. Declaring a method private makes it unavailable to other classes. Declaring a method protected makes it available to methods within the class and to any subclass of that class.

Normally, data members should be made available to outside classes via accessor methods only: methods that read and write that data member.

C# provides for the declaration of class properties that constitute a simplified means of accessing data members without specifically calling the get and set accessor methods.

Quiz Yourself

1. What is a property?
2. What is another name for a static member? Why? (See "Static properties.")
3. What is a virtual property? (See "Virtual properties.")

PART

IV

Saturday Evening
Part Review

1. In what way are name hiding and polymorphism similar? In what way are they different? Provide a few example classes.

2. What is an abstract class?

3. How could we justify declaring a class Dog to be abstract?

4. Why might a class Collie that derives from Dog not be abstract?

5. What is access control of data members? In what ways is access control a good thing?

6. Name and define three of the five access control keywords.

7. Write a short BankAccount class. This class should contain a balance and an account number. An InitBank() function should be available to initialize the BankAccount object. In addition, this BankAccount should provide a Deposit() and Withdrawal() method that contains some form of checking for erroneous input. Include this class in a very short program BankAccount. Write a very short program that makes a deposit and displays the result.

8. Expand your solution by adding a subclass CDAccount that charges a 25 percent penalty on all withdrawals. Rerun your program.

☑ Friday

☑ Saturday

☑ **Sunday**

PART

V

*Sunday
Morning*

Default Constructors

Session Checklist

✔ Allowing an object to initialize itself via the constructor

✔ Defining multiple constructors for the same class

✔ Constructing static or class members

**30 Min.
To Go**

In the three preceding sessions, we examined most of the properties required for a C# class to mimic objects in the real world:

- A class can define itself in terms of more fundamental concepts through the inheritance concept. A Buick is a family sedan that is a car. I can describe a Buick by noting the features it has that are different from those of the standard family sedan.

- A class is responsible for invoking the necessary internal functions in order to perform an operation. I turn the key to make my Buick start. Many of the functions that the Buick performs in order to start are common to all cars; however, the air conditioner controls might be different, the radio isn't quite the same, there are a thousand little things that a Buick must do differently from other cars in order to perform the start operation. I don't know or care what these individual steps are. I want the car to start — it's up to the Buick to know how to perform those operations (otherwise, I'm trading it in for a Jeep).

- A class can protect itself from outside fingers poking in. Opening up the engine voids the warranty. You can change the oil or the battery, but in general you are obliged to use the standard dashboard controls the Buick provides. If you open the hood and start reconnecting wires and hoses in order to "improve" the way the Buick runs and it no longer starts, you can hardly blame the car.

An object cannot be held accountable for its well-being if it is not allowed to create its own initial state. One more property is necessary: the ability for the class to initialize its own state.

The C#-Provided Constructor

C# initializes objects to a value of all zeroes by default. For example, after the declaration

```
int n;
```

n is guaranteed to be zero.

C# is quite good at keeping track of whether or not a variable has been initialized. C# will not allow you to use an uninitialized variable. For example, the following generates a compile time error:

```
public static int Main(string[] args)
{
  int n;
  double d;
  double  dCalculatedValue = n + d;

  return 0;
}
```

C# tracks the fact that neither n nor d has been assigned a value and will not allow them to be used in the expression. Compiling this tiny program generates the following compile time errors:

```
Use of unassigned local variable 'n'
Use of unassigned local variable 'd'
```

References are initialized to null. Consider the following simple example program:

```
namespace Example
{
  using System;

  public class Class1
  {
    public static int Main(string[] args)
    {
      MyObject localObject = new MyObject();

      Console.WriteLine("localObject.n is {0}", localObject.n);

      if (localObject.nextObject == null)
      {
        Console.WriteLine("localObject.nextObject is null");
      }

      // wait for user to acknowledge
      Console.WriteLine("Hit Enter to terminate...");
      Console.Read();
      return 0;
    }
```

```
    public class MyObject
    {
      internal int n;
      internal MyObject nextObject;
    }
  }
}
```

This program defines a class MyObject that contains both a simple variable n of type int and a reference to an object nextObject. The Main() function creates a MyObject and then displays the initial contents of n and nextObject.

Compiling the program generates the following warnings:

```
Field 'Class1.MyObject.n' is never assigned to, and will always have its
default value 0
Field 'Class1.MyObject.nextObject' is never assigned to, and will always
have its default value null
```

 This warning message is a bit misleading — it is still possible to assign a value to an uninitialized class member after the object has been created.

The output from executing the program appears as follows:

```
localObject.n is 0
localObject.nextObject is null
Hit Enter to terminate...
```

When the object is created, C# executes some small piece of code to initialize the object and its members. Left to their own devices, the data members localObject.n and nextObject would contain random "garbage" values.

The code that initializes values when they are created is called the *constructor*. The constructor that C# provides to initialize objects to zero and references to null is sort of an automatic constructor.

The Default Constructor

**20 Min.
To Go**

C# ensures that an object starts life in a known state: all zeroes. However, for many classes (probably most classes), all zeroes is not a valid state. Consider the BankAccount class in Session 16:

```
public class BankAccount
{
  int nAccountNumber;
  double dBalance;
```

```
//...other members
}
```

While an initial balance of zero is probably okay, an account number of zero is definitely not the hallmark of a valid bank account.

Initializing an object using an external Init function

Programs appearing in prior sessions provided many classes with an Init...() method to set the object to a valid initial value. For example, the BankAccount class used the InitBankAccount() method to initialize the object:

```
public int Main(string[] args)
{
  BankAccount ba = new BankAccount();
  ba.InitBankAccount();
}

public class BankAccount
{
  // bank accounts start at 1000 and increase sequentially
  // from there
  static int nNextAccountNumber = 1000;

  // maintain the account number and balance for each object
  int nAccountNumber;
  double dBalance;

  // Init - initialize a bank account with the next
  //        account id and a balance of 0
  public void InitBankAccount()
  {
    nAccountNumber = ++nNextAccountNumber;
    dBalance = 0.0;
  }

  // ...other members...
}
```

The Main() function creates a BankAccount object that is clearly invalid and then immediately invokes the InitBankAccount() method to initialize it to a legal value.

This method has the advantage that the class can initialize itself properly without relying upon external software to set the data members. This also doesn't violate the "rules of limited visibility." The user function doesn't know what operations the Init... method must perform in order to initialize the object properly.

The problem with this approach is that it puts too much responsibility on the application software. If the application fails to invoke the InitBankAccount() function, then the bank account methods may not work through no fault of their own.

Allowing the object to initialize itself

A class should not rely upon external functions to start the object in a legal state.

To get around this problem, C# reserves a function name that it calls whenever an object is created. This method is known as the class constructor. The constructor could have been called Init() or Start() or Create(). Instead, the constructor carries the name of the class. Thus, a constructor for the BankAccount class appears as follows:

```
public int Main(string[] args)
{
  BankAccount ba = new BankAccount();
}

public class BankAccount
{
  // bank accounts start at 1000 and increase sequentially
  // from there
  static int nNextAccountNumber = 1000;

  // maintain the account number and balance for each object
  int nAccountNumber;
  double dBalance;

  // BankAccount constructor
  public BankAccount()
  {
    nAccountNumber = ++nNextAccountNumber;
    dBalance = 0.0;
  }

  // ...other members...
}
```

The contents of the BankAccount constructor are the same as those of the original InitBankAccount() method. The way the method is declared and used is different, however, in the following ways:

- The constructor carries the same name as the class.
- The constructor has no return type, not even void.
- Main() does not need to invoke any extra function in order to initialize the object when it is created.

Initializing an Object Directly

10 Min. To Go

You might think that almost every class must have a constructor of some type, and in a way you would be correct. However, C# allows data members to be initialized as part of the declaration within the class. Thus, I could have written the BankAccount class as follows:

```
public class BankAccount
{
  // bank accounts start at 1000 and increase sequentially
  // from there
  static int nNextAccountNumber = 1000;

  // maintain the account number and balance for each object
  int nAccountNumber = ++nNextAccountNumber;
  double dBalance = 0.0;

  // ...other members...
}
```

Both nAccountNumber and dBalance are initialized a value as part of the declaration. This initialization has the same effect that a constructor would.

Be very clear on exactly what is happening. C# does not set the dBalance to 0.0 directly. Remember that dBalance exists only as a part of an object. Thus, the assignment is not executed until a BankAccount object is created. In fact, this assignment is executed every time an object is created.

C# gathers any initializers that appear in the class declaration and gathers them into an initial constructor.

Initializers are executed in the order of their appearance in the class declaration. If there are both initializers and a constructor, the initializer is executed prior to the execution of the body of the constructor.

Static Constructors

The static (or class) members are shared among all objects of the class. Static members may be initialized via the same initializer method used for object members:

```
class BankAccount
{
  static int nNextAccountNumber = 1000;

  // ...other members...
}
```

The static element nNextAccountNumber is initialized before the first object of class BankAccount is created.

A static constructor is also available. Thus, the previous statement could have been written:

```
class BankAccount
{
  static int nNextAccountNumber;

  static BankAccount()
  {
    nNextAccountNumber = 1000;
```

```
    }

    // ...other members...
}
```

Notice first that the static constructor has no access modifier. All static constructors are private, because they are not invoked by any other function — they are invoked automatically at system startup. Also notice that a static constructor may perform calculations but cannot access any BankAccount object — the static constructor is called before any BankAccount object is created.

 I've been including the static initialization of nNextAccountNumber **for several sessions now.**

Done!

REVIEW

The programs from prior sessions used Init...() functions to initialize newly created objects to a legal state. However, a class must be able to initialize itself if it's to retain responsibility for its own health. To initialize the object properly, C# automatically invokes a special function known as the constructor when an object is created.

QUIZ YOURSELF

1. What is a constructor used for? (See "The C#-Provided Constructor.")

2. What is the default constructor? (See "The Default Constructor.")

3. How do you initialize an object with an external Init function? (See "Initializing an Object Using an External Init Function.")

4. How do you initialize an object with an internal Init function? (See "Initializing an Object Using an External Init Function.")

5. How do you get an object to initialize itself? (See "Initializing an Object Directly.")

SESSION

Multiple Constructors

Session Checklist

✔ Allowing an object to initialize itself via the constructor
✔ Defining multiple constructors for the same class

**30 Min.
To Go**

I n this session we are going to cover how to initialize an object via a constructor and how to define multiple constructors for an object.

Using Constructors to Initialize Objects

Often an object does not know how to construct itself in a legal state without help from the outside. Consider the following simple class:

```
public class Student
{
   string sName;
   int    nStudentID;
   int    nCreditHours;
}
```

In this case, the constructor must know the name of the student and his id (probably his Social Security number) in order to create a legal object. The Student class needs a constructor that can accept the name and id of the student at the time the Student object is created:

```
namespace Example
{
   using System;

   public class Class1
```

```csharp
{
  public static int Main(string[] args)
  {
    // create a student object with a name and id
    Student student = new Student("Stephen Davis", 1234);

    // now output the student data
    Console.WriteLine("Welcome new student {0}",
                      student.GetString());

    // wait for user to acknowledge
    Console.WriteLine("Hit Enter to terminate...");
    Console.Read();
    return 0;
  }
}

// Student - describe a college student
public class Student
{
  string sStudentName;
  int    nStudentID;
  int    nCreditHours;

  // constructor - init the object with a name and
  //               identification and a credit hours of
  //               0 (null name and negative IDs are not
  //               allowed)
  public Student(string sName, int nID)
  {
    // students must have a valid name and id
    if (sName == null)
    {
      sName = "invalid";
    }
    sStudentName = sName;

    if (nID < 0)
    {
      nID = 0;
    }
    nStudentID = nID;

    // students start life with no zero credit hours
    nCreditHours = 0;
  }

  // GetString - return the name and id of the student
  public string GetString()
  {
```

```
        string s = String.Format("{0}({1})",
                                   sStudentName, nStudentID);
        return s;
    }
  }
}
```

The constructor for the class Student is now defined as Student(string, int). The constructor performs a few checks to make sure that the name and student identification are valid. (The checks here are merely demonstrative. A production Student class would undoubtedly take much greater care that the input is correct.)

The class should always defend itself from illegal input. No matter what is thrown at it, the class should not crash.

The function Main() passes the name and identification number to the class when the object is created:

```
Student student = new Student("Stephen Davis", 1234);
```

It is illegal to attempt to create an object without providing those values. The output from executing this small program is as follows:

```
Welcome new student Stephen Davis(1234)
```

Multiple Constructors

*20 Min.
To Go*

It is possible for a single class to have multiple constructors. Suppose, for example, that you provided two means to create a BankAccount object. The constructor you have seen up until now creates an account with a zero balance. However, suppose you wanted to also allow the MultipleConstructor application to provide an initial balance when creating the account:

```
// MultipleConstructor - provides a simple BankAccount class
//                       with multiple, independent constructors
namespace MultipleConstructor
{
  using System;

  public class Class1
  {
    public static int Main(string[] args)
    {
      // create a bank account with valid initial values
      BankAccount ba1 = new BankAccount();
      Console.WriteLine(ba1.GetString());

      BankAccount ba2 = new BankAccount(100);
      Console.WriteLine(ba2.GetString());
```

```
    BankAccount ba3 = new BankAccount(1234, 200);
    Console.WriteLine(ba3.GetString());

    // wait for user to acknowledge
    Console.WriteLine("Hit Enter to terminate...");
    Console.Read();
    return 0;
  }
}

// BankAccount - simulate a simple bank account
public class BankAccount
{
  // bank accounts start at 1000 and increase sequentially
  // from there
  static int nNextAccountNumber = 1000;

  // maintain the account number and balance
  int nAccountNumber;
  double dBalance;

  // provide a series of constructors depending upon the need
  public BankAccount()
  {
    nAccountNumber = ++nNextAccountNumber;
    dBalance = 0.0;
  }

  public BankAccount(double dInitialBalance)
  {
    // repeat some of the code from the default constructor
    nAccountNumber = ++nNextAccountNumber;

    // now the code unique to this constructor
    // starts with an initial balance as long as it's positive
    if (dInitialBalance < 0)
    {
      dInitialBalance = 0;
    }
    dBalance = dInitialBalance;
  }

  public BankAccount(int nInitialAccountNumber,
                     double dInitialBalance)
  {
    // ignore negative account numbers
    if (nInitialAccountNumber <= 0)
    {
      nInitialAccountNumber = ++nNextAccountNumber;
    }
    nAccountNumber = nInitialAccountNumber;
```

```
        // start with an initial balance as long as it's positive
        if (dInitialBalance < 0)
        {
          dInitialBalance = 0;
        }
        dBalance = dInitialBalance;
      }

      public string GetString()
      {
        return String.Format("#{0} = {1:N}",
                             nAccountNumber, dBalance);
      }
    }
  }
```

The complete `MultipleConstructor` **program can be found on the CD.**

This version of BankAccount provides three constructors:

- The first constructor assigns an account ID and sets a balance of 0.
- The second constructor assigns an account ID automatically but initializes the account with a positive balance provided by the application. Negative balances are ignored.
- The third constructor allows the application to specify a positive account number and a positive balance.

The Main() function creates a different bank account using each of the three constructors and then outputs the objects created. The output from executing the program is as follows:

```
#1001 = 0.00
#1002 = 100.00
#1234 = 200.00
Hit Enter to terminate...
```

I want to stress again that a real-world class would perform a good deal more testing of the input parameters to the constructor to make sure that they were legal.

Constructors are differentiated using the same rules that apply to functions. Two constructors may not have the same number of arguments if each is of the same type.

Avoiding Duplication Among Constructors

*10 Min.
To Go*

You can see a significant amount of duplication in the three BankAccount constructors. You can imagine the situation's being much worse in real-world classes that may have a number of constructors and a large number of data elements to initialize. In addition, the tests on input data are generally much more detailed in a real-world class.

Duplicating these business rules is both tedious and error prone. It is far too easy for the checks to get out of synch — through a coding error, one constructor might apply a different set of rules against the balance, for example, than another. Such errors are very difficult to find.

One constructor can invoke another using a variation of the this keyword:

```csharp
// ChainedConstructor - compare this BankAccount class with the
//                      MultipleConstructor version which duplicates
//                      a lot of the constructor code
namespace ChainedConstructor
{
  using System;

// ...same Main() method as in MultipleConstructor example...
// BankAccount - simulate a simple bank account
public class BankAccount
{
    // bank accounts start at 1000 and increase sequentially
    // from there
    static int nNextAccountNumber = 1000;

    // maintain the account number and balance
    int nAccountNumber;
    double dBalance;

    // invoke the more specific constructor by providing
    // default values for the missing arguments
    public BankAccount() : this(0, 0) {}

    public BankAccount(double dInitialBalance) :
                         this(0, dInitialBalance) {}

    // the most specific constructor does all of the
    // real work
    public BankAccount(int nInitialAccountNumber,
                    double dInitialBalance)
    {
      // ignore negative account numbers; a zero account
      // number indicates that we should use the next available
      if (nInitialAccountNumber <= 0)
      {
        nInitialAccountNumber = ++nNextAccountNumber;
      }
      nAccountNumber = nInitialAccountNumber;

      // start with an initial balance as long as it's positive
      if (dInitialBalance < 0)
      {
        dInitialBalance = 0;
```

```
      }
    dBalance = dInitialBalance;
  }

  public string GetString()
  {
    return String.Format("#{0} = {1:N}",
                          nAccountNumber, dBalance);
  }
}
```

The complete ChainedConstructor **program can be found on the CD.**

This version of BankAccount provides the same three constructors; however, rather than repeat the same tests in each constructor, both of the simpler constructors invoke the most flexible constructor, thus providing defaults for the missing arguments.

Creating an object using the default constructor as follows:

```
BankAccount ba1 = new BankAccount();
```

invokes the BankAccount() constructor, which immediately passes control off to the BankAccount(int, double) constructor, passing it the default values 0 and 0.0:

```
public BankAccount() : this(0, 0) {}
```

Control returns to the default constructor once the invoked constructor has completed executing. The body of the default constructor is empty in this case.

The output from the CascadingConstructor example program is the same as that from the prior MultipleConstructor example.

Done!

REVIEW

A class can have multiple overloaded constructors. This allows the programmer to default arguments that are not of interest to the particular application. To avoid duplication of constructor code, C# allows one constructor to invoke others via a new use for the this keyword.

QUIZ YOURSELF

1. How can a single class have more than one constructor? How does the program differentiate among constructors? (See "Multiple Constructors.")

2. Why do such a thing? (See "Multiple Constructors.")

3. How do you avoid duplication in constructors? (See "Avoiding Duplication Among Constructors.")

Constructors and Inheritance

Session Checklist

✔ Including constructors in an inheritance hierarchy

✔ Invoking the base class constructor

**30 Min.
To Go**

Session 21 introduces the constructor, a special method used to give an object a good start in life by initializing it to a legal state. Session 22 describes further constructive considerations. Those sessions dealt with constructing a simple class. Constructing subclasses introduces a few wrinkles you need to consider.

Invoking the Default Base Class Constructor

Constructors are not inherited. Thus, the following is not possible:

```
public class BankAccount
{
  public virtual BankAccount() {}
}

public class SavingsAccount : BankAccount
{
  public override SavingsAccount() {}
}
```

There is a clear reason for this: Each class is responsible for itself. A subclass should not be responsible for initializing the members of the base class. It should not be allowed to override a base class constructor and, thereby, change the way the base class members are initialized.

The constructor for the subclass automatically invokes the constructor for the base class. This is demonstrated in the following simple program:

```
namespace Example
{
  using System;

  public class Class1
  {
    public static int Main(string[] args)
    {
      Console.WriteLine("Creating a BaseClass object");
      BaseClass bc = new BaseClass();

      Console.WriteLine("\nNow creating a SubClass object");
      SubClass sc = new SubClass();

      // wait for user to acknowledge
      Console.WriteLine("Hit Enter to terminate...");
      Console.Read();
      return 0;
    }
  }

  public class BaseClass
  {
    public BaseClass()
    {
      Console.WriteLine("Constructing BaseClass");
    }
  }

  public class SubClass : BaseClass
  {
    public SubClass()
    {
      Console.WriteLine("Constructing SubClass");
    }
  }
}
```

The constructors for BaseClass and SubClass do nothing more than output a message to the command line. Creating the BaseClass object invokes the default BaseClass constructor. When creating a SubClass object, C# invokes the BaseClass constructor before invoking the SubClass constructor.

The output from this program is as follows:

```
Creating a BaseClass object
Constructing BaseClass

Now creating a SubClass object
```

```
Constructing BaseClass
Constructing SubClass
Hit Enter to terminate...
```

A hierarchy of inherited classes is analogous to the floors of a building. Each class is built upon the classes it extends. The BaseClass must be given the opportunity to construct its members before the SubClass members have the opportunity to access them.

Passing Arguments to the Base Class Constructor

20 Min. To Go

The subclass invokes the default constructor of the base class unless specified otherwise. This is demonstrated in the following, slightly updated example:

```csharp
namespace Example
{
  using System;

  public class Class1
  {
    public static int Main(string[] args)
    {
      Console.WriteLine("Invoking SubClass()");
      SubClass sc1 = new SubClass();

      Console.WriteLine("\nInvoking SubClass(int)");
      SubClass sc2 = new SubClass(0);

      // wait for user to acknowledge
      Console.WriteLine("Hit Enter to terminate...");
      Console.Read();
      return 0;
    }
  }

  public class BaseClass
  {
    public BaseClass()
    {
      Console.WriteLine("Constructing BaseClass (default)");
    }
    public BaseClass(int i)
    {
      Console.WriteLine("Constructing BaseClass (int)");
    }
  }

  public class SubClass : BaseClass
  {
    public SubClass()
```

```
    {
      Console.WriteLine("Constructing SubClass (default)");
    }
    public SubClass(int i)
    {
      Console.WriteLine("Constructing SubClass (int)");
    }
  }
}
```

Executing this program generates the following results:

```
Invoking SubClass()
Constructing BaseClass (default)
Constructing SubClass (default)

Invoking SubClass(int)
Constructing BaseClass (default)
Constructing SubClass (int)
Hit Enter to terminate...
```

The program first creates a default object. As expected, C# invokes the default `SubClass` constructor, which first passes control to the default `BaseClass` constructor. The program then creates an object, passing an integer as an argument. Again as expected, C# invokes the `SubClass(int)`. This constructor invokes the default `BaseClass` constructor just as in Session 21 because it has no data to pass to it.

A subclass constructor can invoke a specific base class constructor using the keyword `base`.

This is very similar to the way in which one constructor invokes another within the same class using the `this` keyword.

For example, consider the following small program:

```
// InheritanceConstructor - a subclass uses the keyword
//                          base to invoke a particular
//                          subclass constructor
namespace InheritanceConstructor
{
  using System;

  public class Class1
  {
    public static int Main(string[] args)
    {
      Console.WriteLine("Invoking SubClass()");
      SubClass sc1 = new SubClass();

      Console.WriteLine("\nInvoking SubClass(1, 2)");
```

```csharp
            SubClass sc2 = new SubClass(1, 2);

            // wait for user to acknowledge
            Console.WriteLine("Hit Enter to terminate...");
            Console.Read();
            return 0;
        }
    }

    public class BaseClass
    {
      public BaseClass()
      {
        Console.WriteLine("Constructing BaseClass (default)");
      }
      public BaseClass(int i)
      {
        Console.WriteLine("Constructing BaseClass({0})", i);
      }
    }

    public class SubClass : BaseClass
    {
      public SubClass()
      {
        Console.WriteLine("Constructing SubClass (default)");
      }
      public SubClass(int i1, int i2) : base(i1)
      {
        Console.WriteLine("Constructing SubClass({0}, {1})",
                                              i1, i2);
      }
    }
}
```

The complete InheritanceConstructor **program can be found on the CD.**

The output from this program is as follows:

```
Invoking SubClass()
Constructing BaseClass (default)
Constructing SubClass (default)

Invoking SubClass(1, 2)
Constructing BaseClass(1)
Constructing SubClass(1, 2)
Hit Enter to terminate...
```

This version begins the same as the earlier examples by creating a default SubClass object using the default constructor of both BaseClass and SubClass.

The second object is created with the expression new SubClass(1, 2). C# invokes the SubClass(int, int) constructor, which uses the base keyword to pass one of the values on to the BaseClass(int) constructor. Presumably, SubClass passes the first argument to the base class for processing and continues on, using the second value itself.

The Updated BankAccount Class

The SavingsAccount and BankAccount constructors are repeated here:

```
// BankAccount - simulate a simple bank account
public class BankAccount
{
  // bank accounts start at 1000 and increase sequentially
  // from there
  static int nNextAccountNumber = 1000;

  // maintain the account number and balance
  int nAccountNumber;
  double dBalance;

  // Set of constructors - You can provide an initial
  // balance. The default is 0.
  public BankAccount() : this(0) {}
  public BankAccount(double dInitialBalance)
  {
    // assign an account number
    nAccountNumber = ++nNextAccountNumber;

    // save off non-negative balance
    if (dInitialBalance < 0)
    {
      dInitialBalance = 0;
    }
    dBalance = dInitialBalance;
  }
}

// SavingsAccount - a bank account that draws interest
public class SavingsAccount : BankAccount
{
  double dInterestRate;
  int    nNumberOfWithdrawalsThisPeriod;

  // InitSavingsAccount - input the rate expressed as a
  //                      rate between 0 and 100 (default
  //                      interest is 5%)
  public SavingsAccount() : this(5.0) {}
  public SavingsAccount(double dInterestRate)
                        : this(dInterestRate, 0) {}
```

```
    public SavingsAccount(double dInterestRate,
                          double dInitialBalance)
                            : base(dInitialBalance)
  {
    this.dInterestRate = dInterestRate / 100;
    nNumberOfWithdrawalsThisPeriod = 0;
  }
}
```

CD-ROM

The program ConstructorInheritance **found on this book's CD-ROM is an updated version of the bank account program in which the** SavingsAccount **class is able to pass information back up to the** BankAccount **constructors.**

Garbage collection and the C# destructor

The destructor method in C# is much less useful than it is in some other object-oriented languages such as C++ because C# has what is known as nondeterministic destruction.

The memory for an object is removed from the heap when the program executes the new command. This block of memory remains reserved as long as any valid references to that memory are running around.

The memory is said to be "unreachable" when the last reference goes out of scope. In other words, no one can access that block of memory once there are no more references to it left.

C# doesn't do anything in particular when a memory block first becomes unreachable. A low-priority task executes in the background, looking for unreachable memory blocks. The so-called garbage collector executes at low priority in order to avoid negatively affecting program performance. As the garbage collector finds unreachable memory blocks, it returns them to the heap.

Normally the garbage collector operates silently in the background. The garbage collector takes over control of the program for only a short period when heap memory begins to run out.

The C# destructor is said to be nondeterministic because it is not invoked until the object is garbage collected, and that could be long after the object is no longer being used. In fact, if the program terminates before the object is found and returned to the heap, the destructor is not invoked at all.

The net effect is that the C# programmer cannot rely on the destructor to operate automatically as she can in languages such as C++.

BankAccount defines two constructors, one that accepts an initial account balance and another, the default constructor, that does not. In order to avoid duplicating any code within the constructor, the default constructor invokes the BankAccount(initial balance) constructor using the this keyword.

The SavingsAccount class provides a number of constructors. The default constructor assumes an interest rate of 5 percent. The SavingsAccount(interest rate) constructor invokes the SavingsAccount(interest rate, initial balance) constructor, passing an initial balance of 0. This most general constructor passes the initial balance to the BankAccount(initial balance) constructor using the base keyword.

The Destructor

C# also provides a method that is inverse to the constructor, called the *destructor*. The destructor carries the name of the class with a tilde (~) in front. For example, the ~BaseClass method is the destructor for BaseClass.

C# invokes the destructor when it is no longer using the object. The default destructor is the only destructor that can be created because the destructor cannot be invoked directly. In addition, the destructor is always virtual.

When an inheritance ladder of classes is involved, the destructors are invoked in the reverse order of the constructors. That is, the destructor for the subclass is invoked before the destructor for the base class.

Done!

REVIEW

Constructors are not inherited and cannot be overridden. The constructor for a base class is automatically invoked first so that it has a chance to lay the foundation for the upcoming subclass constructor.

Left to its own devices, C# invokes the default base class; however, the subclass can invoke other base class constructors, passing them whatever information it wants, using the base keyword.

C# also defines a method known as the destructor. This method is not invoked until C# reclaims the memory occupied by the object.

QUIZ YOURSELF

1. Are constructors inherited? (See "Invoking the Default Base Class Constructor.")
2. How do you pass arguments to the base class constructor? (See "Passing Arguments to the Base Class Constructor.")
3. What is the destructor? (See "The Destructor.")

Multimodule Programs

Session Checklist

✔ Breaking a program into more than one source file

✔ Compiling each source file into its own assembly

✔ Assigning each module its own namespace

✔ Controlling access to methods from other classes

**30 Min.
To Go**

The programs that appear in this book are for demonstration purposes only. An industrial program, complete with all of the necessary bells and whistles, can include hundreds of thousands of lines of code spread over dozens of classes.

Storing all of these classes into a single module quickly becomes impractical. First there is the problem of remembering how the classes are organized within the file. Second, combining all of the program classes into one file makes it impossible to divide the programming work among developers. Finally, compiling a large module may take a considerable amount of time. Compiling such a module just because a single line in one class changed becomes intolerable.

For these reasons, C# allows the programmer to divide a single program into a number of .CS source files. Classes can be organized among source files. Changes to a class may involve recompiling a single smaller file that is then combined with the remaining files to form a large program. Finally, sets of source files can be assigned to different programmers for parallel development.

Dividing a Program

The programmer can use different criteria for dividing her classes among .CS source files. About the only limitation is that a single class cannot be divided across files. The most convenient arrangement is to store each class or group of highly related classes in their own source file. By convention, the programmer assigns the same name to the class and the source file. Thus, a class Sort would be contained in Sort.cs. In addition, Sort.cs would not contain classes unrelated to the Sort function. This makes finding classes within a directory containing multiple .CS source files much easier.

Dividing a program's source code introduces the problem of combining the object files back together to produce a single executable. The programs described in earlier sessions involved only a single source file. Although it wasn't obvious in those sessions, the task of building a program actually involves two steps. During the first step, the compilation phase, each C# source file is converted into a machine language object module known as an *assembly*. In a subsequent link phase, the assemblies are combined with the standard C# library to create the executable.

The steps to compile and link separate files into a common program differ depending upon the C# environment. The following two sections describe how to accomplish this using the Microsoft command-line compiler/linker and the Visual Studio .NET environment. The details for other C# environments, as they become available, will differ.

In both cases I will use the source files Baseclass.cs and Subclass.cs. Baseclass.cs. The Baseclass.cs source fileappears as follows:

```
// MultiModuleSameNamespace - Subclass contained in the
//                   Subclass.cs source file extends the
//                   Baseclass found here
namespace MultiModuleSameNamespace
{
  using System;


  public class Baseclass
  {
    // define a public property
    private int nBaseValue = 0;
    public int BaseProperty
    {
      get {return nBaseValue;}
      set {nBaseValue = value;}
    }

    // define a public method
    public void OutputMsg(string s)
    {
      // wait for user to acknowledge the results
      Console.WriteLine(s);
    }
  }
}
```

The complete MultipleModuleSameNamespace **program, including both** Baseclass.cs **and** Subclass.cs, **can be found on the CD.**

The following shows the Subclass.cs file:

```
// MultiModuleSameNamespace - Subclass contained in the
//                       this module extends Baseclass found in
//                       Baseclass.cs. This module also contains
//                       the starting point for execution, Main()
namespace MultiModuleSameNamespace

{
  using System;
  public class Subclass : Baseclass
  {
    // program starts here
    public static int Main(string[] strings)
    {
      // create a baseclass object and set the BaseProperty
      Console.WriteLine
        ("Creating a baseclass object and setting it to 20");
      Baseclass bc = new Baseclass();
      bc.BaseProperty = 10;
      // now invoke the base class method
      String s = String.Format("Baseclass property = {0}\n",
                               bc.BaseProperty);
      bc.OutputMsg(s);
      // repeat the process for this class
      Console.WriteLine
            ("Creating a subclass object and setting it to 20");
      Subclass sc = new Subclass();
      sc.BaseProperty = 20;
      sc.OutputMsg(String.Format("Subclass property = {0}\n",
                                 sc.BaseProperty));
      // wait for user to acknowledge the results
      Console.WriteLine("Hit Enter to terminate...");
      Console.Read();
      return 0;
    }
  }
}
```

The Baseclass module defines a method OutputMsg() and a read-write property BaseProperty. The Subclass module both reads and writes the BaseProperty() property and invokes the OutputMsg() method. The output of the program appears as follows:

```
Creating a baseclass object and setting it to 20
Baseclass property = 10

Creating a subclass object and setting it to 20
Subclass property = 20

Hit Enter to terminate...
```

Using the Microsoft command-line environment

The Microsoft command-line C# compiler is designed to be implemented from MS-DOS. The following command converts the source file Test.cs into the executable Test.exe:

```
PATH_TO_CSC\csc Test.cs
```

where PATH_TO_CSC is the path to the csc compiler. This command generates the executable file Test.exe by converting the Test.cs file into an assembly and then linking that assembly to the standard C# library.

 The Microsoft command-line compiler, which comes with the .NET SDK, is not easy to use. You should undertake this only if you feel very comfortable with MS-DOS.

The PATH_TO_CSC path can be quite lengthy. Early versions of Microsoft's C# compiler used the path %windir%\microsoft.net\framwork\v1.0.2914\csc.exe, where 1.0.2914 is actually the version number of the Visual C# you happened to be using. This version number changes as the compiler is updated. Look in the directory %windir%\microsoft.net\framework to find out the version number that you should use.

 You will want to build a batch (.BAT) file that contains this long and tortured path to csc.exe. You'll avoid a lot of unnecessary typing.

Compiling all source files together

The following, slightly more complicated command compiles both Baseclass.cs and Subclass.cs and then links them to create the executable Test.exe:

```
PATH_TO_CSC\csc /out:Test.exe Baseclass.cs Subclass.cs
```

Listing both source files on the same command line tells the csc tool to compile both files together. The order of the two source files is not important.

By default, csc uses the name of the first module in the command line as the name of the executable it generates. The out: switch instructs the C# tool to name the executable Test.exe no matter what the names of the C# source files are.

Compiling source files separately

Listing all of the file names on a single line is fine for small to moderate-sized applications. As the number of source files increases, however, this approach becomes progressively more impractical because it recompiles all source files even when only one of the files changes. What is needed is the ability to create assemblies separately.

The following command compiles the file Baseclass.cs into an assembly without performing the link step:

```
csc /target:module Baseclass.cs
```

The switch target: instructs the compiler to output an assembly module rather than an executable. The output from this command is the file Baseclass.netmodule.

The following command compiles the Subclass.cs file and links it with the Baseclass assembly:

```
csc /out:Test.exe Subclass.cs /addmodule:Baseclass.netmodule
```

Here, the order of compilation is important. The class Subclass **depends upon** Baseclass. **Thus, it is possible to compile** Baseclass.cs **without any external references. However, C# must have access to** Baseclass **when compiling** Subclass.

Using the Visual Studio .NET environment

Building an executable from multiple C# source files is the same as using Visual Studio .NET to compile and link the single, default Class1.cs module that you have been using in other lessons except that you will now include both the Baseclass.cs and Subclass.cs modules in your program.

Compiling all source files together

Visual Studio .NET uses a "project file" to describe the files that make up the executable file. (The project file determines many other properties of the executable.)

Create a console application in the normal fashion. (Select File ⇨ New... and enter Project. Select Console Application from the options and fill in the name of the program to generate.)

Creating a console application generates a project file with two .CS files: AssemblyInfo.cs and Class1.cs. You can ignore the AssemblyInfo.cs file for now. In this case, we want to add the two files Baseclass.cs and Subclass.cs to the project and remove the Class1.cs file.

Click Class1.cs and press the Delete key to remove Class1.cs from the project. (Alternatively, you can right-click on the source file and select the Delete menu option.) Next, select Project ⇨ Add Class.... Select C# class and enter the name of the class on the Name: line. Enter the Baseclass.cs source code. Repeat the process for the Subclass.cs source code.

Now build the application by selecting the menu option Build ⇨ Build Solution.

Visual Studio .NET recompiles only those files that have been changed since the last build. This speeds the build process by avoiding unnecessary compilations.

Namespaces

C# allows separate source files that make up a single executable to be grouped into a "space" with an assigned name. For example, the programmer may combile all math-related routines into a MathRoutines namespace. The namespace serves a number of purposes:

- A namespace represents a loose coupling of classes. The programmer generally groups related classes into a single namespace.
- Namespaces avoid the possibility of name conflicts. For example, a file input/output library may contain a class Text. At the same time, a translation library might contain a class of the same name. Assigning the namespaces FileIO and TranslationLibrary to the two sets of classes avoids the problem: FileIO.Text is clearly different from the class TranslationLibrary.Text.

In general, each library of classes is assigned its own namespace.

Declaring a namespace

A namespace is declared using the keyword namespace followed by a name and an open and closed parentheses block. The rules for naming a namespace are the same as those for naming a class. You will have noticed that all of the programs you have seen so far in this book have defined their own namespaces.

By default, the Visual Studio .NET environment assigns each project its own namespace to match the name of the program. You may change the namespace in the editor.

Thus, both Baseclass and Subclass in the previous example are a part of the MultiModuleSameNamespace namespace. A class that is not contained within a namespace designator is placed in the global namespace. This is the base namespace for all other namespaces.

Accessing modules in separate namespaces

The namespace containing a class is a part of the extended class name. The namespace of a class name defaults to the "current" namespace. For example, in the following code segment, the C# compiler assumes that Test and Sort are in the same namespace, MathRoutines:

```
namespace MathRoutines
{
  class Test
  {
    static public void function()
    {
      // create an object of type MathRoutines.Sort
      Sort obj = new Sort();

      // ...function continues...
```

```
      }
    }
  }
```

The full class name, including the namespace, must be used when the two classes are not in the same namespace. For example, the following code segment accesses a class Sort contained in a separate Container namespace:

```
// create a sort object of class Sort defined in the
// Container namespace
Container.Sort obj = new Container.Sort();
```

Using a namespace

Referring to a class name by its full name can become a distraction. C# allows the programmer to avoid this tedium with the keyword using. The using command adds the specified class to a list of "default" classes. The C# compiler searches this list when trying to resolve class names.

The using command says, "If you can't find the class specified in the current namespace, then look in that namespace to see if you can find it there." You can specify as many namespaces as you like except that all using commands must appear in a row and at the very beginning of the namespace.

The previous example could have been written:

```
namespace MathRoutines
{
  using Container;

  class Test
  {
    static public void function()
    {
      // create an object of type Container.Sort.
      // note the "using" command above.
      Sort obj = new Sort();

      // ...function continues...
    }
  }
}
```

or:

```
using Container;
namespace MathRoutines
{
  class Test
  {
    static public void function()
```

```
    {
      // create an object of type Container.Sort.
      // note the "using" command above.
      Sort obj = new Sort();

      // ...function continues...
    }
  }
}
```

There is practically no difference between the two versions.

All programs include the command using System;. **This gives the program automatic access to the functions included in the system library such as** WriteLine().

Dividing a program into multiple namespace libraries

A program may be divided into multiple library files, each in its own namespace. As noted previously, for example, the math-based classes might be gathered into a single namespace, MathRoutines. Compiling the source files that make up the MathRoutines namespace generates a MathRoutines library that can be accessed from other programs the programmer might create.

I have created an example program MultipleNameSpaces **consisting of a main program that links with a separate library module contained in a separate namespace. The sources for these modules along with complete instructions for how to build the program are included on the CD-ROM.**

Namespaces and Class Access

**10 Min.
To Go**

Namespaces allow a certain level of "uncoupling" among sets of largely unrelated classes. For example, a person working on the MathRoutines classes tends to use the Container classes without worrying about how they work.

C# allows the programmer to express this uncoupling using the five keywords public, protected, private, internal, and internal protected to control access to class members. The following example program demonstrates how these access controls work. The program AccessControl is made up of Class1 and Class3 contained in the namespace AccessControl and the class Class2 in the namespace AccessControlLib.

The complete AccessControl **program can be found on the CD.**

First create the Command line project `AccessControl` in Visual Studio as per normal. Edit the `Class1.cs` file as follows:

```
// AccessControl - demonstrate the various forms of
//                       access control
namespace AccessControl
{
  using System;
  using AccessControlLib;

  public class Class1 : Class2
  {
    public static int Main(string[] strings)
    {
      Class1 class1 = new Class1();
      Class2 class2 = new Class2();
      Class3 class3 = new Class3();

      // public methods are accessible from other classes
      // in other namespaces
      class2.A_public();

      // protected methods are accessible through the
      // inheritance hierarchy
      class1.B_protected();
      //class3.B_protected();

      // private methods are only accessible from the same
      // class
      //class2.C_private();
      class1.C_private();

      // internal methods are only accessible from a
      // class in the same namespace
      //class2.D_internal();
      class3.D_internal();

      // protected internal methods are accessible
      // either via the inheritance hierarchy or from
      // any class within the same namespace
      class1.E_internalprotected();
      class3.E_internalprotected();

      // wait for user to acknowledge the results
      Console.WriteLine("Hit Enter to terminate...");
      Console.Read();
      return 0;
    }

    public void C_private()
    {
```

```
      Console.WriteLine("Class1.C_private");
    }
  }

  // Class3 - an internal class is accessible to other
  //          classes within the same namespace but
  //          not to external classes that use that
  //          namespace
  internal class Class3
  {
    // declaring a class internal forces all public
    // methods to be internal as well
    public void A_public()
    {
      Console.WriteLine("Class3.A_public");
    }

    protected void B_protected()
    {
      Console.WriteLine("Class3.B_protected");
    }

    internal void D_internal()
    {
      Console.WriteLine("Class3.D_internal");
    }

    public void E_internalprotected()
    {
      Console.WriteLine("Class3.E_internalprotected");
    }
  }
}
```

Now select File ⇨ Add New Item…. From the list of options select C# Class. Visual Studio adds the file Class2.cs to the AccessControl program.Edit Class2 as follows:

```
namespace AccessControlLib
{
  using System;

  public class Class2
  {
    public void A_public()
    {
      Console.WriteLine("Class2.A_public");
    }
    protected void B_protected()
    {
      Console.WriteLine("Class2.B_protected");
    }
    private void C_private()
```

```
    {
       Console.WriteLine("Class2.C_private");
    }
    internal void D_internal()
    {
      Console.WriteLine("Class2.D_internal");
    }
    internal protected void E_internalprotected()
    {
      Console.WriteLine("Class2.E_internalprotected");
    }
  }
}
```

Executing the program generates the following output:

```
Class2.A_public
Class2.B_protected
Class1.C_private
Class3.D_internal
Class2.E_internalprotected
Class3.E_internalprotected
Hit Enter to terminate...
```

The method calls within Class1.Main() demonstrate each of the access types:

- Methods declared public are accessible to all methods in all namespaces. Thus, Class1 can invoke Class2.A_public() directly.

- Methods declared protected are accessible from the class Class2 and any class that inherits from Class1. The call class1.B_protected() is allowed because Class1 inherits from Class2. The call class3.B_protected() is illegal.

- Methods declared private are accessible only to other members of the same class. Thus, the call class2.C_private() is not allowed, but the call class1. C_private() is.

- A method declared internal is accessible to all classes within the same namespace. Thus, the call class2.D_internal() is not allowed. The call class3.C_internal() is allowed because Class3 is a part of the AccessControl namespace.

- The keyword internal protected combines the internal and the protected accesses. Thus, the call class1.E_internalprotected() is allowed because Class1 extends Class2 (this is the protected part). The call class3. E_internalprotected() is also allowed because Class1 and Class3 are part of the same namespace (this is the internal part).

- Declaring Class3 internal has the effect of reducing the access to internal or less. Thus, public methods become internal and protected methods become internal protected.

Methods should be declared with the most restricted access possible. For example, a private method may be modified at will without worrying what effect that might have on other classes. An internal class or method within MathRoutines is used in support of other math classes.

Done!

REVIEW

Large C# programs are often divided into multiple .CS source files, which are combined during the build process. This reduces the time required to rebuild the program after changes to a limited number of source files.

The C# programmer can also create libraries of routines that can be reused in multiple programs. The routines within these libraries are often grouped into namespaces of their own.

Finally, C# allows the programmer to control access to class methods. For example, a method marked `private` can be accessed only from other methods within the same class. The protected, `internal`, and `internal protected` keywords define other types of access limitations compared with the "no holds barred" `public` access.

QUIZ YOURSELF

1. Why divide a program into more than one file? (See the introductory paragraphs.)
2. What is a namespace? (See "Declaring a namespace.")
3. What are the five access control keywords? (See "Namespaces and Class Access.")

Handling Errors: The Exception

Session Checklist

✔ Returning error conditions

✔ Using exceptions, a new error-handling mechanism

✔ Throwing and catching exceptions

**30 Min.
To Go**

The programs that appeared in prior sessions haven't worried too much about errors. (I'm talking about erroneous input, not coding errors.) Even classes that did check for errors didn't quite know what to do when they found one. For example, the BankAccount.Deposit() method simply ignored negative deposits — the calling function had no idea that there was anything wrong.

C# provides a convenient mechanism for reporting error conditions. This mechanism, known as exceptions, is the subject of this session.

Reporting Runtime Errors

The following is an implementation of the common factorial function.

```
public class MyMathFunctions
{
  // Factorial - return the factorial of a value
  //             provided
  public static double Factorial(int nValue)
  {
    // begin with an "accumulator" of 1
    double dFactorial = 1.0;

    // loop from nValue down to one, each time
    // multiplying the previous accumulator value
    // by the result
```

```
    do
    {
      dFactorial *= (double)nValue;
    } while(-nValue > 1);

    return dFactorial;
  }
}
```

The function `factorial(n)` accepts an integer as input. The function returns the factorial of n as a double value.

`factorial()` begins by initializing an accumulator variable. The function then enters a loop, multiplying the accumulator by successively smaller values for `nValue` until `nValue` reaches 1. The resulting accumulator value is returned to the caller.

The following program tests the factorial function by calculating the factorial of 6, followed by 5, 4, 3, and so on down to -6:

```
public class Class1
{
  public static int Main(string[] args)
  {
    // call factorial in a loop from 6 down to -6.
    for (int i = 6; i > -6; i-)
    {
      Console.WriteLine("i = {0}, factorial = {1}",
                   i, MyMathFunctions.Factorial(i));
    }

    // wait for user to acknowledge
    Console.WriteLine("Hit Enter to terminate...");
    Console.Read();
    return 0;
  }
}
```

Executing the function generates the following output:

```
i = 6, factorial = 720
i = 5, factorial = 120
i = 4, factorial = 24
i = 3, factorial = 6
i = 2, factorial = 2
i = 1, factorial = 1
i = 0, factorial = 0
i = -1, factorial = -1
i = -2, factorial = -2
i = -3, factorial = -3
i = -4, factorial = -4
i = -5, factorial = -5
Hit Enter to terminate...
```

While simple enough, this function is lacking a critical feature: The factorial of zero is known to be 1 while the factorial of negative numbers is not defined. The foregoing function should include a test for a negative argument and, if so, indicate an error.

The classic way to indicate an error in a function is to return some value that cannot otherwise be returned by the function. For example, it is not possible for the returned value from factorial() to be negative. Thus, if passed a negative number, the factorial function could return a -1. The calling function can check the returned value — if it's a negative, the calling function knows that an error occurred and can take the appropriate action (whatever that may be).

This is the way that error processing has been done ever since the early days of FORTRAN. Why change it now?

The factorial of an integer N is equal to N * N-1 * N-2 * . . . * 1. For example, factorial 4 is 4 * 3 * 2 * 1 or 24.

Why Do You Need a New Error Mechanism?

20 Min.
To Go

There are several problems with the error return approach to error reporting. First, while it's true that the result of a factorial cannot be negative, other functions are not so lucky. Take logarithm, for example. You can't take the log of a negative number either, but logarithms can be either negative or positive — there is no value that could not be legally returned from the logarithm() function.

Second, there's just so much information you can store in an integer. Maybe -1 for "argument is negative" and -2 for "argument too large," but if the argument is too large, there is no way to store the value passed. Knowing that value might help to debug the problem. There's no place to store any more than the single error return value.

Third, the processing of error returns is optional. Suppose someone writes factorial() so that the factorial function checks the argument and returns a negative number if the argument is out of range. If the code that calls that function doesn't check the error return, the caller doesn't know if the factorial function failed.

Even if you do check the error return from factorial() or any other function, what can your function do with the error? Probably nothing more than output an error message of its own and return another error indication to its calling function.

Pretty soon the code begins to have the following appearance:

```
public class MyMathFunctions
{
  // common "no error" response
  public const int OK = 0;

  // BaseFunction - performs some operations; negative input
  //                value is illegal
  public const int NEGATIVE_VALUE = -1;
  public static int BaseFunction(int nDerived)
```

```
{
  // if input is negative...
  if (nDerived < 0)
  {
    // ...return some error condition
    Console.WriteLine(
                "BaseFunction() passed negative argument");
    return NEGATIVE_VALUE;
  }
  // ...
  return OK;
}

// SomeOtherFunction - performs a number of operations.
//                     Returns two error indications:
//                     "illegal input value" and "other error"
public const int INVALID_INPUT = -1;
public const int OTHER_ERROR = -2;
public static int SomeOtherFunction(int nValue)
{
  // ... perform some calculations ...
  int n = BaseFunction(nValue);

  // a negative return value indicates an error
  if (n < 0)
  {
    if (n == NEGATIVE_VALUE)
    {
      Console.WriteLine
      ("Negative argument error returned from BaseFunction()");
      return INVALID_INPUT;
    }

    Console.WriteLine
        ("Some type of error returned from BaseFunction()");
    return OTHER_ERROR;
  }

  return OK;
}
```

This mechanism has several problems:

- it's highly repetitive
- it forces the user to invent and keep track of numerous error return indications
- it mixes the error-handling code into the normal code flow, thereby obscuring both

These problems don't seem so bad in this simple example, but the overhead rises rapidly as the complexity of the calling code increases. The complexity also increases the "deeper" you work your way into the code. In other words, f1() calls f2(), which calls f3(), which calls f4() — by this time, the error handling gets very involved.

After a while, there's actually more code written to handle errors and checking return values than there is "real" code.

The net result is that error-handling code doesn't get written to handle all the conditions it should. (That is, if it gets written at all.) Some function calls one of the class methods with an illegal value, the method returns an error indication that the caller ignores, and the program continues off on some unpredictable path.

What is needed is a way to generate an error message and pass it up the chain of called functions automatically.

Exception Mechanism

C# introduces a totally new mechanism, called exceptions, for capturing and handling errors. This mechanism is based on the keywords try, catch, throw, and finally. In outline it works like this: A function trys to get through a piece of code. If the code detects a problem, it throws an error indication that the calling functions can catch, and no matter what happens the function executes a special block of code finally.

The exception mechanism is easier explained by example.

Demonstrating the exception mechanism

The following program demonstrates the key elements of the exception mechanism:

```
namespace ExceptionDemo
{
  using System;

  class Class1
  {
    public static int Main()
    {
      try
      {
        // invoke a function to throw an exception
        Console.WriteLine("Calling f1()");
        f1();
        Console.WriteLine("Returning from f1()");
      }
      // catch any exception thrown during execution
      catch(Exception exception)
      {
        Console.WriteLine("\nException! Message is: {0}",
                          exception.Message);
      }
      finally
      {
        Console.WriteLine("The finally block is executed" +
                " no matter what else happens");
      }
```

```
    // lines after the try block are executed, whether
    // f1() throws an exception or not
    Console.WriteLine("Execution continues");

    // wait for user to acknowledge
    Console.WriteLine("Hit Enter to terminate...");
    Console.Read();
    return 0;
}

public static void f1()
{
    Console.WriteLine("Entering f1()");
    f2();
    Console.WriteLine("Returning from f1()");
}

public static void f2()
{
    // function f2() performs some valid work
    Console.WriteLine("Entering f2()");

    // based upon some error detected, the f2() function
    // decides to report an error by throwing an exception
    Exception e =
         new Exception("This exception thrown from f2()");
    throw e;

    // function would continue processing if
    // there were no error
    Console.WriteLine("After the exception is thrown");
    }
  }
}
```

Main() starts by wrapping its work in a try block in order to catch any unhandled errors that might be detected during the execution of the program.

I'll explain in the next section why I say "unhandled errors."

**10 Min.
To Go**

Main() then starts its normal processing, first calling the WriteLine() function, followed by a call to f1() and a final call to WriteLine(). Normal execution of the program resumes with the final WriteLine() after the end of the try/catch/finally blocks.

The function f1() performs some processing, calls f2(), and then continues by outputting a final message. The function f2() creates an object of class Exception. The argument to the Exception constructor is a string describing the nature of the exception. The f2() function throws the exception, which is caught back in Main().

The catch block back in Main() outputs the message thrown. It then executes the code within the finally block before continuing.

The output from executing the program appears as follows:

```
Calling f1()
Entering f1()
Entering f2()

Exception! Message is: This exception thrown from f2()
The finally block is executed no matter what else happens
Execution continues
Hit Enter to terminate...
```

Notice the progression of output messages, with each one following the path of functions being called. However, none of the messages following the throw is executed. Instead, control passes from the throw in f2() directly back to f1(). Because f1() has no catch waiting to handle the exception, control passes on to Main(), where C# does find a matching catch block. This block outputs the message contained within the exception object passed it. The code within the finally block completes before the program moves on. Execution continues after the end of the try/catch/finally block.

The demonstration program generates the following output if the throw is commented out:

```
Calling f1()
Entering f1()
Entering f2()
After the exception is thrown
Returning from f1()
Returning from f1()
The finally block is executed no matter what else happens
Execution continues

Hit Enter to terminate...
```

Notice that the program now continues up through the calls to f2() and back down the returns to Main(). The code within the catch block is not executed, because no exception was generated. The code within the finally block is executed before control passes out of the try.

Done!

REVIEW

Historically, error conditions were reported to calling functions by returning some value. Often, zero meant that all worked okay, whereas other values indicated different types of errors: 1 for argument out of range, 2 for data not available, and so forth. These values were hard to interpret because they were left up to the individual programmer to make up and thus completely arbitrary. In addition, it is impossible to report any detail in an error return such as this. If 1 means "argument out of range," which argument, what was its value, and what's the legal range?

This session discussed the C# exception, a superior means for handling errors than relying on some return value from a function. An exception object is created at the point that the error is detected and "thrown" up the path of calling functions until one of the calling functions is prepared to handle the problem. Exception objects extend the class `Exception` by providing whatever unique information is needed to describe the problem. Thus, a user-defined `ArgumentOutOfRangeException` class could include the name of the argument, its value, and the legal range.

QUIZ YOURSELF

1. Why do we need error handling? (See "Why Do You Need a New Error Mechanism?")
2. What new mechanism does C# introduce for error handling? (See "Exception Mechanism.")
3. What are the key elements of an exception handler? (See "Demonstrating the exception mechanism.")

Extending the Exception Mechanism

✔ Overriding the exception class

✔ Tracing back to the location of the error

**30 Min.
To Go**

T he C# exception mechanism can be extended in a number of ways. This session examines a few of them.

Extending the Exception class

You can extend the Exception class with your own subclass, and doing so provides further details concerning the nature of an error that your program might encounter. For example, the following TimedStampException flags the date and time when the exception object was created (presumably this is the same as the time when the error occurred):

```
public class TimeStampedException: Exception
{
  public DateTime dateTime;
  public TimeStampedException(string sMessage)
    : base(sMessage)
  {
    // record the current date and time
    dateTime = DateTime.Now;
  }
}
```

The constructor for TimeStampedException accepts a message string that it passes on to the Exception base class for processing. TimeStampedException then creates and stores the current date and time using the DateTime class and its Now static property.

Multiple catch blocks

A single try block may be followed by a number of catch blocks:

```
try
{
  // ...whatever processing...
}
catch(TimeStampedException tse)
{
  // ...TimeStampedExceptions come here...
}
catch(Exception e)
{
  // ...generic exceptions caught here...
}
```

In this case, an exception generated from within the try block is compared with the first catch statement. If the exception object is a TimeStampedException (or one of its subclasses), control passes to the contents of the first catch block. If there is no match, control passes to the second catch statement, where the comparison is repeated. The catch(Exception) command catches all exceptions because Exception is the base class for all exceptions thrown.

A catch appearing without any arguments is the same as catch(Exception).

 The comparisons are performed in a serial fashion. catch **phrases must be lined up starting with the most specific and working toward the most general. Were I to reverse the two** catch **phrases in the earlier example, the** catch(TimeStampedException) **block would become unreachable because** catch(Exception) **intercepts all exception types.**

Cascading exceptions

A given try block is not compelled to handle all the different types of exceptions that a function might throw at it. In other words, the following code snippet is legal C#:

```
void GenericFunction()
{
  MathFunction();
}

void MathFunction()
{
  try
  {
    // ...whatever...
  }
  catch(DivideByZeroException dbze)
```

```
  {
    // ...handle the divide by zero case...
  }
}
```

The function MathFunction() has set itself up to handle the exception that C# generates when you attempt to divide any number by zero. GenericFunction() does not "see" the DivideByZero exception. Any other type of exception passes through MathFunction().

In this case, we say that DivideByZero **is a handled exception with respect to** MathFunction() **because it is handled at that level. Any other type of exception is considered unhandled.**

There are little or no restrictions as to what the code within a catch block can perform. In fact, a catch block may throw its own exception. There are two common reasons why a catch might do this.

An individual catch block might "generalize" an exception in some way by catching a specific exception and rethrowing a more general exception. For example, MathFunction() might handle the DivideByZero exception via some mathematical routines but then rethrow a generic Exception object to let the parent function(s) know that some type of error had occurred. This is far preferable to forcing the same mathematical code into the higher-level GenericFunction(), which may have no idea of the calculations going on within the MathFunction().

In addition, a function might need to perform its own processing in the event of an exception without actually handling the exception. Consider the following example function:

20 Min. To Go

```
public static void BufferString(string s)
{
  StreamWriter sw = null;
  try
  {
    // create a file
    sw = new StreamWriter("FileBuffer.txt");

    // ...perform more computing...

    // write the string out to the buffer file
    sw.WriteLine(s);

    // ...perform even more computing...

    // close the file now that we're done
    sw.Close();
  }
  catch
  {
    // be sure to close the temp file
    if (sw != null)
    {
      sw.Close();
```

```
    }

    // rethrow the same exception
    throw;
  }
}
```

The BufferString() function is designed to write to a file FileBuffer.txt whatever text string you give it. The StreamWriter() constructor creates the file and leaves it in the open state ready for writing.

If BufferString() does not call sw.Close() at the end, the FileBuffer.txt file will be left locked open. The blank catch at the end of the function intercepts any exceptions that might be thrown to make sure the file is properly closed. The blank throw rethrows the same object just as if BufferString() had not gotten in the way at all.

Extending the exception program example and updated Factorial function

The exception mechanism can be extended to perform detailed error handling. I have provided an ExceptionDemo program that extends the earlier exception demonstration program by creating a custom exception class, using multiple catch blocks to differentiate the nature of the induced error and cascading exceptions to allow problems to be handled at multiple levels.

Because of its imposing length, I have not listed this program here. Return to ExceptionDemo after Sunday when you feel a little more comfortable with C#.

 The complete ExceptionDemo **program can be found on the CD-ROM.**

Extending the Factorial function

The following program contained on the CD-ROM revisits the Factorial() function by adding error checking:

```
// FactorialExceptions - demonstrate the exception
//                       mechanism by throwing an exception
//                       from factorial() when passed a
//                       negative argument
namespace FactorialExceptions
{
  using System;

  public class Class1
  {
    public static int Main(string[] args)
    {
      // call factorial in a loop from 6 to -6.
      // Catch any exceptions that the function
```

```
      // might generate
      try
      {
        for (int i = 6; i > -6; i-)
        {
            Console.WriteLine("i = {0}, factorial = {1}",
                        i, MyMathFunctions.Factorial(i));
        }
      }
      catch(Exception e)
      {
        Console.WriteLine("Exception message:{0}",
                        e.Message);
        Console.WriteLine("Stack trace:\n{0}",
                        e.StackTrace);
      }

      // wait for user to acknowledge
      Console.WriteLine("Hit Enter to terminate...");
      Console.Read();
      return 0;
    }
}


// MyMathFunctions - a set of arithmetic functions
public class MyMathFunctions
{
  // Factorial - return the factorial of a value
  //             provided
  public static double Factorial(int nValue)
  {
    // if nValue is negative...
    if (nValue < 0)
    {
      // ...bundle the value up in the exception
      // message so that the caller knows the value
      // passed
      string s = String.Format(
        "Factorial passed negative value of {0}",
        nValue);

      // now throw the message to the caller
      throw new Exception(s);
    }

    // --factorial code from here down--
    // begin with an "accumulator" of 1
    double dFactorial = 1.0;

    // loop from nValue down to one, each time
    // multiplying the previous accumulator value
    // by the result
```

```
        do
        {
          dFactorial *= (double)nValue;
        } while(-nValue > 1);

        return dFactorial;
      }
    }
  }
```

The complete FactorialException **program can be found on the CD-ROM.**

**10 Min.
To Go**

Once again Main() invokes the Factorial() function with the numbers 6 down through -6. This time, however, Main() encloses the call in a block beginning with the keyword try.

The Factorial() function itself includes a check for a negative argument. If nValue is less than zero, Factorial() creates a string s describing the nature of the problem, including the actual value of nValue. Finally, Factorial() throws the error message back out to Main(). Main() catches the exception object and displays both the message and the stack trace.

Executing the program now generates the following output:

```
i = 6, factorial = 720
i = 5, factorial = 120
i = 4, factorial = 24
i = 3, factorial = 6
i = 2, factorial = 2
i = 1, factorial = 1
i = 0, factorial = 0
Exception message:Factorial passed negative value of -1
Stack trace:
    at FactorialExceptions.MyMathFunctions.Factorial(Int32 nValue)
          in c:\c#programs\factorialexceptions\class1.cs:line 62
    at FactorialExceptions.Class1.Main(String[] args)
          in c:\c#programs\factorialexceptions\class1.cs:line 20
Hit Enter to terminate...
```

Done!

REVIEW

In this session, we discussed how to extend the exception handler with multiple catch blocks and cascading exception handlers. We also took a look at a revised Factorial() function for error handling with extended exceptions.

QUIZ YOURSELF

1. How can we extend the exception class? (See "Extending the Exception class.")
2. How can we use multiple `catch` blocks for error handling? (See "Multiple `catch` blocks.")
3. What are the key elements of an exception handler? (See "Multiple `catch` blocks.")
4. What are cascading exceptions? (See "Cascading exceptions.")

PART

V

Sunday Morning
Part Review

1. Why is the capability of defining a constructor critical to the object-oriented programming concept?

2. What is the default constructor, and where does it come from?

3. Give an example of a static constructor.

4. Create a class `MyClass` that consists of nothing but a default constructor and a constructor that accepts an integer argument. Output an identifying message from each constructor. Invoke each constructor within a small program to prove that your class works.

5. Extend your program by adding a `SubMyClass` which has a single constructor that takes a string and an integer. Output the string and pass the integer portion to the proper base class constructor.

6. What is the full name of a method `MemFun()` that is a member of the class `MyClass` that itself is part of the namespace `MyNamespace` and accepts an `int` argument and returns a `double`?

7. How can you avoid specifying the namespace name when using the `MemFun()` function?

8. Under what conditions are both the namespace and class portion of the name unnecessary? Is there any condition under which you don't need the `int` argument?

9. Write a small function `CheckArgs(int)` that throws an exception any time it is passed a negative value. Include the function in a program that catches the exception and displays the error message.

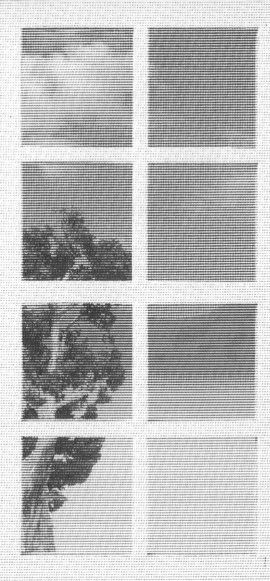

PART

VI

Sunday Afternoon

The C# struct

Session Checklist

✔ Examining the C# struct

✔ Using struct as the glue to unify the C# typing system

✔ Boxing and unboxing variables

In this session we are going to take a look at the C# struct. We are also going to discuss "boxing" and "unboxing" values.

Declaring Variables

There appears to be a dichotomy in the way variables are declared in C#. Intrinsic variables such as `int` and `double` are declared as follows:

```
int n;
n = 1;
```

This code segment creates a simple variable n and assigns it the value 1. By comparison, class objects are declared like this:

```
public class MyClass
{
   public int n;
}

MyClass mc = new MyClass();
mc.n = 2;
```

The variable mc contains a reference to an object that must subsequently be allocated out of an external area known as the heap, using the keyword new, before a value can be stored in its data member n.

C# defines a third structure type called struct that bridges the gap between these two variable types and binds them together into a neat package.

Declaring a C# struct

The syntax of a struct declaration looks like that of a class:

```
public struct MyStruct
{
  internal int n;
  internal double d;
}

public MyClass
{
  int o;
  double e;
}
```

A struct object is used the same as a class as well:

```
MyStruct ms = new MyStruct();
ms.n = 3;
ms.d = 3.0;
```

Despite the similarity in the way it is declared, a struct object is stored more like an intrinsic variable internally. The variable ms is not a reference to some external memory block allocated off the heap; instead, ms occupies the same local memory that the variable n occupies.

Consider the following declarations:

```
int m = 1;
double c= 1.0;

MyStruct ms = new MyStruct();
ms.n = 2;
ms.d = 2.0

MyClass mc = new MyClass();
mc.o= 3;
mc.e = 3.0;
```

Their layout in memory is shown graphically in Figure 27-1.

Memory

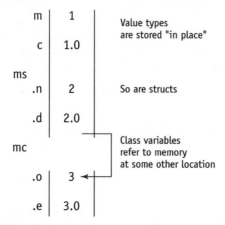

Figure 27-1 *The struct variable ms "lives" within the same memory space as the simple variables m and c.*

The variables m and c are allocated space first. The struct ms is allocated memory for its variables second. The memory for the reference mc comes third; however, the MyClass object is likely in some separate memory location.

Reference versus value type

The distinction between reference and value type is made more explicit in the following example. Allocating an array of 100 class objects requires the program to invoke new 101 times (once for the array and once for each object):

**20 Min.
To Go**

```
MyClass[] mc = new MyClass[100];
for(int i = 0; i < mc.Length; i++)
{
   mc[i] = new MyClass();
}
mc[0].n = 0;
```

However, the memory for the struct objects is allocated as part of the array:

```
MyStruct[] ms = new MyStruct[100];
ms[0].n = 0;
```

Properties of a struct

A struct object looks and acts like a class in use. A struct can have methods in addition to its data members. A struct can (and should) have one or more constructors.

However, a struct cannot extend any class other than object. You can override the methods of object — the main method you might want to override is ToString() in order to give your struct object a reasonable string representation.

Unified Type System

The comparison between struct objects and the intrinsic variables extends beyond the fact that both are value types: For every intrinisic type, there is a corresponding struct. For the standard int, the corresponding struct is Int32 (the 32 refers to the fact that the standard int variable occupies 32 bits). For double, the corresponding struct is Double.

Boxing variables

The relationship between the intrinsic and the corresponding struct is strikingly close, as the following code snippet makes clear:

```
int i = 0;
Int32 i32 = i;
```

This assignment creates a new object i32 of struct type Int32 that is a copy of the original value i. This automatic conversion from value type to struct type is known as *boxing*. The boxed struct object can continue to be used much like the original object:

```
Int32 j32 = i32 + 1;
```

**10 Min.
To Go**

In fact, struct objects demonstrate the same value semantics when being passed interchangeably to fn_int(int) and fn_int32(Int32) in the program PassingStructToFunctions:

```
// PassingStructToFunctions - struct objects have the
//                            same pass by value semantics
//                            as simple intrinsics
namespace PassingStructToFunctions
{
  using System;

  class Class1
  {
    public static int Main(string[] args)
    {
      int i = 0;
      Console.WriteLine("Initial value of i = {0}", i);
      fn_int(i);
      Console.WriteLine("i after fn_int() = {0}", i);
      fn_Int32(i);
      Console.WriteLine("i after fn_Int32 = {0}", i);

      Console.WriteLine();

      Int32 i32 = 1;
      Console.WriteLine("Initial value of i32 = {0}", i32);
      fn_int(i32);
      Console.WriteLine("i32 after fn_int() = {0}", i32);
      fn_Int32(i32);
      Console.WriteLine("i32 after fn_Int32 = {0}", i32);
```

```
        // wait for user to acknowledge the results
        Console.WriteLine("Hit Enter to terminate...");
        Console.Read();
        return 0;
    }

    public static void fn_Int32(Int32 k)
    {
      k = 10;
    }


    public static void fn_int(int k)
    {
      k = 20;
    }
  }
}
```

The output from this program is as follows:

```
Initial value of i = 0
i after fn_int() = 0
i after fn_Int32 = 0

Initial value of i32 = 1
i32 after fn_int() = 1
i32 after fn_Int32 = 1
Hit Enter to terminate...
```

Notice that both the int variable i and the Int32 variable i32 are passed to both functions by value. (Changes to their value in the functions do not affect the value of the object in the calling routine.)

Unboxing variables

A variable may be *unboxed* implicitly via a simple assignment, as in the following example:

```
Int32 i32 = 1;
int i = i32;
```

However, the types must match exactly. An explicit cast is required when the types are not identical.

Unification side-effects

The boxing and unboxing of intrinsic variables to and from struct objects tie the world of simple intrinsic variables to class objects in a tidy fashion: Simple variables can be used as objects in most cases. This extends to seemingly meaningless expressions, such as the following:

```
string s = 1.ToString();
```

Here the `ToString()` method is invoked on the `Int32` object resulting from boxing the `int` 1. The result is the string 1.

Done!

REVIEW

In this session, we examined the C# struct data type. We also discussed values and references types and what is meant by boxing and unboxing a value. Finally, we discussed some of the side effects that can occur when we box and unbox a value.

QUIZ YOURSELF

1. What is the difference between a reference type and a value type? (See "Declaring a C# struct.")

2. What is meant by *unifying types,* and how is boxing involved? (See "Unified Type System.")

The Interface

Session Checklist

✔ Investigating the CAN_BE_USED_AS relationship

✔ Defining an interface

✔ Using the interface to perform common operations

✔ Implementing an interface with an abstract class

**30 Min.
To Go**

You have seen in earlier sessions how inheritance can be used to help programs mimic the world. This session concentrates on one final type of class relationship: the *interface*. An interface describes a property of the class.

Examining an Interface

A reference within an object allows a class to mimic the HAS_A relationship, as in a car has a motor, as shown here:

```
class Car
{
  Motor motor;

  // ...other properties of the class...
}

class Motor
{
  // ...properties of the class...
}
```

At the same time, *inheritance* describes the all-important IS_A relationship, as in a car is a type of vehicle:

```
class Vehicle
{
  // ...properties of the class...
}

class Car : Vehicle
{
  // ...includes the properties of a Vehicle...
}
```

What is still missing is the not-so-obvious but equally important CAN_BE_USED_AS property. For example, if I want to jot down a note I can either scribble it on a piece of paper with a pen, stroke it into my personal digital assistant (PDA), or type it on my laptop.

Thus, I can say that all three objects — the paper, the PDA and the laptop — implement the TakeANote operation. I could implement this in C# as follows:

```
abstract class ThingsThatRecord
{
  abstract public void TakeANote(string sNote);
}

public class Pen : ThingsThatRecord
{
  override public void TakeANote(String sNote)
  {
    // ...scribble a note with a pen...
  }
}

public class PDA : ThingsThatRecord
{
  override public void TakeANote(String sNote)
  {
    // ...stroke a note on the PDA...
  }
}

public class Laptop : ThingsThatRecord
{
  override public void TakeANote(String sNote)
  {
    // ...whatever...
  }
}
```

This solution seems to work fine as far as the TakeANote() operation is concerned. A function such as RecordTask() can use the TakeANote() method to write down a shopping list without regard to the type of device supplied:

```
void RecordTask(ThingsThatRecord things)
{
  things.TakeANote("things to do");
  // ...and so on...
}
```

However, this solution suffers from two very big problems. The first is fundamental: One cannot really claim that the pen, PDA, and laptop have any type of IS_A relationship. Knowing how a pen works and how it takes notes gives me no information as to what a laptop is or how it records information. The name ThingsThatRecord is more of a description than a base class.

The second is purely technical. One might better describe Laptop as some subclass of Computer. While one could reasonable extend PDA off of the same Computer base class, the same cannot be said of the Pen. A pen would have to be characterized as some type of MechanicalWritingDevice. However, a C# class cannot inherit from two different classes at the same time — a C# class can be only one type of thing.

Some languages, most notably C++, do allow a single class to inherit from multiple base classes. C++ would solve the problem being described by basing Laptop on both ThingsThatRecord and Computer. However, this so-called multiple inheritance brings along additional complexity both in the language syntax as well as in the code it generates. The unwitting C++ programmer can stumble into some very difficult-to-solve multiple-inheritance-related problems.

Returning to the initial three classes, the only thing that the classes Pen, PDA, and Laptop have in common is that all three can be used to record a note. The interface feature allows us to communicate this without implying any inherent relationship among the three classes.

Implementing an Interface

An interface description looks much like a data-less class in which all of the methods are abstract. The interface description for "things that record" might look like the following:

```
interface IRecordable
{
  void TakeANote(String sNote)
}
```

By convention the names of interfaces begin with the letter I. In addition, the names of interfaces tend to be adjectives.

The following declaration indicates that the class PDA implements the IRecordable interface.

```
public class PDA : IRecordable
{
```

```
   public void TakeANote(string sNote)
   {
     // ...do something to record the note...
   }
}
```

There is no difference in the syntax of a declaration that extends a base class ThingsThatRecord and that which implements an interface IRecordable. This is the main reason for the naming convention for interface names.

A class implements an interface by providing a definition for every method of the interface, as shown here:

```
public class Pen : IRecordable
{
  public void TakeANote(string sNote)
  {
    // ...record the note with a pen...
  }
}
public class PDA : ElectronicDevice, IRecordable
{
  public void TakeANote(string sNote)
  {
    // ...graffiti write the note...
  }
}
public class Laptop : Computer, IRecordable
{
  public void TakeANote(string sNote)
  {
    // ...type in the note...
  }
}
```

**20 Min.
To Go**

The Pen, PDA, and Laptop classes each extend a different base class but implement the same Irecordable interface. IRecordable indicates that each of the three classes can be used to jot down a note using the TakeANote() method. This relationship is not as fundamental as the inheritance relationship. Nevertheless, it can be very useful.

Consider the following function:

```
static public void RecordShoppingList(IRecordable recordObject)
{
  // create a shopping list
  string sList = GenerateShoppingList();

  // now jot it down
  recordObject.TakeANote(sList);
}

public int Main(string[] args)
{
```

```
    PDA pda = new PDA();
    RecordShoppingList(pda);
}
```

In effect, this code snippet says that the function RecordShoppingList() will accept as its argument any object that implements the TakeANote() method (in human terms, "any object that can record a note"). RecordShoppingList() does not make any assumptions about the exact type of recordObject — the fact that the object is actually a PDA or that it is a type of ElectronicDevice is not important as long as it can take a note.

An example interface program

The following IDisplayable interface is satisfied by any class that contains a GetString() method. The interface doesn't know what GetString() does — each class is on its honor to fulfill the requirements described in the comment.

```
// IDisplayable - an object which implements the
//                GetString() method
interface IDisplayable
{
    // return description of yourself
    string GetString();
}
```

The following familiar class implements IDisplayable:

```
class Student : IDisplayable
{
    private string sName;
    private double dGrade = 0.0;


    // access read-only methods
    public string Name
    {
        get
        {
            return sName;
        }
    }
    public double Grade
    {
        get
        {
            return dGrade;
        }
    }

    // GetString - return a representation of the student
    public string GetString()
    {
```

```
      string sPadName = Name.PadRight(9);
      string s = String.Format("{0}:{1:N0}",
                                    sPadName, Grade);
      return s;
   }
}
```

Given this declaration, I can now write the following:

```
// IDisplayArray - display an array of objects which
//                 implement the IDisplayable interface
public static void IDisplayArray
                   (IDisplayable[] displayables)
{
   int length = displayables.Length;
   for(int index = 0; index < length; index++)
   {
      IDisplayable displayable = displayables[index];
      Console.WriteLine("{0}", displayable.GetString());
   }
}
```

The `IDisplayArray` **program on the CD-ROM uses the** `IDisplayArray`
function to display an array of `Student` **objects.**

This `DisplayArray()` method is capable of displaying any type of array as long as the members of the array define a `GetString()` method.

Predefined interfaces

The C# system library defines a number of interfaces. For example, the `IComparable` interface is defined as follows. (For a more thorough discussion of interfaces, please review the .NET SDK documentation. From within Visual Studio .NET, select Help ⇨ Index and enter **IComparable** in the Look for window.)

```
interface IComparable
{
   // compare the current object to the object 'o'; return
   // a 1 if larger, -1 if smaller and 0 otherwise
   int CompareTo(object o);
}
```

A class implements the `IComparable` interface with a `CompareTo()` method. For example, we might say that one `Student` object is "greater than" another `Student` object if its student id is greater or, perhaps, if its grade point average is greater.

Implementing the `CompareTo()` method implies that there is a sorting order to the objects. If one student is "greater than" another, then it must be possible to sort the students from "least" to "greatest."

In fact, the Array class implements the following method:

```
Array.Sort(IComparable[] objects);
```

This method will sort an array of objects of any class that implements the IComparable interface — for example, the following version of Student:

```
// Student - description of a student with name and grade
class Student : IComparable
{
  private double dGrade;

  public Student(double dGrade)
  {
    this.dGrade = dGrade;
  }

  // access read-only methods
  public double Grade
  {
    get
    {
      return dGrade;
    }
  }

  // CompareTo - compare another object (in this case,
  //             Student objects) and decides which
  //             one comes after the other in the
  //             sorted array
  public int CompareTo(object rightObject)
  {
    Student leftStudent = this;
    Student rightStudent = (Student)rightObject;

    // now generate a -1, 0 or 1 based upon the
    // sort criteria (the student's grade)
    if (rightStudent.Grade < leftStudent.Grade)
    {
      return -1;
    }
    if (rightStudent.Grade > leftStudent.Grade)
    {
      return 1;
    }
    return 0;
  }
}
```

Sorting an array of Students is reduced to a single call:

```
void SortStudents(Student[] students)
{
  // sort the array of IComparable objects
  Array.Sort(students);
}
```

The program SortInterface **included on the CD-ROM demonstrates the principle by sorting the two classes** Student **and** Bird, **which although different both implement the** IComparable **interface.**

Abstract Interface

**10 Min.
To Go**

A class must override every method of an interface in order to implement the interface. However, a class may override the method of an interface with an abstract method (such a class is abstract, of course), as shown here:

```
// AbstractInterface - this simple program demonstrates
//                how the abstract BaseClass can interface.
//                The concrete SubClass automatically inherits
//                the interface implementation.
namespace AbstractInterface
{
  using System;

  public interface ICompare
  {
    int GetValue();
    int Compare(ICompare ic);
  }

  abstract public class BaseClass : ICompare
  {
    int nValue;

    public BaseClass(int nInitialValue)
    {
      nValue = nInitialValue;
    }

    // provide two methods for accessing the Value
    // property
    public int Value
    {
      get {return GetValue();}
    }
    public int GetValue()
    {
      return nValue;
    }
```

```
      // complete the ICompare interface with an abstract method
      abstract public int Compare(ICompare bc);
  }

  public class SubClass: BaseClass
  {
    public SubClass(int nInitialValue) : base(nInitialValue)
    {
    }

    override public int Compare(ICompare ic)
    {
      return GetValue().CompareTo(ic.GetValue());
    }
  }

  public class Class1
  {

    public static int Main(string[] strings)
    {
      SubClass sc1 = new SubClass(10);
      SubClass sc2 = new SubClass(20);

      MyFunc(sc1, sc2);

      // wait for user to acknowledge the results
      Console.WriteLine("Hit Enter to terminate...");
      Console.Read();
      return 0;
    }

    public static void MyFunc(ICompare ic1, ICompare ic2)
    {
      Console.WriteLine("bc1.Compare(bc2) returned {0}",
                        ic1.Compare(ic2));
    }
  }
}
```

The complete AbstractInterface **program can be found on the CD-ROM.**

The ICompare interface describes a class that can compare two objects. The GetValue() method returns some int value that the Compare() method can use to generate a comparison of two ICompare objects.

The class BaseClass implements the ICompare interface — the GetValue() method returns the data member nValue, which is initialized in the constructor. However, the Compare() method, which is also required by the ICompare interface, is declared abstract. The class SubClass extends BaseClass by implementing Compare().

SubClass implements the ICompare interface because it extends a class that implements the interface. This is demonstrated in the lower part of the program. Main() creates two objects sc1 and sc2 of class SubClass. It then passes these objects to a method MyFunc(), which is declared to accept two objects that implement ICompare.

This program outputs this short but sweet output:

```
bc1.Compare(bc2) returned -1
Hit Enter to terminate...
```

Done!

REVIEW

The interface represents a promise. When a class implements the IComparable interface, it is in effect promising that it can perform the CompareTo() method. Other functions can rely on this promise. For example, the System method Sort() can sort any arrays whose objects implement the IComparable interface.

The interface relationship need not get in the way of an inheritance "tree." For example, an abstract class must overload every function in the interface, but it may do so with an abstract method..

QUIZ YOURSELF

1. What is the CAN_BE_USED_AS relationship? How does it differ from the IS_A relationship? (See "The Interface.")

2. What is an interface? (See "Examining an Interface.")

3. What are predefined interfaces? (See "Predefined interfaces.")

4. What is an abstract interface? (See "Abstract Interface.")

Method Delegates

Session Checklist

✔ Defining and invoking a method delegate

✔ Adding delegates to a structure

✔ Using delegates to handle events

**30 Min.
To Go**

This session discusses an advanced topic, function delegates.

A *delegate* is an object that references an object/method combination. This reference allows application software to *register* a method so that it can be called later. This would not be interesting were it not for the fact that a delegate does not know or care about the type of the object that it references. Any object and any method will do as long as the method signature matches that of the delegate.

Creating and Using a Delegate

A delegate class must be declared as follows:

```
public delegate int CallbackDelegate(int i);
```

This rather unusual declaration defines a special class known as CallbackDelegate, which extends the class System.Delegate. C# automatically adds a constructor to a delegate that receives a reference to a method whose signature matches that of the declaration. In other words, the argument to CallbackDelegate's constructor is a reference to an object method of the form int MyFunction(int).

The program uses the delegate's constructor to create an object that can be used to invoke a function at some later date. The following example code segment declares and uses an object that implements the example CallbackDelegate:

```
using System;

// define a delegate class which can be used to reference
// a function of the format int class.method(int)
public delegate int CallbackDelegate(int i);

class DelegateMain
{
  public static void Main()
  {
    // invoke the Class1.Function() directly as
    // a demonstration
    Class1 c = new Class1();
    int nValue = c.Function(0);

    // now invoke the method via a delegate object
    CallbackDelegate cbd =
                    new CallbackDelegate(c.Function);
    nValue = cbd(100);
  }
}

// define a couple of class.methods which fit the
// declaration of the CallbackDelegate
public class Class1
{
  public int Function(int i)
  {
    Console.WriteLine("Class1.Function() = {0}",
                       i);
    return 0;
  }
}
```

This example first invokes the method int Class1.Function(int), passing it the value 0 and storing the value returned. The code segment then creates a delegate object cbd that references the Function() method on the object c of type Class1.

Finally, the example invokes the method c.Function() via the delegate cbd(). The delegate object acts as a proxy for the Function() method.

Example Delegate Program

**20 Min.
To Go**

There is little point in creating and immediately using a delegate object. However, the power of a delegate is that it allows the program to save off references to different methods on different objects (as long as that method fits the proper function signature) for later use.

The program DelegateTest **can be found on the CD-ROM.**

The following example program demonstrates how delegates can be used:

```
// DelegateTest - demonstrate the use of delegates
//                 to serve as references to methods
//                 which can be stored for later use
namespace DelegateContainer
{
  using System;
  using System.Collections;

  // declare the delegate CallbackDelegate
  // - by default it extends the class System.Delegate
  public delegate int CallbackDelegate(int i);

  class DelegateMain
  {
    public static int Main(string[] args)
    {
      // invoke the Class1.Function1() directly
      // (like any other method)
      Class1 c = new Class1("invoked directly");
      c.Function1(0);

      // now create a queue of delegate objects, each
      // pointing to a different object.method pair
      Queue queue = new Queue();
      Class1 c1 = new Class1("invoked via delegate");
      CallbackDelegate cbd1 =
                      new CallbackDelegate(c1.Function1);
      queue.Enqueue(cbd1);
      queue.Enqueue(new CallbackDelegate(c1.Function2));
      Class2 c2 = new Class2();
      queue.Enqueue(new CallbackDelegate(c2.Function1));

      // pass the queue to some other function
      Callbacks(queue);

      // wait for user to acknowledge
      Console.WriteLine("Hit Enter to terminate...");
      Console.Read();
      return 0;
    }

    // Callbacks - invoke the list of callback objects
    //             which have been registered earlier
    public static void Callbacks(Queue queue)
    {
      int nCount = 1;

      // foreach object...
      foreach(CallbackDelegate cbd in queue)
      {
```

```
                // ...invoke the delegate
                int i = cbd(nCount++);
            }
        }
    }

    // define a couple of class.methods which fit the
    // declaration of the CallbackDelegate
    public class Class1
    {
        private string sMessage;
        public Class1(string sMessage)
        {
            this.sMessage = sMessage;
        }

        public int Function1(int i)
        {
            Console.WriteLine("Class1.Function1(){0} = {1}",
                              sMessage,
                              i);
            return 0;
        }
        public int Function2(int i)
        {
            Console.WriteLine("Class1.Function2() = {0}", i);
            return 0;
        }
    }
    public class Class2
    {
        public int Function1(int i)
        {
            Console.WriteLine("Class2.Function1() = {0}", i);
            return 0;
        }
    }
}
```

**10 Min.
To Go**

This program first defines CallbackDelegate, a delegate to a method that takes a single int argument and returns an int. The definition of two dummy classes, Class1 and Class2, appears at the bottom of the listing. Class1 defines two functions cleverly named Function1() and Function2(); Class2 defines the single method Function1().

The Main() function begins by invoking Class1.Function1() just to demonstrate that the function can be invoked directly, like any other method. The next few lines are critical and repeated here:

```
        Queue queue = new Queue();
        Class1 c1 = new Class1("invoked via delegate");
        CallbackDelegate cbd1 =
                    new CallbackDelegate(c1.Function1);
        queue.Enqueue(cbd1);
```

Why bother?

Why worry about delegates? True, you can define a delegate that points to an object/method pair that you can later invoke; however, why bother when you can invoke the method directly?

Delegates enable scenarios that C++ and some other languages have addressed with function pointers. Specifically, a program can register a delegate with the Windows operating system as an *event handler*. (An event is an asynchronous event such as the press of a key, the movement of the mouse, or the alarm associated with a timer.) Once the registration has taken place, Windows invokes the delegate when the event occurs. This gives the application software the ability to process the event.

C++ function pointers are extremely flexible but prone to error. Unlike function pointers, delegates are object-oriented, type-safe, and secure.

The delegate construct is not the only way to register event handlers. Java makes use of a different, incompatible process to achieve the same end. However, a Java event handler cannot be registered directly with Windows. In addition, the Java event handler approach is not compatible with the limitations of other programming languages such as Visual Basic and Visual C++.

This section creates a queue-type container. It continues by creating a delegate cbd1, which points to Function1() invoked on the object c1. Rather than invoke the function, Main() adds this callback to the queue. Main() adds a number of other delegates.

The queue of delegates is passed to the function Callbacks(). This function iterates through the queue container using the foreach control. The function then invokes each delegate that it finds in the queue. The output from the program appears as follows:

```
Class1.Function1()invoked directly = 0
Class1.Function1()invoked via delegate = 1
Class1.Function2() = 2
Class2.Function1() = 3
Hit Enter to terminate...
```

Done!

REVIEW

The *delegate* is a class with a unique declaration format. The application program creates an object of class delegate with an object and a method. Invoking the resulting delegate object has the same effect as invoking the original object/method.

This construct has the advantage that the delegate object can be stored off or passed to a function no matter what object or method the delegate contains. This can be especially useful in providing a *function callback*, an application-defined function that is invoked when a specified event occurs. The delegate callback is considerably safer than the equivalent C++ pointer scheme.

QUIZ YOURSELF

1. What is a delegate? (See the introduction to this session.)
2. What is the relationship between a delegate and the System.Delegate base class? (See "Creating and Using a Delegate.")
3. What is a callback function? (See the "Why bother?" sidebar.)

Collections

Session Checklist

✔ Introducing collections of objects

✔ Using iterators to access some types of collections

✔ Defining indexers to ease access to collections

✔ Implementing collection-based interfaces to provide additional capabilities

✔ Using the foreach control to increment through a collection

An array is one type of collection, but there are others. This session introduces some of the other collection types. The second section in the session, "Linked List Example," describes the manual implementation of one of these collection types. This final session wraps up by describing a few of the collection-based interfaces that provide extra capabilities to any collection class you might create.

30 Min.
To Go

Types of Collections

A group of objects of the same type is known generically as a collection of objects or, more commonly, as *a collection*. The collection actually contains references to objects. However, programmers often simply say that the collection "contains" the objects themselves. This section contrasts the array collection, the most common, to the linked list collection. You'll also find a discussion of some other collection types.

Some advantages and disadvantages of the array

The most common collection type is the array. Arrays have one extreme advantage over other types of collections: They allow a program to access random elements quickly and efficiently. The simple expression x[i] accesses the ith element in the collection. This expression is not only easy to write but also quick to execute. An expression such as x[i] takes not more than three or four computer instructions, far less than any other collection type.

The array collection also has at least two disadvantages. A program must declare the size of the array when it is created. This size cannot change once declared. Second, it is wildly inefficient to insert an object in the middle of an array. To insert an object into the insertHereth slot, the program must copy every object from i to i+1, starting at insertHere and continuing to the end of the array. One of the elements (usually the last) must be thrown away in order to make room for the new object.

The linked list

The second most common collection type after the array is the linked list. In the linked list, each object refers to both the next and the previous object in the list. A separate variable, commonly known as the *head* reference, points to the first object of the list while the *tail* points to the last element in the list.

The linked list has the following advantages and disadvantages compared with the array:

- It is easy to insert an element into the middle of a linked list. The program need only change the value of four variables in order to add an object.
- It is also easy to remove an element from a linked list.
- Linked lists can grow and shrink as necessary. The program declares the linked list empty and then adds and removes elements as needed.
- Accessing sequential elements in the list is quick and easy. However, elements within a linked list are not indexed — accessing data elements within the list is time-consuming.

Linked lists are ideal for containing a sequence of data especially when the program does not know how much data it is to receive.

 An implementation of a linked list appears on the CD-ROM as part of the LinkedListCollection **program. This program is described in more detail later in this session under "Linked List Example."**

Other collection types

It is instructive to write your own collection once or twice; however, it is not easy to write a good, error-free collection type. C# provides a number of collection types to choose from, including the following:

- ArrayList: An array that grows automatically as necessary. When the size of the array is exceeded, the array list allocates a second, larger array. It then copies the contents of the original array to the duplicate. That done, the array list puts the original, smaller block of memory back on the heap.
- Queue: A very fast, fixed-length collection. An add method adds objects to the end of the queue. A remove method retrieves the oldest member of the queue. This is the so-called first-in-first-out (FIFO) capability. Queues are ideal for storing input

data where new data is added to one end of the queue while older data is being worked off the other end.

- Stack: The reverse of the queue. The stack implements the last-in-first-out (LIFO) property. The push() method adds an object to the top of the stack. The pop() method pulls the first object off the top of the stack. In other words, pop() retrieves the most recently pushed object.

- Dictionary: A collection of objects that is keyed for quick lookup. The dictionary is useful for database-type applications where the program needs to quickly find an entry based upon some key.

Each of these classes is defined in the namespace System.Collection.

 Don't forget to add the uses System.Collection; **command at the top of any program that makes use of one of the collection classes; if you don't, you will need to refer to each class by its full namespace — for example,** System.Collection.ArrayList.

Indexers

The command collection[n] accesses the nth element of the collection array. It would be convenient if you could access the members of other types of collections just as easily.

C# allows the programmer to write her own implementation of the index operation on a class she has defined. In addition, a user-defined index operator is not limited to accessing via an index.

Indexer format

The indexer looks much like a property except for the appearance of the index operator: [] instead of the property name, as shown here:

```
class MyArray
{
  public string this[int index]
  {
    get
    {
      return array[index];
    }
    set
    {
      array[index] = value;
    }
  }
}
```

In practice, the expression s = myArray[i]; invokes the get function, passing it the value of i as the index. In addition, the expression myArray[i] = "some string"; invokes the set function, passing it the same index i and some string as value.

Example index program

The index type is not limited to int. (You might choose to index a house by the owner's name, by house address, or by any number of other indices.) In addition, the indexer property can be overloaded with multiple index types.

The following Indexer program generates a virtual array class MyArray. This virtual array looks and acts like an array except that it uses a string value as the index. (An int index is also allowed.)

```
// Indexer - this program demonstrates the use of the
//           index operator
namespace Indexer
{
  using System;

  public class MyArray
  {
    private string[] sArray;
    private object[] oArray;

    // MyArray - Create a fixed size MyArray.
    public MyArray(int nSize)
    {
      sArray = new string[nSize];
      oArray = new object[nSize];
    }

    // Find - find the index of the record
    //        corresponding to the string s
    //        (return a negative if can't be found)
    private int Find(string s)
    {
      for(int i = 0; i < sArray.Length; i++)
      {
        if (String.Compare(sArray[i], s) == 0)
        {
          return i;
        }
      }
      return -1;
    }

    // FindEmpty - find room in the array for a new
    //             entry
    private int FindEmpty()
    {
      for (int i = 0; i < sArray.Length; i++)
      {
        if (sArray[i] == null)
        {
          return i;
```

```
          }
      }

      throw new Exception("Array is full");
  }

  // look up contents by index
  public object this[int index]
  {
    set
    {
      sArray[index] = (string)value;
    }
    get
    {
      return sArray[index];
    }
  }

  // look up contents by string index
  public object this[string s]
  {
    set
    {
      // see if the string isn't already there
      int index = Find(s);
      if (index < 0)
      {
        // it isn't -  find a new spot
        index = FindEmpty();
        sArray[index] = s;
      }

      // save the object off in the corresponding spot
      oArray[index] = value;
    }

    get
    {
      int index = Find(s);
      if (index < 0)
      {
        return null;
      }
      return oArray[index];
    }
  }
}
}
```

The class MyArray holds two arrays. The sArray member holds an array of strings that act as indices into MyArray. The oArray array holds the corresponding object value for that index.

MyArray defines two indexers. The more useful accepts a string as its index and an object as its argument. The set[string] indexer starts by checking to see if the specified index already exists by calling the function Find(). If it does not, set[] finds a new, empty element where it stores both the indexing string and the object passed it.

The Find() method loops through the members of MyArray looking for the sArray element with the same value as the string s passed in. Find() returns the index of the element found (or a -1 if none could be found).

The get[] portion of the indexer searches through the list using the Find() method. get[] returns the corresponding oArray object at the same index. If no element with the same string index is found, get[] returns a null.

The following trivial program demonstrates the use of MyArray:

```
// Indexer - this program demonstrates the use of the
//             index operator
namespace Indexer
{
  using System;

  public class Class1
  {
    public static int Main(string[] args)
    {
      // create an array with enough room
      MyArray ma = new MyArray(100);

      // save off the ages of the Simpsons kids
      ma["Bart"] = 8;
      ma["Lisa"] = 10;
      ma["Maggie"] = 2;

      // look up the age of Lisa
      int age = (int)ma["Lisa"];
      Console.WriteLine("Lisa is {0}", age);

      // wait for user to acknowledge the results
      Console.WriteLine("Hit Enter to terminate...");
      Console.Read();
      return 0;
    }
  }
}
```

 The complete Indexer **program can be found on the CD-ROM.**

The program creates a MyArray object ma of length 100 (that is, with 100 free elements). It continues by storing the ages of the Simpson children indexed by each child's name. Finally, the program retrieves Lisa's age using the expression ma["Lisa"] and displays the result.

Notice that the program has to cast the value returned from ma[] because MyArray is written to hold any type of object. The cast would not be necessary were the indexer to be written to handle only int values.

Collection Interface Definitions

Different collection types may have different accessing schemes. For example, arrays are accessed with an index, and a linked list via a GetNext() method. These differences make it impossible to write a function such as the following without special provisions:

```
void myClearFunction(Collection collection, int index)
{
  collection[index] = 0; // index doesn't work for all
                         // types of collections

  // ...continues...
}
```

There are essentially two ways around this problem. Both are described by the IList interface.

The IList interface

One approach is to force all collection types to look like an array. Classes that implement the IList interface provide an arraylike integer indexer of the form object this[int]. This allows the programmer to write the following no matter what type of collection:

```
void MyFunction(IList ilCollection)
{
  // calculate an index
  // ...

  // retrieve a value from the collection
  object o = ilCollection[index];

  // ...continue...
}
```

Here the programmer is assured that the access to the index operator in MyFunction() is allowed because the collection passed to it implements the IList interface.

The IEnumerator interface

A second approach to defining a common access implementation for all collection types is known as the *enumerator technique*. This technique uses a second object called the *iterator* as a pointer into the collection.

The iterator method offers a number of advantages:

- Each class can define its own iteration class.

- The application code does not need to know the internals of the collection code. As long as the programmer understands how to use the iterator, the iteration class can handle the details.

- The application code can create multiple independent iterators. Because the iterator contains the state information, each iterator can navigate through the collection independently.

Unfortunately, with only a limited number of methods, the iterator is not easy to manipulate. The programmer can move the iterator back and forth through the collection; however, the iterator must support different types of collections — for example, the programmer cannot use the iterator to access locations within the collection class randomly.

Specifically, let's call our collection class Collection. The programmer of the Collection class creates a corresponding iterator class, say CollectionIterator. This iterator class implements the following methods, which are described by the IEnumerator interface:

- Reset(): Sets the enumerator to point to the beginning of the array.
- MoveNext(): Moves the enumerator from the current object in the collection to the next one.
- Current: Retrieves the object located at the current position of the enumerator.

 An iterator could implement a different set of methods; however, C# iterators implement the above three methods by convention.

The application programmer uses these three methods to navigate the Collection class as follows:

```
// the Collection class holds ContainedObject type objects
void MyFunction(Collection collection)
{
  // the programmer which created the Collection class also
  // creates an iterator class CollectionIterator;
  // the application program creates an iterator object
  // in order to navigate through the collection object
  IEnumerator iterator = new CollectionIterator(collection);

  // move the enumerator to the "next location" within the
  // collection
  while(iterator.MoveNext())
  {
    // fetch a reference to object at the current location
    // in the collection
    ContainedObject contained;
    contained = (ContainedObject)iterator.Current;

    // ...use the collection object...
  }
}
```

The function MyFunction() accepts as its argument a collection of ContainedObjects. MyFunction() creates an object iterator of class CollectionIterator. (Presumably the programmer of the Collection class had also created the CollectionIterator class.) The function continues by invoking the MoveNext() method. On this first call, MoveNext() moves the iterator to the first element in the collection. On each subsequent call, MoveNext() moves the pointer over one position. MoveNext() returns a false when the collection is exhausted and the iterator cannot be moved any further.

The Current property returns a reference to the object at the current location of the iterator. Calls to Current are invalid if the MoveNext() method did not return a true on the previous call.

The foreach control

**10 Min.
To Go**

A class implements IEnumerable by defining the method GetEnumerator(). Any class that implements IEnumerable can be accessed via the foreach command as follows:

```
void MyFunction(IEnumerable collectionOfStrings)
{
  foreach(string s in collectionOfStrings)
  {
    Console.WriteLine("The next string is {0}", s);
  }
}
```

foreach invokes the GetEnumerator() method to retrieve an iterator. It uses this iterator to make its way through the collection. Each element it retrieves is cast appropriately before continuing into the block of code contained within the braces.

Thus, the foreach control

```
foreach(int nValue in myCollection)

{
  // ...
}
```

is equivalent to the for loop, as shown here:

```
for(IEnumerator i = myCollection.GetEnumerator(); // initializer
       i.MoveNext();        // conditional also increments
       )                    // increment does nothing
{
  int nValue = (int)i.Current     // retrieve the current element
  // ...
}
```

The initializer section of the foreach control retrieves an iterator. The conditional section uses the MoveNext() method to look for the end of the collection. The MoveNext() increments the pointer. The first line in the loop fetches the next object and casts it to an int. If the object is not actually an int, C# throws an exception.

The String **class implements** Ienumerable, **which allows you to use** foreach
to enumerate each item.

Linked List Example

The following program demonstrates the methods that make up the internals of the doubly
linked list:

```
// LinkedListCollection - demonstrate a "home grown" linked.
//       This collection implements the IEnumerable
//       to support operators such as foreach. This
//       example also includes an iterator which
//       implements the IEnumerator interface
namespace LinkedListCollection
{
  using System;
  using System.Collections;

  // LinkedListClass -
  public class LinkedListClass : IEnumerable
  {
    // AddObject
    public LLObject AddObject(object objectToAdd)
    { ... }

    // RemoveObject
    public void RemoveObject(LLObject currentNode)
    { ... }


    // GetEnumerator -
    public IEnumerator GetEnumerator()
    {
      return new LinkedListIterator(this);
    }

    // Indexer - access elements in the array by index
    public object this[int nIndex]
    {
      get
      {
        IEnumerator iterator = GetEnumerator();

        while(iterator.MoveNext())
        {
          if (nIndex- == 0)
          {
            break;
```

```
          }
        }

      return iterator.Current;
    }
  }
}

// LinkedListIterator -
class LinkedListIterator : IEnumerator
{
  //LinkedListIterator -
  internal LinkedListIterator(LinkedListClass linkedList)
  {
    // ...
  }

  // Current
  ///    return the object at the current location
  public object Current
  {
    get{ ... }
  }

  //  Reset -
  public void Reset()
  { ... }

  // MoveNext - move forward; return true if the
  //            operation is executable
  public bool MoveNext()
  { ... }
}
```

The program is too large to include here in its entirety — the full
`LinkedListCollection` **program is contained on this book's CD-ROM. This
listing includes the function names but not the actual code itself.**

The basis of this program is the LinkedListClass and the LinkedListIterator classes.
The AddObject() and RemoveObject() methods allow user code to add objects to and
remove them from the list. The GetEnumerator() method returns an object of class
LinkedListIterator() (thereby fulfilling the IEnumerable interface).

The object this(int) indexer allows the user to access the nth element of the linked
list. It does this by creating an iterator to point at the beginning of the list and counting
out n elements from the beginning using the MoveNext() method.

**This inefficient algorithm is necessary because the linked list is not
amenable to being accessed with that type of reference. This highlights one
of the dangers with the generic indexer: An extremely inefficient operation
may be hiding behind a simple operator.**

The `LinkedListIterator` class implements the `Current`, `Reset()`, and `MoveNext()` properties to satisfy the `IEnumerator` interface. Declaring the constructor `internal` keeps user code from creating a `LinkedListIterator` object other than via the `LinkedListCollection.GetEnumerator()` method.

The following example program demonstrates how to use these two classes:

```
// LinkedListCollection - adds an indexer to the LinkedList class
//                        to allow elements to be indexed with a
//                        string
namespace LinkedListCollection
{
  using System;
  using System.Collections;

  public class Class1
  {
    public static int Main(string[] args)
    {
      // add elements to the collection
      LinkedListClass llc = new LinkedListClass();
      LLObject first = llc.AddObject("This is first");
      LLObject second = llc.AddObject("This is second");

      // we can manipulate the iterator "manually"
      Console.WriteLine("Access the collection manually");
      LinkedListIterator lli
              = (LinkedListIterator)llc.GetEnumerator();
      lli.Reset();
      while(lli.MoveNext())
      {
        string s = (string)lli.Current;
        Console.WriteLine(s);
      }

      // or we can let the foreach do it for us
      Console.WriteLine("Access using the foreach");
      foreach(string s in llc)
      {
        Console.WriteLine(s);
      }

      // finally we can use the indexer provided to
      // output the i'th string
      Console.WriteLine("Access the second string directly");
      Console.WriteLine((string)llc[1]);

      // wait for user to acknowledge the results
      Console.WriteLine("Hit Enter to terminate...");
      Console.Read();
      return 0;
    }
```

```
        }
    }
```

The output from this program is as follows:

```
Access the collection manually
This is first
This is second
Access using the foreach
This is first
This is second
Access the second string directly
This is second
Hit Enter to terminate...
```

The program begins by creating a collection 11c and calling the AddObject() method to add two strings. The program then uses the newly created 11i to iterate through the list. The object returned by Current must be cast from class object to string before it can be used. The test program performs the same iteration operation with the foreach command. Finally, the program accesses a location at random using the indexer.

Done!

REVIEW

In this final session you saw that an array is one type of collection. It has the advantage that elements can be accessed quickly and at random. There are other types of collections, each with its own set of advantages and disadvantages.

The C# indexer allows the programmer creating a collection to provide the application program with a generic access method using the array-type syntax.

The C# programmer can also provide an iterator. This generic approach allows the programmer of the collection to define an access object. The application programmer uses this object to retrieve elements from the collection. The iterator approach is not as clean but generally more efficient.

Finally, you saw how C# provides the foreach function to iterate through the collection.

QUIZ YOURSELF

1. What is a disadvantage of an array? (See "Some advantages and disadvantages of the array.")
2. Name an alternative collection that does not suffer from the disadvantages of an array (it may carry its own disadvantages). (See the section after "Some advantages and disadvantages of the array.")
3. Name a third type of collection. (See "Other collection types.")
4. What is an indexer? (See "Indexers.")

PART

VI

Sunday Afternoon
Part Review

1. What is actually happening in the following small code segment?

```
int i = 10;
Int32 i32 = i;
int j = (int)i32;
int k = i32;
```

2. Explain the following interface definition:

```
interface IAddable
{
int Add(int n1, int n2);
}
```

3. Create a class that implements the IAddable interface.

4. Of the following collections:
   - Array
   - LinkedList
   - Dictionary
   - Stack
   - Queue

   which collection is best suited for the following tasks?

   a. The user enters an 8-digit ID number that the program uses to look up a name.

   b. The program accepts a stream of data from the Internet and holds it until the browser can get around to displaying it. It's important that the browser receive the data in the order the same order in which it was sent.

   c. The program reads a file with an unspecified number of student records. The program must then sort the students by name before displaying their names on the console.

d. A function holds a fixed number of names that it displays on the screen. The user enters the index of the record that he wants to change. The changed record is placed back in the same slot as the original.

Answers to Part Reviews

Following are the answers to the review questions at the end of each part in this book. Think of these reviews as mini-tests that are designed to help you prepare for the final — the Skills Assessment Test on the CD.

Friday Evening Review Answers

1. A warning often indicates that C# doesn't really "understand" your intentions. If you can't fix a warning, you should at least understand what's causing it. (By the way, I don't think I've ever met a warning message that couldn't be addressed.)

    A computer program is a complicated piece of art. Even a good program can be difficult to understand, even for the author. Comments included with the source code help programmers who try to read and understand the program perhaps years after it was written.

2. Writing comments helps me collect my thoughts. As I begin to write the next block of code, writing out the comment encourages me to think about what I am trying to accomplish in this next bit of source code.

3. The following declares an `int` variable `nVar1` and a `double` variable `var2`:

    ```
    int nVar1;
    double var2;
    ```

    The floating point `var2` could also have been declared:

    ```
    float var2;
    ```

    The `float` type has a smaller range and less accuracy but takes up less memory.

4. An integer variable is used primarily to count things. The set of all integer variable types is also known as the "counting types." Floating variables are used to measure things. My height or weight would be stored in a floating point variable. (Use an integer a "measurement" like the number of people in Europe since this is actually a count of the number of people in Europe.)

5. Here is my program for converting the number of feet entered at the console into meters:

```
public static int Main(string[] args)
{
    // prompt user to enter feet
    Console.Write("Enter feet:");


    // read the feet entered

string sFeet = Console.ReadLine();
double dFeet;
dFeet = Double.Parse(sFeet);

// convert feet to meters
double dFeet;
dFeet = (dFeet * 3.3);

// output the result
Console.WriteLine("Feet in meters = "
                 + dFeet);

// wait for user to acknowledge the results
Console.WriteLine("Hit Enter to terminate...");
Console.Read();
return 0;

}
```

6. An expression x in a control if(x) is of type bool, which stands for Boolean, the inventor of the logical calculus. A bool variable can have the value true or false.

7. My version of the absolute value is as follows:

```
// Abs - return the absolute value of the argument passed it
double Abs(double x)
{
    double dAbs = x;
    if (x < 0)
    {
        dAbs = -x;
    }
    return dAbs;
}
```

8. The IsEven(x) function returns a true if its argument is even and a false if not. It works by first dividing x by two. It then strips off the integer portion of x. If the result is zero, then x must be divisible by two.

9. A calculated floating point value may not have exactly the value you think. For example, the expression 3.0 * (x / 3) may not be exactly equal to x because of roundoff.

10. The following version of IsEven(x) works as expected for all values of x.

```
bool IsEven(double x)
{
  // calculate the fractional part (the part to the
  // right of the decimal point) of x / 2
  double dHalf = x / 2;
  double dModulo = dHalf - (int)dHalf;
small
  // value)
  return (dModulo < 0.10)
}
```

11. The following function displays the numbers 1 through 10 on the console.

```
namespace CountTo10
{
  using System;

  public class Class1
  {
    public static int Main(string[] args)
    {
      int i = 1;
      while(i <= 10)
      {
        Console.WriteLine(i);
        i = i + 1;
      }

      // wait for user to acknowledge the results
      Console.WriteLine("Hit Enter to terminate...");
      Console.Read();
      return 0;
    }
  }
}
```

12. Programmers often say that while(IsEven(dValue)) loops as long as dValue is even. This isn't an accurate description. In fact, the function CountUntilOdd() loops forever because dValue is always even at the beginning of the loop even though dValue becomes odd somewhere in the middle of the while().

13. The calculation is not performed even once if the condition is false in the `while` loop. The `do...while()` always performs the calculation at least once.

Saturday Morning Review Answers

1. The `while` loop equivalent of `for(int n = 0; n < 10; n++) { nSum = nSum + 1;}` is

```
int n = 0;
while(n < 10)
{
  nSum = nSum + 1;
  n++;
}
```

2. The following function uses the `break` statement to test the loop condition in the middle of the loop.

```
void CountUntilOdd()
{
  double dValue = 0;
  while(IsEven(dValue))
  {
    Console.Write("x = " + dValue);
    dValue = dValue + 1.0;

    // recheck the while loop condition in the
    // middle of the loop
    if (IsEven(dValue) == false)
    {
      break;
    }

    Console.WriteLine(" and then " + dValue);
    dValue = dValue + 1.0;
  }
}
```

3. The following program first prompts the user for a value. It then indicates whether the user enters a zero, one, two, three, or something else.

```
namespace SwitchProgram
{
  using System;
```

```csharp
public class Class1
{
  public static int Main(string[] args)
  {
    // prompt the user for an integer value
    Console.WriteLine("Enter value:");
    string s = Console.ReadLine();
    int n = Int32.Parse(s);

    // display appropriate message based on value
    switch(n)
    {
      case 0:
        Console.WriteLine("Value entered is zero");
        break;

      case 1:
        Console.WriteLine("Value entered is one");
        break;

      case 2:
        Console.WriteLine("Value entered is two");
        break;

      case 3:
        Console.WriteLine("Value entered is three");
        break;

      default:
        Console.WriteLine("Value entered is something else");
        break;
    }

    // wait for user to acknowledge the results
    Console.WriteLine("Hit Enter to terminate...");
    Console.Read();
    return 0;
  }
}
```

4. The following program prompts the user for five integer values. The program first displays the values in order and then in reverse order.

```
namespace Reverse
{
  using System;

  public class Class1
  {
    public static int Main(string[] args)
    {
      int[] nArray = new int[5];

      // tell the user what to do
      Console.WriteLine("Enter 5 integers:");

      // now input 5 integers
      for(int i = 0; i < 5; i++)
      {
        Console.Write("Enter [" + i + "] - ");
        string sValue = Console.ReadLine();
        nArray[i] = Convert.ToInt32(sValue);
      }

      // and output them backwards
      Console.WriteLine("The sequence backwards is:");
      for(int i = 0; i < 5; i++)
      {
        // the index of the last element is 4; therefor
        // 4 - 0 is 4, 4 - 1 is 3, etc. until 4 - 4 is 0
        int nIndex = 4 - i;
        Console.WriteLine(nArray[nIndex]);
      }

      // wait for user to acknowledge the results
      Console.WriteLine("Hit Enter to terminate...");
      Console.Read();
      return 0;
    }
  }
}
```

5. In order to process a variable number of integer values, the Reverse program would need to first ask the user how many values he intends to enter. The program would then allocate the array dynamically as `int[] nArray = new Int[nNumberOfInts]`.

6. The `class` structure allows the programmer to combine the relevant properties of an object. This includes both passive (data) and active (method) properties.

7. The following code segment allocates a `Person` object and initializes its members:

```
Person person = new Person;
person.sFirstName = "Friendly";
person.sLastName  = "Reader";
person.nID = 1234;
```

8. The static function `StaticFunc()` accepts its `SomeClass` object explicitly as an argument. The `Method()` accepts its `SomeClass` object implicitly. `Method()` assigns this implicit object the name `this`.

9. The following version of `Person` provides its own initialization method.

```
public class Person
{
   public string sFirstName;
   public string sLastName;
   public int nID;

   public void InitPerson(string sFName, string sLName, int nInitialID)
   {
      sFirstName = sFName;
      sLastName  = sLName;
      nID = nInitialID;
   }
}
```

10. The following version of `InitPerson()` is slightly more readable by giving the function arguments the same name as the corresponding data members.

The following version of `Person` provides its own initialization method.

```
public class Person
{
   public string sFirstName;
   public string sLastName;
   public int nID;

   public void InitPerson(string sFirstName , string sLastName , int nID)
   {
```

```
      this.sFirstName = sFirstName ;
      this.sLastName = sLastName ;
      this.nID = nID;
   }

}
```

11. The following Pool class defines a DeeperPool() method that returns the deeper
    of two pools, one the current object and the other a Pool object passed in as its
    argument. The small program exercises the method.

```
namespace DeeperPool
{

  using System;

  public class Pool
  {

    public int nDepth;    // depth of the pool [meter]
    public double dArea;  // surface area of the pool [meter2]

    public Pool DeeperPool(Pool otherPool)
    {
      if (this.nDepth > otherPool.nDepth)
      {
        return this;
      }
      else
      {
        return otherPool;
      }
    }
  }

  public class Class1
  {
    public static int Main(string[] args)
    {
      Pool pool1 = new Pool();
      pool1.nDepth = 2;
      pool1.dArea  = 20;

      Pool pool2 = new Pool();
```

```
        pool2.nDepth = 3;
        pool2.dArea  = 50;

        Pool deeperPool = pool1.DeeperPool(pool2);
        Console.WriteLine("surface area of the deeper pool is " +
                        deeperPool.dArea);

        // wait for user to acknowledge the results
        Console.WriteLine("Hit Enter to terminate...");
        Console.Read();
        return 0;
      }
    }
  }
```

Saturday Afternoon Review Answers

1. A static function is not called with an object. Therefore, it has no current object (and, therefore, no this reference).

2. The following program SeeingSpots uses the function Replace() to replace every space with a period in a string input from the console.

```
namespace SeeingSpots
{
  using System;

  public class Class1
  {
    public static int Main(string[] args)
    {
      // prompt the user for a string
      Console.Write("Enter a sentence containing spaces:");
      string s = Console.ReadLine();

      // replace evey occurence of ' ' with '.'
      s = s.Replace(' ', '.');

      // output the result
      Console.WriteLine("Output: {0}", s);
```

```
      // wait for user to acknowledge the results
      Console.WriteLine("Hit Enter to terminate...");
      Console.Read();
      return 0;
    }
  }
}
```

3. The following version of the SeeingSpots program does not rely on Replace().

```
namespace SeeingSpots
{
  using System;

  public class Class1
  {
    public static int Main(string[] args)
    {
      // prompt the user for a string
      Console.Write("Enter a sentence containing spaces:");
      string s = Console.ReadLine();

      // iterate through the string looking for spaces;
      while(true)
      {
        // find the index of the next space
        int nIndex = s.IndexOf(' ');

        // exit when there are no more
        if (nIndex == -1)
        {
          break;
        }

        // remove the space at that location
        s = s.Remove(nIndex, 1);

        // insert a '.' at the previous location of the space
        s = s.Insert(nIndex, ".");
      }
```

```
        // output the result
        Console.WriteLine("Output: {0}", s);

        // wait for user to acknowledge the results
        Console.WriteLine("Hit Enter to terminate...");
        Console.Read();
        return 0;
    }
  }
}
```

4. The `String.Format()` control `{0:F1}` outputs the double 123.456 as "123.4."

5. Consider the following declarations:

```
char[] cName = {'S', 't', 'e', 'p', 'h', 'e', 'n'};
string sName = "Stephen";
string[] sNames = new String[] {"Stephen"};
```

The variable `cName` is an array of characters that happen to spell out my first name (and a glorious name it is, too). `cName` has array semantics in that characters within the array can be accessed via an index. Thus, `cName[1]` is equal to the character t. However, `cName` does not have access to any of the string manipulation functions.

The variable `sName` is an object of class `string`. `sName` is manipulated like an object — it has access to a number of methods that are specialized to operate on strings of characters. However, individual characters within the string are difficult to access.

The variable `sNames` is actually an array of strings consisting of a single member, "Stephen." `sNames[0]` is a `string` and has the same semantics as `sName`.

6. The C# environment stores any arguments passed to the program as an array of strings in the variable `args` in the declaration of `Main()`. This makes the name `args` very descriptive, though any variable name is equally valid: `public static int Main(string[] someOtherName)`.

7. An object-oriented language must provide:

- **a well-defined interface.** A C# class can define public data members and methods that describe the properties of the real-world class of objects.

- **access control.** A C# class must be able to expose members that are visible to the outside world while hiding data members that, though critical to the internal workings of the class, are of no interest to application functions that use the class.

- **specialization.** One C# class can provide subtypes of another class via the wonders of inheritance. For example, a class `Harley` can extend a class `Motorcycle` by describing only the properties that are unique to a Harley-Davidson motorcycle (in particular, its masculine, rumbling idle).

- **polymorphism.** A function must respond accordingly depending upon which variation of a base class is being used. For example, the program must decide on its own the proper method `GetIn()` of an object to invoke when that object may be of class `LeftHandDriveCar` or `RightHandDriveCar`.

Saturday Evening Review Answers

1. In both name hiding and polymorphism, a method in a subclass has the same name (including arguments to the function) as a method in a base class. A program decides which hidden method to call based upon the declaration of the object. A program decides which virtual (polymorphic) method to call based upon the actual or runtime type of the object.

2. An abstract class is a base class which represents a concept that unifies two or more subclasses. For example, the class Boat is abstract because there is no such thing as a "boat," but it serves to describe the common properties of a MotorBoat and a SailBoat. The class Boat is abstract because there is no such thing as a Boat, only types of boats. In particular, the method GetUnderway() is implemented completely differently in the two subclasses. A MotorBoat gets underway by starting the engine while a Sailboat raises and sets its sails.

3. There is no such thing as a "dog," only types of dogs, and yet the term *dog* has considerable meaning. When one speaks of a dog, he means a furry, four-legged mammal that barks all the time, begs for food, and makes a mess on your carpet.

4. A collie is a type of dog. For example, all dogs bark, but different species of dog bark differently. Ignoring any individual peculiarities, all collie dogs bark the same way. Thus the class Collie might extend the abstract base class Dog by providing an implementation of the method Bark().

5. An access control method exposes some property of the class. Access control allows the class to project a given, hopefully simple interface that represents a potentially complicated set of internal properties. For example, the public method Sailboat.GetUnderway() invokes the private methods StartMotor(), MotorFromHarbor(), HoistSails(), and StopMotor() while changing the state of the mainSail, jib, and sheet data members. The simple GetUnderway() provides the application programmer with what she needs without boring or confusing her with the details.

6. The four access keywords are:
   - a public member is accessible to all classes
   - a private member is accessible only to other members in the same class
   - a protected member is accessible to members of the class and subclasses
   - an internal member is accessible to other classes within the same namespace, essentially within the same group or modules
   - a protected internal member is accessible to both other classes within the same namespace as well as to a class that might extend the class

7. The following is my version of a BankAccount program that creates a simple bank account class:

```
namespace BankingAccount
{
  using System;
```

```
// BankAccount - simulate a bank account each of which
//               carries an account id (which is assigned
//               upon creation) and a balance
public class BankAccount
{
  // bank accounts start at 1000 and increase sequentially
  // from there
  public static int nNextAccountNumber = 1000;

  // maintain the account number and balance for each object
  public int nAccountNumber;
  public double dBalance;

  // Init - initialize a bank account with the next
  //        account id and a balance of 0
  public virtual void InitBankAccount()
  {
    nAccountNumber = ++nNextAccountNumber;
    dBalance = 0.0;
  }

  // Balance - retrieve the balance of the current account
  public double Balance()
  {
    return dBalance;
  }

  // Account - return the account number
  public int Account()
  {
    return nAccountNumber;
  }

  // Deposit - any positive deposit is allowed
  public void Deposit(double dAmount)
  {
    if (dAmount > 0.0)
    {
      dBalance += dAmount;
```

```
    }
  }

  // Withdraw - you can withdraw any amount up to the
  //            balance; return the amount withdrawn
  public double Withdraw(double dWithdrawal)
  {
    if (dBalance <= dWithdrawal)
    {
      dWithdrawal = dBalance;
    }

    dBalance -= dWithdrawal;
    return dWithdrawal;
  }
}

public class Class1
{
  public static int Main(string[] args)
  {
    // create a bank account object
    BankAccount ba = new BankAccount();
    ba.InitBankAccount();

    // start out with a balance of 100
    Console.WriteLine("Deposit 100");
    ba.Deposit(100);

    // now withdraw 50
    Console.WriteLine("Withdraw 50");
    ba.Withdraw(50);

    // output the balance
    Console.WriteLine("Resulting balance is " + ba.Balance());

    // wait for user to acknowledge the results
    Console.WriteLine("Hit Enter to terminate...");
    Console.Read();
```

```
      return 0;
    }
  }
}
```

The method `InitBankAccount()` sets the bank account number to the next available id.

8. I expanded the `BankAccount` by adding the following `CDAccount` class, which provides a 25 percent penalty for early withdrawal.

```
public class CDAccount: BankAccount
{
  public override double Withdraw(double dWithdrawal)
  {
    double dPenalty = dWithdrawal * 0.25;
    base.Withdraw(dPenalty);

    return base.Withdraw(dWithdrawal);
  }
}
```

In addition, I modified the `Withdraw()` method in `BankAccount` by adding the `virtual` descriptor. This allows C# to invoke the `BankAccount.Withdraw()` method when dealing with simple bank accounts while automatically invoking the `CDAccount.Withdraw()` method when handling CD accounts.

Sunday Morning Review Answers

1. An object-oriented class must be self-sufficient. The class must have some way to initialize these internal elements. The class cannot rely upon external code to initialize its data elements properly. The class must provide an initialization function that C# can call when an object is created. The constructor is this initialization function.

2. Every class must have a constructor even if this constructor does nothing more than zero out the data members. C# removes this requirement by providing a default constructor if the user has not already defined a constructor of his own.

3. Oftentimes, the constructors do nothing more than set data members to some initial, legal value. This could be handled in a constructor; however, the following initialization construct is both easier to write and more intuitive.

The following constructor:

```
public class BankAccount
{
  public static int nNextAccountNumber = 1000;
```

```
   public int nAccountNumber;
   public double dBalance;

   public BankAccount()
   {
     nAccountNumber = ++nNextAccountNumber;
     dBalance = 0.0;
   }
 }
```

can be replaced with the more intuitive:

```
public class BankAccount
{
   public static int nNextAccountNumber = 1000;

   public int nAccountNumber = ++nNextAccountNumber;
   public double dBalance = 0;
}
```

4. My version of the `MyClass` program appears as follows:

```
namespace MyClass
{
   using System;

   public class MyClass
   {
     public MyClass()
     {
       Console.WriteLine("A MyClass object constructed"+
         "using default constructor");
     }
     public MyClass(int n)
     {
       Console.WriteLine("A MyClass object constructed"+
         "using (int) constructor");
     }
   }

   public class Class1
   {
```

```
            public static int Main(string[] args)
            {
                // create a container object
                Console.WriteLine("Generate default MyClass object");
                MyClass cc1 = new MyClass();

                // now use the other constructor
                Console.WriteLine("\nGenerate specific NyClass object");
                MyClass cc2 = new MyClass(0);

                // wait for user to acknowledge the results
                Console.WriteLine("Hit Enter to terminate...");
                Console.Read();
                return 0;
            }
        }
    }
```

The output from executing this program appears as follows:

```
Generate default MyClass object
A MyClass object constructedusing default constructor

Generate specific NyClass object
A MyClass object constructedusing (int) constructor
Hit Enter to terminate...
```

5. My version of the MySubClass program appears as follows:

```
namespace MySubClass
{
    using System;

    public class MyClass
    {
        public MyClass()
        {
            Console.WriteLine("A MyClass object constructed"+
                "using default constructor");
        }
        public MyClass(int n)
        {
            Console.WriteLine("A MyClass object constructed"+
```

```
                      "using (int) constructor");
        }
    }

    public class MySubClass : MyClass
    {
        public MySubClass(int i, string s) : base(i)
        {
            Console.WriteLine("A MySubClass object created with " +
                              "an (int) and a (string)");
        }
    }

    public class Class1
    {
        public static int Main(string[] args)
        {
            // create a container object
            Console.WriteLine("Generate a MySubClass object");
            MySubClass sc = new MySubClass(1, "a string");

            // wait for user to acknowledge the results
            Console.WriteLine("Hit Enter to terminate...");
            Console.Read();
            return 0;
        }
    }
}
```

The output from this program appears as follows:

```
Generate a MySubClass object
A MyClass object constructedusing (int) constructor
A MySubClass object created with an (int) and a (string)
Hit Enter to terminate...
```

6. The full name of a method MemFun() that is a member of the class MyClass that itself is part of the namespace MyNamespace and accepts an int argument is:

```
MyNamespace.MyClass.MemFun(int)
```

Notice that double is not part of the function's name.

7. Including the command using MyNamespace tells C# to look in MyNamespace automatically for the function.

8. You do not need to specify a function's class when the function is invoked from another function in the same class, as in the following:

```
namespace MyNamespace
{
  class MyClass
  {
    double MemFun(int i)
    {
      // ...
    }

    void SomeOtherFun()
    {
      // the class name for MemFun is understood
      // to be current class
      double d = MemFun(1);
    }
  }
}
```

9. The following `CheckArgs(int)` function throws an exception when the argument passed it is negative:

```
using System;

public class Class1
{
  public static int CheckArgs(int i)
  {
    if (i < 0)
    {
      throw new Exception("Negative argument passed to CheckArgs");
    }
    return i;
  }

  public static int Main(string[] args)
  {
    try
    {
```

```
    int nReturnValue = CheckArgs(-1);
  }
  catch(Exception e)
  {
    Console.WriteLine(e.Message);
  }

  // wait for user to acknowledge the results
  Console.WriteLine("Hit Enter to terminate...");
  Console.Read();
  return 0;
  }
}
```

The output from this program is as follows:

```
Negative argument passed to CheckArgs
Hit Enter to terminate...
```

Sunday Afternoon Review Answers

1. The problem was to explain the following code segment:

   ```
   int i = 10;
   Int32 i32 = i;
   int j = (int)i32;
   int k = i32;
   ```

   The first line declares an int variable i, initializing it to 10 just as in all previous sessions. The second line creates a struct object i32 of class Int32. The i32 object shares the properties of both value type variables and class objects. For example, the WriteLine() function uses the ToString() method to display the i32 object as a string. The next line uses the (int) cast to convert the Int32 object back into an int so that it can be stored in j. In fact, the cast is not actually necessary — C# knows when to create an Int32 object for an int and when to convert it back as demonstrated in the assignment to k.

   This automatic conversion is known as *boxing*. The ability to box connects the value type variables to class objects.

2. Any class that wants to implement IAddable must provide a function int Add(int, int).

3. The following class implements IAddable:

   ```
   public class MyClass : IAddable
   {
     // define unrelated members
   ```

```
int nMember = 0;
static int nStaticMember = 0;

// the Add method is required
public int Add(int n1, int n2)
{
  return n1 + n2;
}
```

4. The following collections are best suited for the cases listed:

   a. The user enters an 8-digit ID number for a set of records stored in a Dictionary for lookup. A Dictionary collection can be keyed for almost any type of object. In this case, the lookup key would be the ID number. The records stored would be the name records.

   b. A Queue is best suited for storing data to be passed on to another application when it gets around to it. The Queue provides a method for storing data going in and another method for retrieving the oldest data.

   c. A LinkedList is the best choice for storing data when you intend to perform a sort. Reordering a record in a LinkedList requires very few operations. In addition, a LinkedList works well in applications where you don't know how many objects you will be asked to store.

   d. The Array is by far the best choice for applications in which the records are indexed. The Array provides random access to members as well. However, the Array does not work well if you do not know in advance how many object you will be storing.

What's on the CD-ROM?

What You'll Find

The CD-ROM contains the programs you find in this book. These programs are oriented into directories by program name. Each directory contains all of the files that go with a single example program and nothing more. In general, that means that each directory contains one or more C# source files.

These source files are intended to save you from typing in sometimes-lengthy programs. In addition, the CD-ROM may contain programs that do not appear in the book because of their length. The contents of the CD-ROM are documented in the TableOfContents.txt file.

A self-assessment test, to help you measure how much you have learned, can also be found on the CD.

A README.TXT file is present as well. Read this file first for the latest information.

System Requirements

The main system requirement is that you must have a C# development environment such as Microsoft's Visual Studio .NET installed on your computer before you can build and execute the example programs. This book does not supply a C# development environment.

Refer to the Visual Studio system requirements for details concerning the hardware requirements for Visual Studio .NET. In general ,for adequate performance you will need:

- A 500MHz Pentium II processor (you can get by with less, but the response time may become intolerable).
- At least 256MB of internal RAM memory, more if you can get it — Visual Studio .NET has a large appetite for memory.
- 2 GB of free disk storage space. Visual Studio .NET seems much less sensitive to available disk space. The example programs contained on the CD-ROM take up a minimal amount of space.
- A CD-ROM drive.

As of this writing, an alternative C# development tool comes bundled in the .NET Software Development Kit (SDK) MS-DOS command line. The .NET SDK may be available for download from Microsoft's Web site. The hardware requirements for the .NET SDK are less than those for Visual Studio .NET. Check the SDK documentation for details.

The C# language has become an industry standard. It is possible that other C# environments will appear, each with their own requirements. However, you can be assured that they will be similar to or greater than those listed above.

Using the CD with Microsoft Windows

The programs in this book are contained in a folder \C#Programs. Follow these instructions to make use of these source files:

1. Create your program framework in the normal way. For Visual C# this means selecting File ➪ New ➪ Project... from the Visual Studio user interface. In the dialog box that appears, enter the name of the program in the text field labeled Name and the directory that you want to use in the Location text field. Select ConsoleApp from the list of possible templates. Select OK.
2. For purposes of discussion, let's assume that you created the application HelloWorld in the C:\C#Programs directory.
3. Copy the file Class1.cs from the *D*:\C#Programs\HelloWorld directory on the CD-ROM (where *D* is the letter corresponding to your CD-ROM drive) into your newly created C:\C#Programs\HelloWorld directory.
4. If you are using Visual Studio .NET, a warning dialog box will pop up informing you that someone has changed the Class1.cs file and asking if you want to reload it. Click Yes.
5. The Class1.cs file that appears in your editor window should already be populated with source code identical to that in the book.
6. Proceed on as if you had typed in the Class1.cs file yourself.

Some folders on the CD-ROM may have special README.TXT **text files describing some particular considerations associated with that program. You should read that file before using the source files contained there.**

If You've Got Problems (of the CD Kind)

I've tried my best to recompile the programs contained on this CD-ROM on a computer with the minimum system requirements. Alas, your computer may differ and some programs may not work for some reason or they may work but very slowly.

The most likely problem is that you do not have the .NET environment installed. Programs created in C# require that a set of .NET libraries be installed on your computer. At this writing, these libraries did not come preinstalled, though versions of Windows after Windows 2000 were purported to do so. If you have installed Visual Studio or the .NET SDK on your computer, you will definitely have the necessary .NET libraries. Otherwise, you may be able to download them from www.microsoft.com.

Another possible problem is that your computer does not have enough memory (RAM). Visual Studio itself is very memory hungry, although the programs that it generates are not.

- **Close unnecessary running programs.** The more programs you have running, the less memory you have to execute Visual Studio.

- **Have your local computer store add more RAM to your computer.** This is admittedly a drastic and potentially expensive step. However, the more memory that you can throw at Visual Studio, the better, especially when using Windows NT, Windows 2000, or later.

If you continue to have problems, check out `www.stephendavis.com` for a list of known issues.

Index

Symbols & Numbers

Continued

Hungry Minds, Inc.
End-User License Agreement

READ THIS. You should carefully read these terms and conditions before opening the software packet(s) included with this book ("Book"). This is a license agreement ("Agreement") between you and Hungry Minds, Inc. ("HMI"). By opening the accompanying software packet(s), you acknowledge that you have read and accept the following terms and conditions. If you do not agree and do not want to be bound by such terms and conditions, promptly return the Book and the unopened software packet(s) to the place you obtained them for a full refund.

1. **License Grant.** HMI grants to you (either an individual or entity) a nonexclusive license to use one copy of the enclosed software program(s) (collectively, the "Software") solely for your own personal or business purposes on a single computer (whether a standard computer or a workstation component of a multi-user network). The Software is in use on a computer when it is loaded into temporary memory (RAM) or installed into permanent memory (hard disk, CD-ROM, or other storage device). HMI reserves all rights not expressly granted herein.

2. **Ownership.** HMI is the owner of all right, title, and interest, including copyright, in and to the compilation of the Software recorded on the disk(s) or CD-ROM ("Software Media"). Copyright to the individual programs recorded on the Software Media is owned by the author or other authorized copyright owner of each program. Ownership of the Software and all proprietary rights relating thereto remain with HMI and its licensers.

3. **Restrictions On Use and Transfer.**

    (a) You may only (i) make one copy of the Software for backup or archival purposes, or (ii) transfer the Software to a single hard disk, provided that you keep the original for backup or archival purposes. You may not (i) rent or lease the Software, (ii) copy or reproduce the Software through a LAN or other network system or through any computer subscriber system or bulletin-board system, or (iii) modify, adapt, or create derivative works based on the Software.

    (b) You may not reverse engineer, decompile, or disassemble the Software. You may transfer the Software and user documentation on a permanent basis, provided that the transferee agrees to accept the terms and conditions of this Agreement and you retain no copies. If the Software is an update or has been updated, any transfer must include the most recent update and all prior versions.

4. **Restrictions on Use of Individual Programs.** You must follow the individual requirements and restrictions detailed for each individual program in Appendix B of this Book. These limitations are also contained in the individual license agreements recorded on the Software Media. These limitations may include a requirement that after using the program for a specified period of time, the user must pay a registration fee or discontinue use. By opening the Software packet(s), you will be agreeing to abide by the licenses and restrictions for these individual programs that are detailed in Appendix B and on the Software Media. None of the material on this Software Media or listed in this Book may ever be redistributed, in original or modified form, for commercial purposes.

5. **Limited Warranty.**

   (a) HMI warrants that the Software and Software Media are free from defects in materials and workmanship under normal use for a period of sixty (60) days from the date of purchase of this Book. If HMI receives notification within the warranty period of defects in materials or workmanship, HMI will replace the defective Software Media.

   (b) HMI AND THE AUTHOR OF THE BOOK DISCLAIM ALL OTHER WARRANTIES, EXPRESS OR IMPLIED, INCLUDING WITHOUT LIMITATION IMPLIED WARRANTIES OF MERCHANTABILITY AND FITNESS FOR A PARTICULAR PURPOSE, WITH RESPECT TO THE SOFTWARE, THE PROGRAMS, THE SOURCE CODE CONTAINED THEREIN, AND/OR THE TECHNIQUES DESCRIBED IN THIS BOOK. HMI DOES NOT WARRANT THAT THE FUNCTIONS CONTAINED IN THE SOFTWARE WILL MEET YOUR REQUIREMENTS OR THAT THE OPERATION OF THE SOFTWARE WILL BE ERROR FREE.

   (c) This limited warranty gives you specific legal rights, and you may have other rights that vary from jurisdiction to jurisdiction.

6. **Remedies.**

   (a) HMI's entire liability and your exclusive remedy for defects in materials and workmanship shall be limited to replacement of the Software Media, which may be returned to HMI with a copy of your receipt at the following address: Software Media Fulfillment Department, Attn.: *C# Weekend Crash Course*, Hungry Minds, Inc., 10475 Crosspoint Blvd., Indianapolis, IN 46256, or call 1-800-762-2974. Please allow four to six weeks for delivery. This Limited Warranty is void if failure of the Software Media has resulted from accident, abuse, or misapplication. Any replacement Software Media will be warranted for the remainder of the original warranty period or thirty (30) days, whichever is longer.

   (b) In no event shall HMI or the author be liable for any damages whatsoever (including without limitation damages for loss of business profits, business interruption, loss of business information, or any other pecuniary loss) arising from the use of or inability to use the Book or the Software, even if HMI has been advised of the possibility of such damages.

   (c) Because some jurisdictions do not allow the exclusion or limitation of liability for consequential or incidental damages, the above limitation or exclusion may not apply to you.

7. **U.S. Government Restricted Rights.** Use, duplication, or disclosure of the Software for or on behalf of the United States of America, its agencies and/or instrumentalities (the "U.S. Government") is subject to restrictions as stated in paragraph (c)(1)(ii) of the Rights in Technical Data and Computer Software clause of DFARS 252.227-7013, or subparagraphs (c) (1) and (2) of the Commercial Computer Software - Restricted Rights clause at FAR 52.227-19, and in similar clauses in the NASA FAR supplement, as applicable.

8. **General.** This Agreement constitutes the entire understanding of the parties and revokes and supersedes all prior agreements, oral or written, between them and may not be modified or amended except in a writing signed by both parties hereto that specifically refers to this Agreement. This Agreement shall take precedence over any other documents that may be in conflict herewith. If any one or more provisions contained in this Agreement are held by any court or tribunal to be invalid, illegal, or otherwise unenforceable, each and every other provision shall remain in full force and effect.

Get Up to Speed
in a Weekend!